esc

Written by Lewis Blackwell
Designed by Angus Hyland / Pentagram
Published by Laurence King

20th-Century Type

revised edition

Contents

1

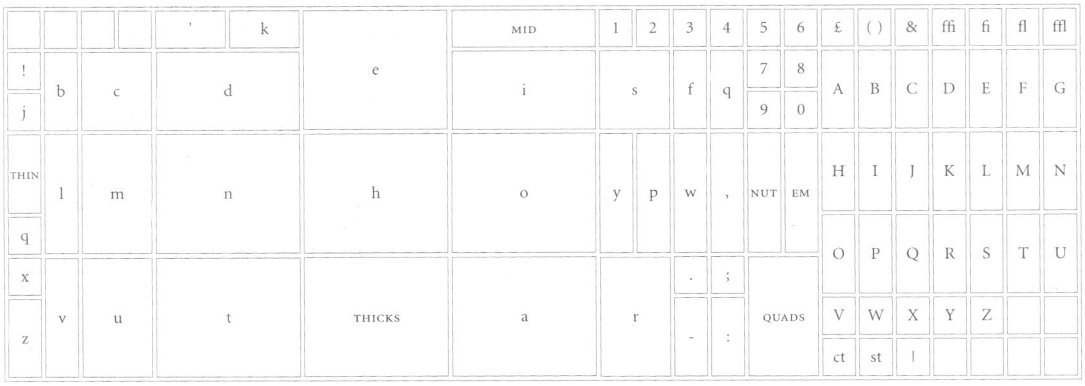
' k MID 1 2 3 4 5 6 £ ( ) & ffi fi fl ffl
! j b c d e i s f q 7 8 9 0 A B C D E F G
THIN l m n h o y p w , NUT EM H I J K L M N
q x z v u t THICKS a r . ; - : QUADS O P Q R S T U
V W X Y Z
ct st !

2

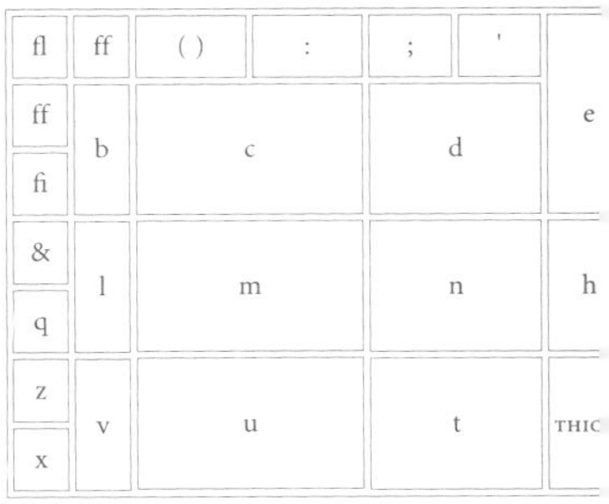
fl ff ( ) : ; '
ff fi b c d e
& q l m n h
z x v u t THIC

3

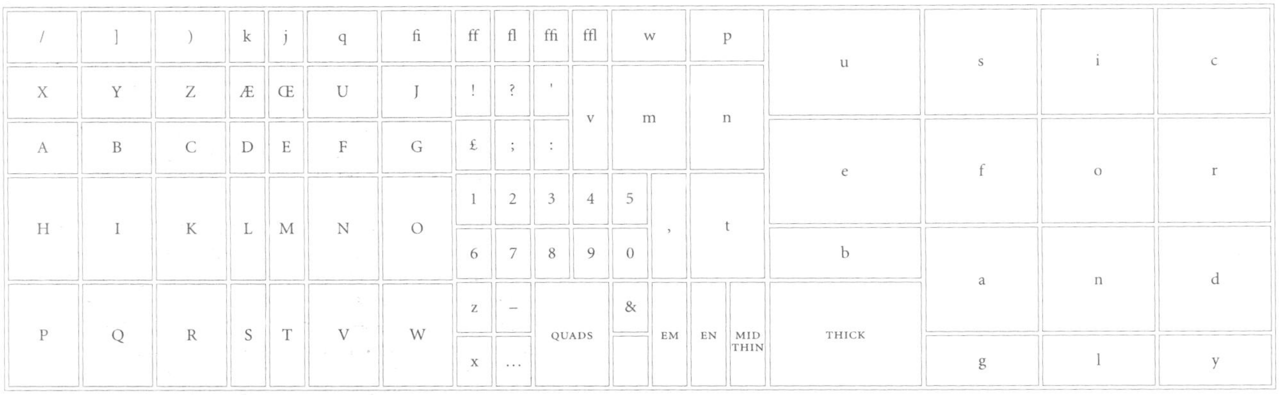
/]) k j q fi ff fl ffi ffl w p u s i c
X Y Z Æ Œ U J ! ? ' v m n
A B C D E F G £ ; : e f o r
H I K L M N O 1 2 3 4 5 6 7 8 9 0 , t b a n d
P Q R S T V W z – x … QUADS & EM EN MID THIN THICK g l y

4

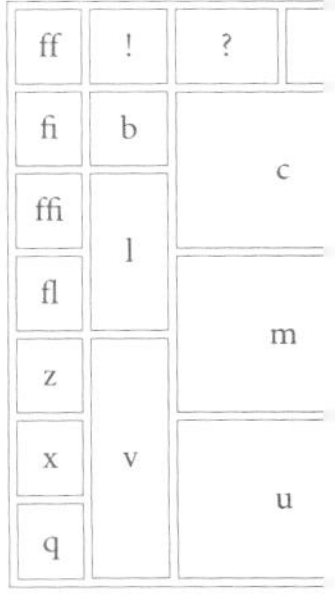
ff ! ?
fi b c
ffi l
fl m
z x v u
q

5

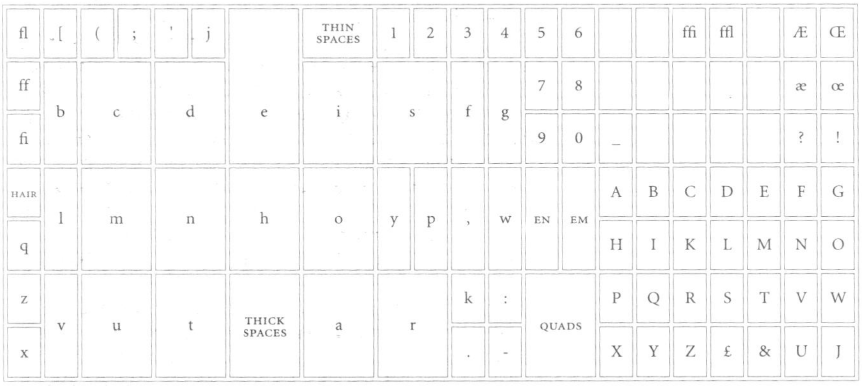
fl [(; ' j THIN SPACES 1 2 3 4 5 6 ffi ffl Æ Œ
ff b c d e i s f g 7 8 æ œ
fi 9 0 _ ? !
HAIR l m n h o y p , w EN EM A B C D E F G
q H I K L M N O
z v u t THICK SPACES a r k : QUADS P Q R S T V W
x . - X Y Z £ & U J

6

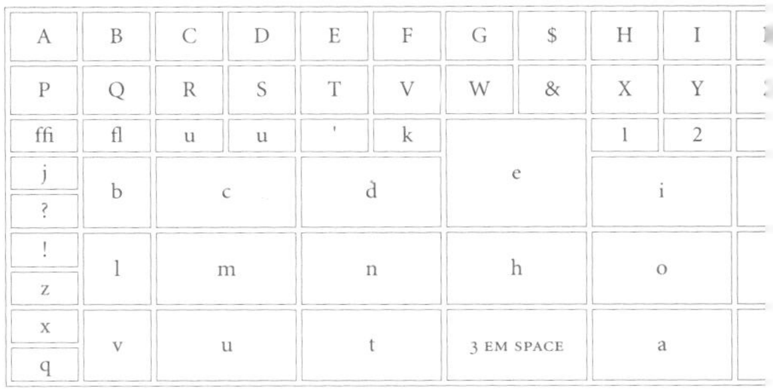
A B C D E F G $ H I
P Q R S T V W & X Y
ffi fl u u ' k e 1 2
j ? b c d i
! l m n h o
z x q v u t 3 EM SPACE a

7

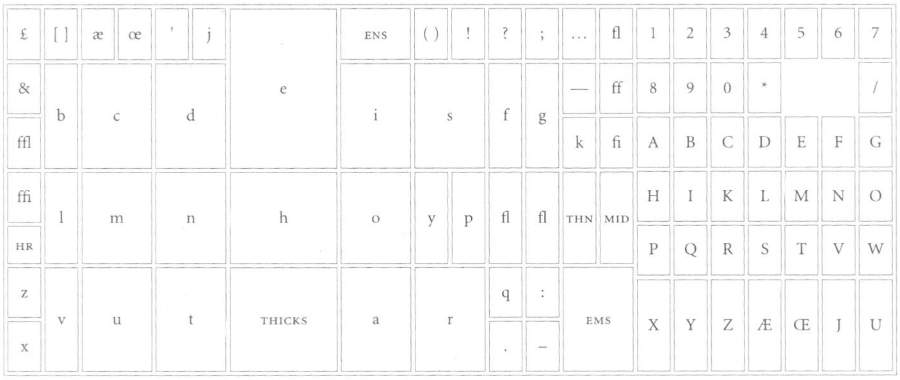
£ [ ] æ œ ' j ENS ( ) ! ? ; … fl 1 2 3 4 5 6 7
& b c d e i s f g — ff 8 9 0 * /
ffl k fi A B C D E F G
ffi l m n h o y p fl fl THN MID H I K L M N O
HR P Q R S T V W
z v u t THICKS a r q : EMS X Y Z Æ Œ J U
x . —

8

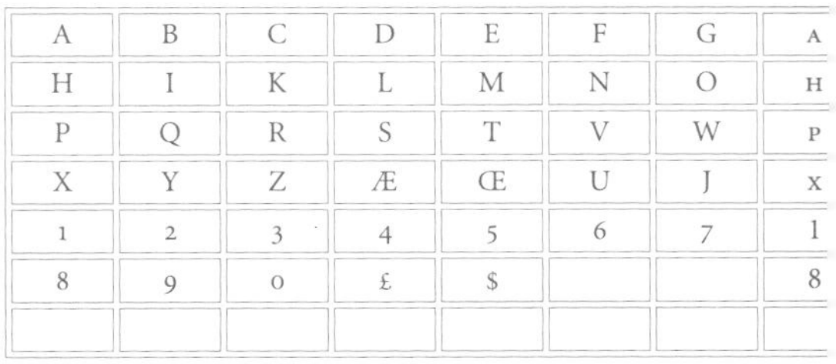
A B C D E F G A
H I K L M N O H
P Q R S T V W P
X Y Z Æ Œ U J X
1 2 3 4 5 6 7 1
8 9 0 £ $ 8

Introduction

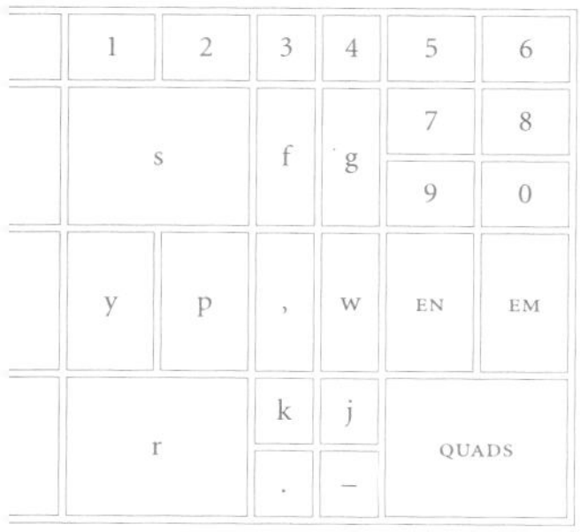

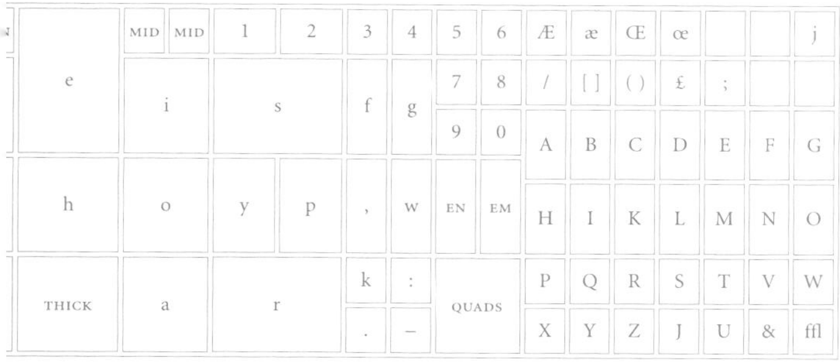

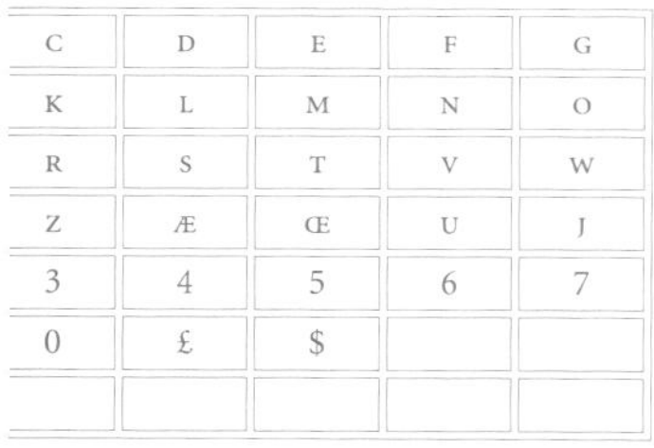

This is a book about typography. For our purposes, typography is the subject of typefaces and the matters involved in their creation and application.

The arrangement of letters on a page is an arcane corner of interest. In general, it has not proven a route to great individual advancement in a single lifetime. We know this from the biographies of typographers throughout the ages, who at best have been temporarily fêted, but have rarely benefited from the glamour or the income to match the creatives and industries that depend on their endeavours. John Baskerville's corpse took some time before it found a respectable grave.

Why, then, are so many people interested in typography? The fascination of the subject itself would seem to be the answer. It is a subject that quickly gets its devotees into uncharted depths, where aesthetics meet engineering, where art meets maths, where the strictly ephemeral and decorative meets a quest for timeless values and transparent functionalism. With this going on, typography becomes something you can believe in as a good cause. Typographers are not without all hope of worldly gain, but they suspend disbelief in the face of the evidence of predecessors who failed to achieve much more than the respect of some of their own kind. And this persists. So clearly it can be enough. Perhaps typography is a noble calling, or a self-deluding one.

The growing interest and dedication of many to this subject can be best explained by its rising stature as an area of study, rather than as a trade discipline. It is a growth industry – at least in the sense that there is a growing amount of work; it is a debatable point (which we will address later) as to what greater value is being created by that explosion of typographic familiarity, certainly in financial terms. While once it was craft-based, largely in the pragmatic, fast-moving hands of the compositor, over the past century it has moved out of the print shop and become a subject with close connections to the development of art, technology and literacy. That typography is now associated with some of the more avant-garde activities in communication and innovation, with the more expressive dimensions of graphic design, also makes it a subject likely to appeal to new designers seeking to make their mark. At least we can now see that typography is no backwater: it is a nexus of thought, and can claim to be the architecture of our written language, which is no small thing given that our language is one of the key definers of our humanity. So typography may be arcane, but it is not immaterial. It can even be said to be at the centre of culture.

This is the third edition of a book that began life in 1990. This writer and publisher's interests and enthusiasms synchronized with rapid changes in the digital world of communication. We heard much about the desktop publishing model, and talk was rife of a "revolution" in how we would all work in the future. At that time, the activity and output of most "dtp" left much to the imagination. Pundits spoke of "wysiwyg" – "what you see is what you get" – on-screen display through to hard-copy delivery, but the reality was a very slow process resulting in a high error rate and often inferior results when compared with those produced by the technology that was being supplanted.

1 Improved Double Case / Talbot Press, Essex (late 1960s)
2 English Lower Case / Southward: *Modern Printing* (6th ed., 1933)
3 Double Case / Caslon & Co: *Printing Types and Catalogue of Materials* (1925)
4 Double Case / Dorset House School of Occupational Therapy, Oxford (1976)
5 Double Case / Atkins: Art & Practice of Printing (1930)
6 Yankee Job Case / American Type Founders: *American Line Type Book* (1906)
7 Double Case / The Curwen Press (1968)
8 Upper Case / Heffer & Sons of Cambridge (1970s)

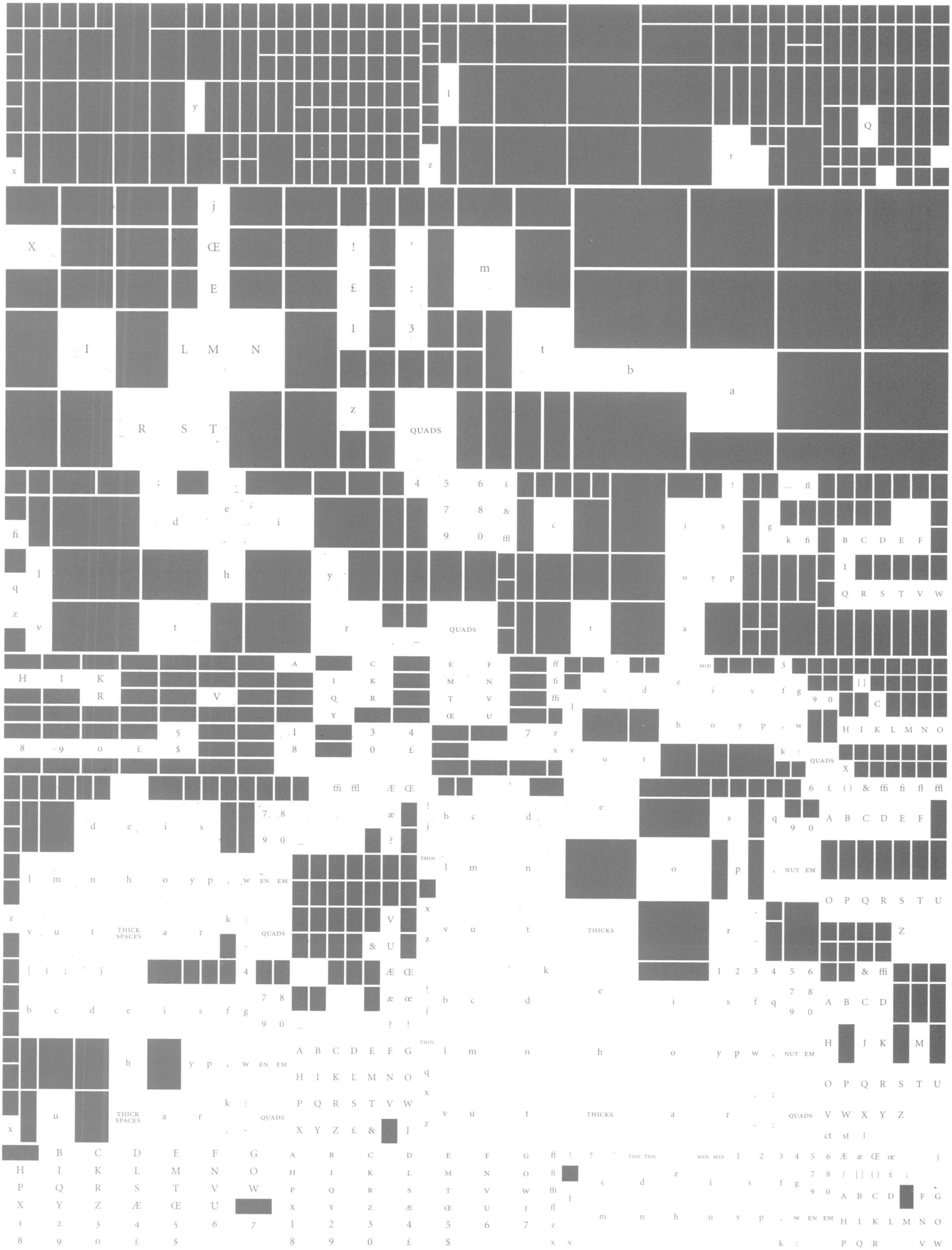
QUADS
THICK SPACES
THICKS
THIN
MID
NUT
EN
EM

Time has rapidly erased that experience of intermediate technology: only the lovers of old-print process can still envisage an alternative to the world of fully digital creation and output. We are now so immersed in the environment those "dtp" pioneering days envisaged that we easily forget the great change that has rapidly come to pass. For many of us working in the field today, the technology shift was mostly past by the time we came into typography, design and art direction. Every office and many a home in the wealthier nations now has equipment capable of printing layouts generated on the screen. Often an individual will have two or more tools (personal computer, laptop, handheld device) configured to be a typographic input and output device.

Let's jump into a quick case study to reinforce that point: this text is being written in a program that offers a range of typographic features, and then invites sharing of the resulting file with many other graphic applications before outputting in a selection of media. It is a world that only the wilder pundits would have proposed 20 years ago. To go from ideas to characters to pages here involves a merging of noting and writing sessions that took place using several of the above-mentioned devices. Indeed, not just one PC, laptop and handheld, but a Mac and a Windows-based laptop. Files are seamlessly pushed around, with copies stored in many places, the master version being as likely to be on a "remote server" that is not easily traceable as it is to be inside the machine my fingers are running across right now. The files are accessible by authorized users over the internet from the remote storage, which may be in London or just outside Seattle (I have reason to believe that it is likely to be one of those two data-storage centres, but it could have been moved to anywhere else in the world). The resulting text was sent to the designer and the publisher over the web, was edited and laid out in further programs and on other machines, then viewed and proofed through other tools, and finally sent to the printer as pages fully locked. No design input invited from the printer. The printer is now an output unit, and has a creative role in the finessing of execution, but not in owning the typographic arrangement as it once did when our story began, back in the late 19th century.

The problem of execution on the digital vision has been mostly resolved. The sci-fi future has come to pass. So where to now?

It is time to build the understanding anew. There are strong comparisons to be made between 2003 and a hundred or so years earlier. Just over a century ago, a new technology was lifting off, driven by an exploding demand for print, but the vision and skill as to how these communications could best be created and executed was lacking. There was a general lament by the aesthetes of typography that standards were appalling. From artist and writer William Morris to the printer and type historian Daniel Berkeley Updike, anybody who cared about type only had bad things to say about it. Many designers and typographic specialists today and over the past decade have sounded similar Jeremiah-like pronouncements about the work around them.

Today, we have a media landscape that has recently transformed itself and that is continuing to evolve apace. And there is a general lamentation by experts of type tradition at the debasement of much communication, and the horrors that pass for "typography". Sound familiar? They are not all reactionaries: in many cases in 1903 and 2003 it is also radicals who protest and resist. Some even propose alternatives, and meanwhile some of the best work comes from the centre of the global capitalism driving the global technologies driving the global typographic machine. At this time, Microsoft has arguably the largest, most expert typographic unit in the world. With responsibility for the functionality and output of the great majority of type-generating devices, it is no surprise that they should have that, but it is not a fact that is celebrated or much investigated. That the Apple Macintosh platform is more celebrated and is widely supported by creative designers obscures the prevalence of Microsoft technology in generating the typography that the world sees – even if many of its smartest ideas came from elsewhere.

We have a landscape in which typography is dominated at the generating point by a technology that sees it as a by-product of its own desire to control the operating system of the modern computer. A questionable position from which to promote high typographic standards, especially when these really are a very insignificant concern in the technology war.

That said, perhaps this is the time we should expect to see typographers marshalling the defence. As in 1903, when newfangled mechanized machines were mangling the finer points of traditional typesetting, so today we may lament the rough edges left by software and hardware companies' lack of concern for typographic control. Whenever they do show some consideration, whenever they see some financial benefit from improving the typographic machine in their tools, they tend to hand it to everybody to use and abuse. Type was initially crudely generated for the machine possibilities of both the hot-metal age at the beginning of the 20th century and again for the digital age at the end of it.

What a state for experts to find things in, their expertise handled crudely and cheaply. But it is a state in which problems can be turned to solutions. Put simply, there is now more need for typographic expert help than ever before, and the democratization of who holds the tools (everybody with a keyboard) means many more people are able to consider upgrading their typographic knowledge. It is not for a few businesses to change their practices, it is for the whole population of computer-users, now potential typographers, to learn about this discipline to a higher level. To some level. Typography was a key element in the introductory course at the Bauhaus: might it not be so for all schools today, already widely teaching design courses as part of the general-studies stream? A study of typography brings together questions of language, technology, art and philosophy, and links in with the practical skills of keyboard use, basic design and software operation.

Opposite Illustration: Deconstructed typecase

THIN SPACES
THICK SPACES
QUADS
HAIR
EN
EM
MID
NUT
THICKS
ENS
EMS
THN
HR

That is for the more distant future. It is a vision in which typography is embraced as something approaching a "life skill". It is not too fanciful, given that many people taking their place in the modern work world will be expected to make typographic decisions that will help or hinder their successful communication with others. Typography is not just for professionals – although more generalized access and interest should also increase the opportunity for and quality of professional work. Already the computer interface and the web throb with amateur as well as professional tips on how to use type. There's a typographic self-help culture out there in a way that has never existed before.

The nearer-term situation is darker, but easier to see. Right now there are some basic issues that need to be addressed if typography, and in particular type design, is not to fall into decay – or, depending on how dispirited you already are, further decay.

The key issues to tackle in the short term are:

The prevalence of choice over quality, which has confused understanding and direction in typography.
The loss of control in the typographic process.
The poor investment potential of type as an intellectual property.

Choice Versus Quality

Who dares say that choice is not a wonderful thing? Who even dares think, in the post-Communist era, in the age of free-market determinations, that choice is not an almost sacred given? And yet, faced with a mass of choice and little that you need or desire, who can get that excited about it? Such is perhaps the state of mind of the modern designer considering typeface choice, or even the newly enfranchised amateur typographer, the desktop computer-user hard at work on jazzing up his or her powerpoint presentation. What are they to make of the drop-down menus of faces and effects? Who told them what to do with all those options and buttons that can shift and distort type in the twinkling of an eye?

There is a wealth of choice and a poverty of understanding of what to do with the type gizmos (or why they were created in the first place?). In the midst of all this, all typefaces are treated as commodities – piled high and sold cheap; in fact, given away in the eyes of most of us, so that there is little perceived value in a typeface. For example, 27 typefaces (often confused with "fonts" in the jargon of the desktop) are loaded as standard in the Windows interface used for this text and 120 in the Macintosh one that was also used. The selection is not made on the basis of what you might need most, otherwise why offer Wingdings? Or to say that in Wingdings: ◆♒⍓ □♐♐♏❒ ⌖♓■♑♎♓■♑⬧✍

The selection is made in part as an advertisement for the typographic range now available. It is part of the culture of choice, rather than a culture of functionality. In the same standard Windows software, the Help menu gives only one typographic pointer, on how to embed Truetype fonts. There is no advice on what to do with the multitude of typographic features and functions that have been stacked up.

"You need more" – that is the basic message of having upgrade after software upgrade that adds features both obscure and usually of questionable value. A range of "effects" are available that outline, shadow, emboss or engrave characters – these should really come with a "handle with care, can be highly toxic" notice, but instead they are offered as standard features that can be slapped on anywhere. Even more visually dangerous fun can be had if the medium is available to animate the effects. Many a document or presentation past has borne tragic witness to the uses made of these tools by inexperienced hands.

Once again, it is rewarding to look back and examine the type sample books of the early part of the 20th century. There are remarkable variations in quality, drawing on the wilder shores of 19th-century display demands to suggest that all could be accommodated in the type of the new mechanized processes. It would be reassuring to say that these gimmicks subsequently just passed away and the underlying strengths of "good" typeface design came through – hence the survival of the Akzidenz Grotesks over the not-yet-revived inlined and drop-shadow Cheltenham. But that would be to read history with a propagandist intent. The reality of the Windows interface is that the coarse, expressive choices evolve and change and reassert themselves. They have been there with every previous type-creation system.

What may evolve is the controls and focus determining the usage. Hence the cause for concern at the way more and more people are…

Seizing the Controls

When printers and compositors, and then graphic designers, controlled the typographic process, some rules were built into the system by which type choice and application were delivered. A level of formal education lay behind the practice, involving indentures and lengthy practical study. As a result, to sample the everyday output of a jobbing printer from the 1950s is probably to experience some typographic basics done quietly and well. The communication strategy of the piece may be otherwise flawed, but the kerning and leading have been treated with the benefit of generations of craft expertise. To disrupt this, first came photosetting, and then the freedom of the digital age, all of which left few people in jobs plying the old craft skills at the core of typography: the old fundamentals governing the putting of one character after another and of one line next to another line were mostly abandoned. Designers are popularly celebrated to such a degree that "designer" is now used adjectivally to suggest a kind of chic refinement, but today everybody has a little knowledge of the typographic process. Often the "designer" is actually the engineer who put the settings in QuarkXPress, while the client also knows they have the freedom to be involved to an unprecedented extent. With all this freedom

Opposite Illustration: From typecase to keyboard

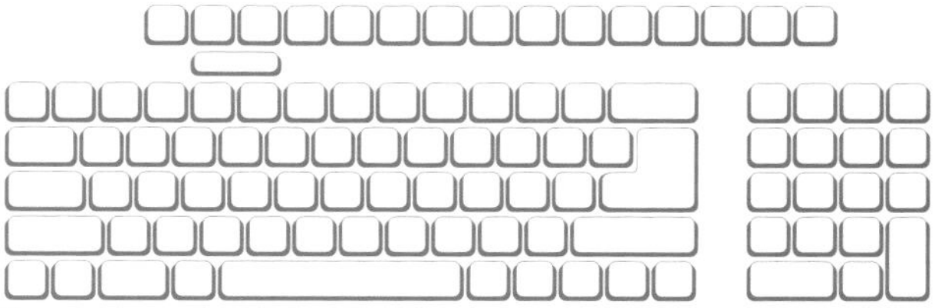
9

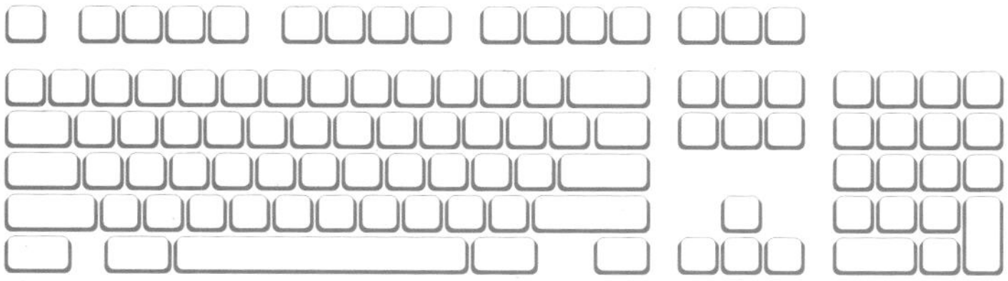
10

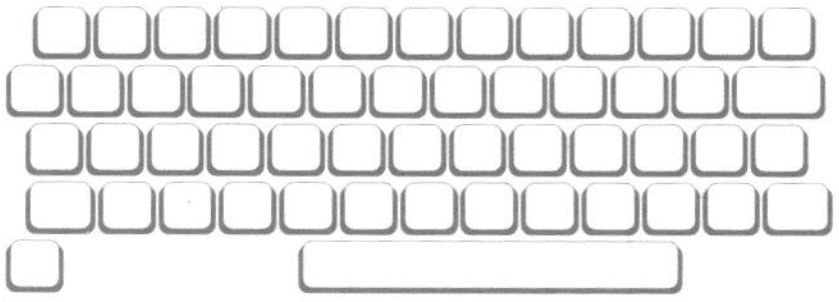
11

12

13

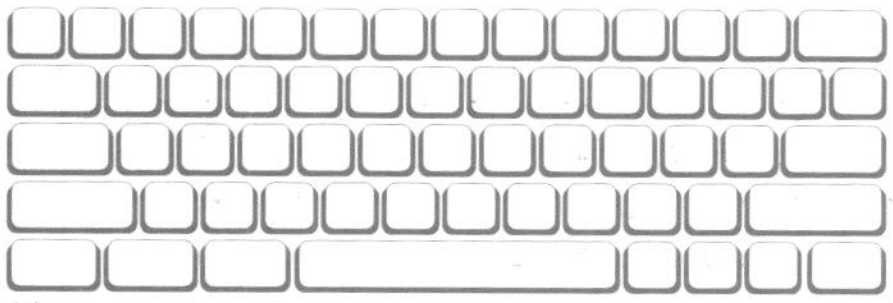
14

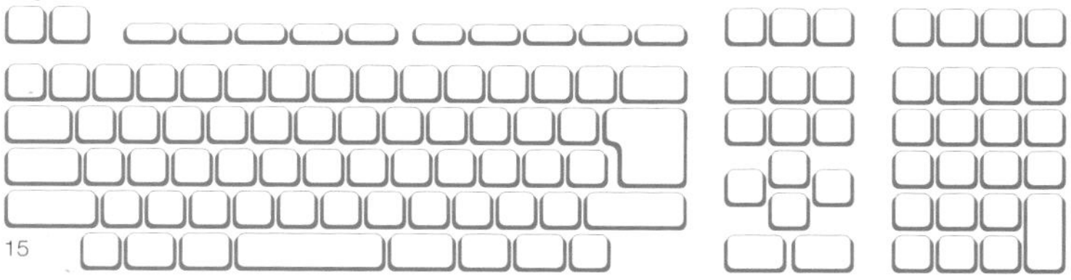
15

16

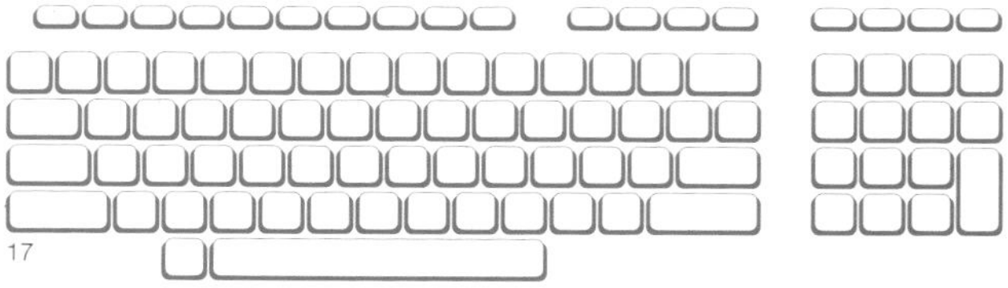
17

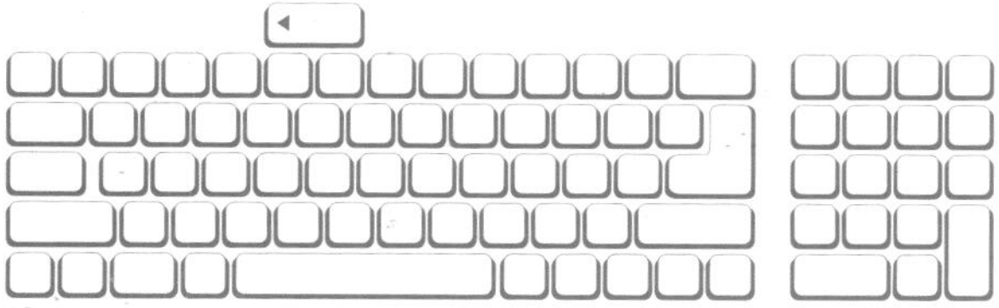
18

19

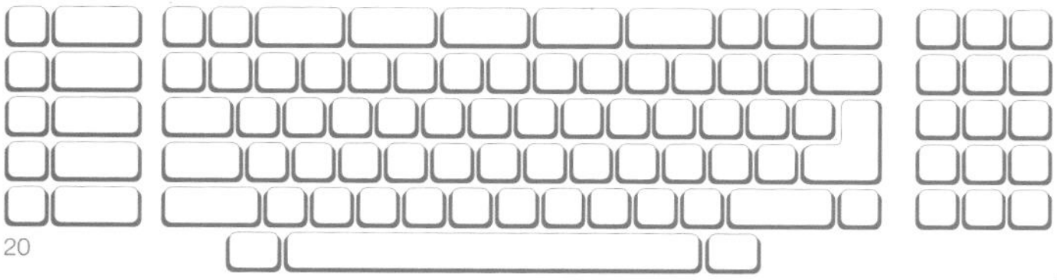
20

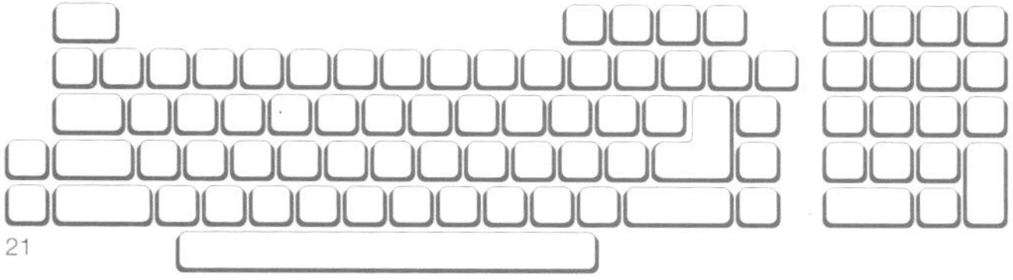
21

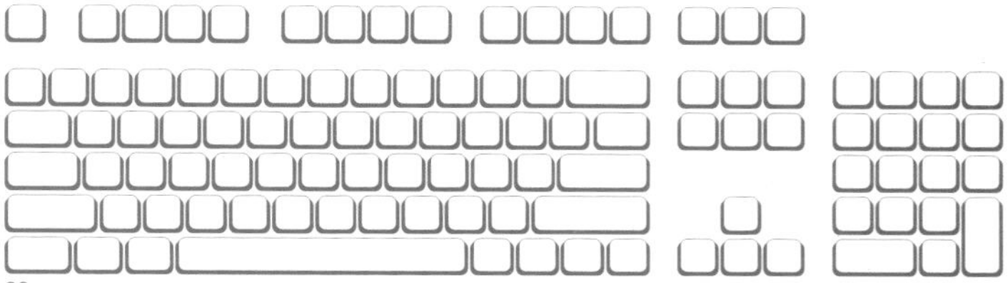
22

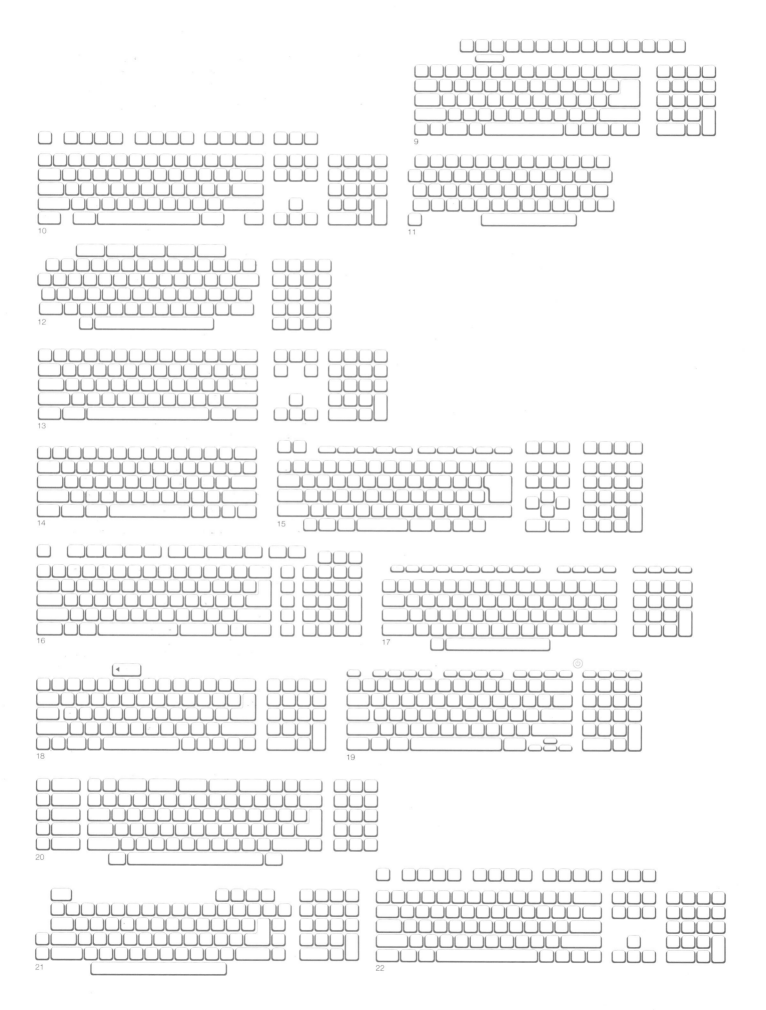

and so little focus on the core requirements, it is no wonder words and paragraphs can literally fall apart on the page for lack of real craft.

Today, the client of a designer does not just ask for the logo to be larger (though this is always demanded), but is also likely to question whether it can be centred instead of set left, reversed out of a colour, or made bold, or say that they would like to see the text otherwise "pop" a little louder. Everybody can do type... they can change the size and arrangement: once that would have been forbiddingly expensive and time-consuming, now it is known to be easy and is done with a freedom that shows all the disrespect usually afforded things that don't cost much. The result has not been to free professionals from laborious processes, but often to reduce them to little more than artworkers for the client, with their own lack of expertise and that of the client's ultimately resolved in a general muddle of confusion. Beware the designer and client who have some understanding of the typographic engine at their disposal, but only a little knowledge. This is a dangerous thing.

We cannot return to the earlier state, which was anyway fraught with its own problems. Undoubtedly, the digital age has brought immense benefits to designers and their clients. But to accompany these new freedoms we clearly need new forms of education. The knowledge built up by generations of compositors has vanished from our society. We should not grieve for the job of the compositor, which was skilled, but often repetitive and monotonous. But we must respect the expertise that that trade had and recognize that its value needs now to be embedded in basic life skills, given that everybody who can write is likely to some extent to be exercising those skills. We all need a course in typography along with the other basics of language – it is, after all, one of the basics of visual language, and visual language is ever more the common tongue.

The "RoI" of Type

The greatest problem standing in the way of the type design and typographic research community is the broken licensing model for type design. Quite simply, to set yourself up as an independent type designer today is to invite the theft of your intellectual property. As a result, the return on investment (RoI) is less than compelling. The profession requires that you create something of value and then promote and distribute it with little or no safeguards to stop people taking it from you for free. Sometimes they do this accidentally, and sometimes deliberately. And mostly you never know when they do.

This is how it works. You design a typeface. You distribute it via your own small company, or you license it to a major distributor and they sell it. If you are lucky, somebody notices you have designed the most usable font since Helvetica and Times Roman rolled into one, and they start using it. They buy it in every weight available. Wow! You could be in the money if this carries on. Which it looks like doing. Especially as your fans use it on every job they have and they tell their friends. Every printer of every job they do gets sent it with the artwork. By and by some less scrupulous friends get hold of it. It finds its way into a college. Everybody uses it, and everybody's friend soon has it. Think Napster, MP3 players and the whole piracy debacle that has afflicted the music industry. Only here there are no big music companies making it difficult for intellectual-property theft to take place.

Art may be its own reward, but even artists need to eat. At present, it is very difficult to live off the design and distribution of your typefaces, even very successful ones. Erik Spiekermann, one of the most successful type designers of the 1990s and a founder of Fontshop International and the design group MetaDesign, told me that FSI "estimate that for every font sold, at least ten others are being used as illegal copies, stolen from friends', colleagues', and employers' hard drives." Spiekermann, designer of a highly successful font in FF Meta, gets a 20 percent royalty back from whatever is retailed worldwide. This adds up to a useful sum, but with royalties at a one-tenth reflection of the scale of success, it makes type design and distribution a less appealing business than its cultural significance suggests.

As a result of this inability to build a credible return on investment, it is not surprising that type design continues to be a cottage industry. (An industry that would seem in need of consolidation and re-energizing with investment, but who would bother?) Few designers stick at a career in pure applied typography. Teaching, the wider fields of graphic design and other creative areas are seductive, if not essential, associated fields of endeavour if you want to secure an income and a little self-fulfilment.

Part of the problem is the nature of intellectual property. It is a concept scarcely recognized by many, including designers who instinctively understand its application to their own work. If something is not well understood, it is hard to respect. Hence creatives who would complain bitterly if somebody copied their ideas, or did not pay them enough for their work, are happy to steal a typeface or collaborate in its illegal distribution. Many highly respected organizations, perhaps clients of such uneducated designers, are inadvertently perpetuating the problem by going about their business using unlicensed fonts.

The ignorance surrounding the property status of typefaces is further clouded by a cultural problem. The technology revolution and dotcom era of the late 1990s often encouraged a disrespect for intellectual property, with the computer hackers and the "free music" bandwagon attacking those who sought to defend private property. There was an irony in this, in that while they were ostensibly attacking the large corporations, their victims were usually the individual artists who did not see the royalties from those who benefited from access to their work for free. Indeed, the new businesses distributing tools that enabled the stealing of other people's intellectual property were the real capitalist bad guys, but were often acclaimed as somehow doing it for the wider benefit. For a while, business journalists were more interested in writing about the potential of a company like

9 Pioneer MPC-KP2 Keyboard / Apple
10 IBM 101 Keyboard / PC
11 Apple II Keyboard / Apple
12 PC8001 Keyboard / NEC
13 NeXTstation Keyboard / NeXT
14 Apple Newton Keyboard
15 X68000 Keyboard / Sharp
16 Sony News NWP-5461 Keyboard / Sony
17 MZ 80B Keyboard / Sharp
18 Mac 0116 Keyboard / Apple
19 iMac Keyboard / Apple
20 Type2 Keyboard / Sun
21 VT100 Keyboard / DEC
22 Microsoft 104 Keyboard / PC

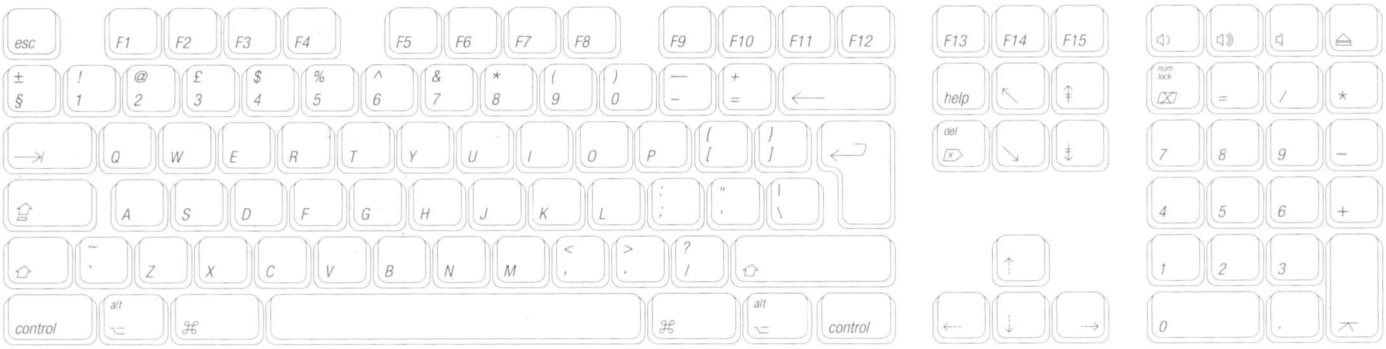

23

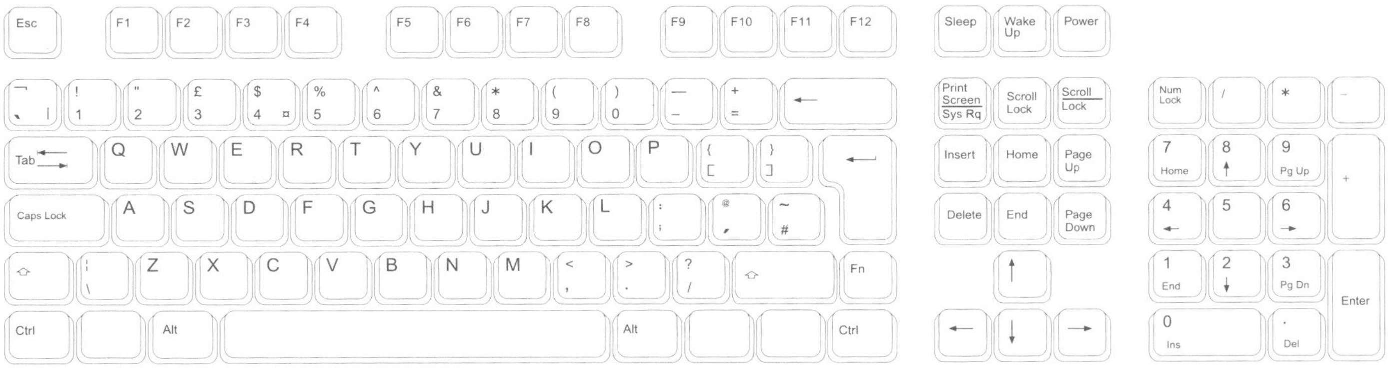

24

23 Pro Keyboard / Apple 2002
24 PC Keyboard / Date unknown

Napster (in 1999 and 2000, the leading provider of software for "exchanging" music files) than respecting the original property holders – whose investment value was increasingly being written down. The whole debate was conducted under the spurious banner of "freedom" – freedom to appropriate other people's property. At this time a new-technology stockdealer told me that intellectual property in the arts was a dead concept. His attitude was shared by many, and was part of the reason for the depression of stocks that were connected with valuing intellectual property. "The future method of an artist gaining reward will be through performance and the products sold, not the licensing rights of the creative work," he argued. Composers, typeface designers and all other kinds of artists affected by the digital delivery of their product were expected to accept the erosion of their royalties and to carry on working for the common good. They were challenged to find other means than licensing for generating income.

"Live performance" and collectible objects seemed a limited option for rewarding type design – although that is in effect how type designers do hit paydirt, applying their skills to the dedicated "performance" involved in creating a corporate-identity typeface. This is the equivalent of a rock band playing a private gig for a billionaire, with the difference that for the rock band the pay is jam on top of the recording-income cream, whereas for the type designer it's the whole deal.

Royalties from the sale of a typeface are the only way designers are going to get paid for their work, and thereby be encouraged to invest in greater innovation and refinement in their products. Fortunately, the notion of intellectual property as both socially acceptable and defensible appears to be in the ascendant. While illegal copying of everything from music to movies to entire databases continues apace, there is no longer a fashion to see it as somehow acceptable.

The challenge is no longer the "why?" but the "how?" of protecting files that are so easily distributed. The pioneer model may be produced by the music industry, where the property owners or representatives (the large music labels) are working with the new method of distribution via the web to charge for downloads. The type industry needs to follow suit. Its activities through type industry bodies such as the Federation Against Software Theft (FAST) have won some battles, but they do little to prevent common piracy.

The inability to earn a fair income is a problem that extends beyond the small pockets of most individual type designers and the accounts of the many struggling type vendors. It is a wider business and cultural issue.

If type is a low-value activity, then few people are going to invest in it – that goes for talented designers, as well as financiers and software companies. The result is that type design will decay, that the resources to develop and defend intellectual property will further dwindle and type design will decline. After a period in the 1990s when the subject was enthusiastically embraced, there will be a hangover as individuals and businesses realize it is an activity with no long-term reward. That is the situation we are perhaps in now, where both designers and companies seem to be looking elsewhere. While it has never been easier to set up a font company and proudly make your creations available for purchase over the web, it has perhaps never been harder to ensure a good and lasting return from a robust, innovative design. The lack of any vision for a lasting, growing market is counter to the logic that should be there for the market: larger but more diverse audiences viewing more fragmented media should be demanding more and more varied communications, greater variety in the expression of words... more type. But it does not seem to follow that any more funds flow to type design.

That is the current state of the industry – a worldwide industry that would seem to be worth a lot less than $100 million in revenue, and yet is integral to just about every medium, and nearly every communication at some point. Type design is mostly a by-product of other activities. Most designers and vendors look to branch out into other areas for revenue, as they struggle to grow their activities in the world of type. Many type companies move into other software or intellectual property, such as images.

The conclusion to all this has to be that type is in demand and *must* become more valued. With the access to and interest in typographic issues at its greatest, with the demand for the type product and typographic knowledge at its height (if not realized by the licensing model or the education systems), it follows that at some point the structure and the rewards should come.

Welcome to the opportunities and the challenges facing typography in the early 21st century. If the above makes a case for increasing our typographic knowledge today, where will that come from? We can learn much from the previous century of radical typographic experimentation, a century still so close that we can handle its products, breathe its energy, resolve its problems.

It is not for the purpose of reviving old or making new rules that these facsimiles have been reproduced. One might as well try to provide models for unalterable fashions in garments, houses, furniture, or decoration. However pleasing a new fashion may be, that pleasure does not entirely suppress the desire for change, and that desire was never greater than it is now.[25] / Less is more.[26] / Catalogues, posters, advertisements of all sorts. Believe me, they contain the poetry of our epoch.[27] / Build a book like a body moving in space and time, like a dynamic relief in which every page is a surface carrying shapes, and every turn of a page a new crossing to a new stage of a single structure.[28] / A photograph neither lies nor tells the truth.[29] / Colour is a creative element, not a trimming.[30] / The words on the printed surface are taken in by seeing, not by hearing.[31] / The more uninteresting a letter, the more useful it is to the typographer.[32] / For the modern exponent of form the artist's 'own touch' – is of absolutely no consequence.[33] / Typography must be clear communication in its most vivid form… Clarity is the essence of modern printing.[34] / Contrast is the mark of our age.[35] / I am the leaden army that conquers the world: I AM TYPE.[36] / All the old fellows stole our best ideas.[37] / Type production has gone mad, with its senseless outpouring of new types… Only in degenerate times can 'Personality' (opposed to the nameless masses) become the aim of human development.[38] / Contrast is perhaps the most important element in all modern design.[39] / A layout man should be simple with good photographs. He should perform acrobatics when the pictures are bad.[40] / Simplicity of form is never a poverty, it is a great virtue.[41] / Art is a noun, and design is a noun and also a verb.[42] / Typography is an art, good typography is art.[43] / Art in any form is a projected emotion using visual tools.[44] / … a study of typography must include a study of the meaning of 'text'.[45] / Typography fostered the modern idea of individuality, but it destroyed the medieval sense of community and integration.[46] / Type can be a tool, a toy and a teacher.[47] / Everything under the sun is art![48] / Communication should be entertaining.[49] / You read best what you read most.[50] / In order for language to function, signs must be isolable one from another (otherwise they would not be repeatable). At every level (phonetic, semantic, syntactic, and so on) language has its own laws of combination and continuity, but its primary material is constructed of irreducible atoms (phonemes for spoken language, and for written, signs…) … Language is a hierarchical combination of bits.[51]

Quotes

25 Theodore Low De Vinne / preface to *A Treatise on Title Pages* / 1902
26 Ludwig Mies van der Rohe / 1912
27 Guillaume Apollinaire / 1913
28 El Lissitzky / 1920
29 John Heartfield / 1921
30 Piet Zwart / 1922
31 El Lissitzky / 1923
32 Piet Zwart / 1924
33 El Lissitzky / 1926
34 László Moholy-Nagy / 1926
35 Theo van Doesburg / 1926
36 Frederic Goudy / 1927
37 Frederic Goudy / date unknown
38 Jan Tschichold / *The New Typography* / 1928
39 Jan Tschichold / 1928
40 Alexey Brodovitch / 1930
41 Jan Tschichold / 1930
42 Paul Rand / 1960
43 Paul Rand / 1960
44 Lester Beall / 1964
45 Wolfgang Weingart / 1972
46 Neil Postman / *Amusing Ourselves to Death* / 1985
47 Bradbury Thompson / 1986
48 Joseph Beuys / 1988
49 Neville Brody / 1991
50 Zuzana Licko / 1995
51 Yve Alain-Bois / *Formless* / Zone Books / 1997

Monograms

52 Piet Zwart
53 Max Burchartz
54 El Lissitzky
55 Herbert Bayer
56 Max & Walter Huber
57 Wolfgang Weingart
58 Antonio Boggeri
59 Hans Neuburg
60 Alexander Rodchenko
61 Joost Schimidt

52

53

el

54

55

56

57

58

61

60

59

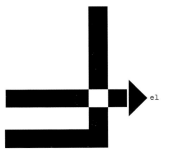

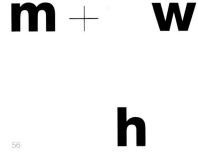

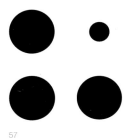

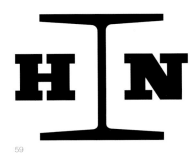

Points in time, be they 2000, 2001, 1990, 1900 – or whatever is deemed significant – provoke reflection on the past and the future. As the ancient Greeks pictured it, our notion of the future is of something sneaking up behind us, while the past recedes in front – and so we dream the future with the materials accumulated from our present culture.

The years around 1900 saw anticipation of change and proposals for it, along with some fundamental shifts in the technology of typography. There were intellectual and artistic responses, involving radical visions of how the new century should take shape, along with a yearning for lost values. These dreams – of futures based on the past – projected futures based on fears as much as hopes. These conflicting concerns were the seeds of Modernism – the over-arching name that we give to a movement across many disciplines (from psychoanalysis to architecture) which is central to the story in these pages, too.

A long period of relative peace between the leading nations had helped lay the basis for waves of industrialization and social change. Not far into the new century, it was the outbreak of the First World War in 1914 that finally brought an end to the period of growth and unprecedented riches in the world's most powerful economies. Before that happened, the first fourteen years of the twentieth century allowed the bedding-in of crucial technological change in print and the fomenting of aesthetic issues that were to underlie the coming decades in typographic thought.

Tension between the old and new technology took a number of forms. First there was a looking back at and reviving of lost values and lost modes of expression, a nostalgia that is apparent in the work of the small presses in Britain and the United States and the artist-craft groups such as the Secession movements in Austria and Germany. In contrast, there were new practices derived from the new print methods (notably developments in colour lithography and breakthroughs in machine-set type), and there were also pressures from the changing technologies and mass production. This search for and questioning of "the new" underlay movements such as the *Neue Sachlichkeit*, or "new objectivity", in Germany. Involved in this was a revising of typography, along with a general distinguishing of the significance of design in industrial processes from the earlier embodiment of the design process within craft practices.

The notion of typography was something largely different from the meaning carried today: then typography embraced much that is now within the job description of the printer, or has simply ceased to exist. The printer was the overriding figure, uniting the various processes in manufacturing the printed object, and graphic design had yet to emerge fully as a separate skill. The typesetter was one with the typographer.

The Arts and Crafts Movement in Britain was a key manifestation of craft revivalism that helped spawn an awareness of the space for design. It attacked the low standards of print and the aesthetic it saw as a product of modern industrial culture. William Morris (1834–96) had a wide influence through his work at the Kelmscott Press in the 1890s. His colleague in that enterprise, Emery Walker, set up the Doves Press in 1900 with Thomas Cobden-Sanderson. Together they designed the one type that the press held, a roman cut in one size only by Edward Prince (who had worked with Morris); like Morris's Golden, Troy and Chaucer faces this was based on a fifteenth-century model from Jenson. Cobden-Sanderson's axiom on typography displays the quest for a functional but interpretative form for the characters, pointing the way towards Modernist thought to come. In it he asserts that the only duty of typography is "to communicate to the imagination, without loss by the way, the thought or image intended to be communicated by the author". The Walker/Cobden-Sanderson face had a brief, but glorious, life: it was used by the Doves Press for the finest of private press books, peaking with the Doves' Bible. However, the matrices came to a violent end when Cobden-Sanderson smashed them and threw the lot into the Thames after a row with Walker – reputedly over who had the better claim to having created the face.

The manner in which the private press books conceived of the various elements of a page as parts of a whole finds a strong echo in the work of the group of artists and designers in Vienna who formed the Secession group (from 1897). Some of them later went on to set up the Wiener Werkstätte (from 1903). The distinctive development of Arts and Crafts and Art Nouveau ideas that this group showed was apparent in the typographic exercises of Koloman Moser. His illustrative calligraphy for the Secession magazine *Ver Sacrum* and his logotypes explored letterforms beyond the rigidity of established foundry faces. Initially his work was florid, organic, Art Nouveau-influenced, but it became more geometric. A masterpiece of the Secession/Wiener Werkstätte's print output is the luxurious commemorative book for the Austro-Hungarian royal print works, produced in 1904, featuring a typeface by Rudolf von Larisch, a title page and initial letters by Moser, and woodcuts by Czeschka. The similarities with Kelmscott work are apparent – the typeface is drawn from fifteenth-century Venetian precedents, and the text is set into wide decorated margins.

In Germany a similar mixing of ideas was present: between notions initially connected with the Art Nouveau style (here, called Jugendstil) moving on to less decorative work. The most distinctive of Art Nouveau typefaces was designed by Otto Eckmann for the Klingspor foundry in 1900; Eckmann was available in two weights, both relatively heavy. It mixed the organic themes of the Jugendstil with the black-letter tradition of Germany, reflecting the medieval pen in the open bowls of letters. It was a distinctive display face, but low on legibility thanks in part to the poor letterforms derived from the overwhelming styling. Producing such sports in metal required considerable investment in time and money, but this perhaps paid off for Klingspor as Eckmann proved to be the definitive Art Nouveau face. Eckmann did not reap much benefit: he died of tuberculosis in 1902, aged 37.

Peter Behrens (1868–1940) is the German designer who travelled furthest in his ideas in this decade. His interests

Left: from *Schriften und Ornamente*, issued in 1900 by the Klingspor foundry in Germany to promote the release of Otto Eckmann's eponymous type. One of the better known Jugendstil/Art Nouveau faces, the soft forms of its characters are not derived from calligraphy so much as brush-strokes imitative of organic forms, such as plants and trees. Scorned by later generations as too decorative and so consigned to signal a period and style, this face typifies the Art Nouveau reference to Nature, finding in it a quasi-spiritual touchstone for type form. Eckmann was a painter whose career ranged across the applied arts.

went from type design through to architecture, and could claim credit for helping found the notion of "corporate identity". From mixing traditional German gothic (also called black-letter, or *textur*) type with Jugendstil illustrative work, he moved on to question the ornamental, working to a logic derived from modern industrial methods. Around 1900 his typographic ideas can be seen in the face he designed for Klingspor, Behrens Roman, which like Eckmann's, is a pen-drawn roman but less florid and more related to the German black-letter tradition. At about the same time, Behrens designed a book set in sans serif: Feste des Lebens was an abrupt break with the expected gothic of the *textur* variety, but can be seen as a precursor of the German evolution from black-letter to a reliance on bold sans serifs. Behrens's most famous work came in 1907 when he was commissioned to review the visual identity of AEG. It is a large multinational today, and still has an identity derived from the logotype of Behrens. From the graphic identity and how this should be applied, Behrens's work progressed through the products to buildings: the turbine factory of 1909 represented a seminal development in architecture in its extensive use of glass. His approach indicates how typography goes well beyond concerns about legibility/readability; it illustrates a wider purpose for typeface character.

The German interest in sans serif, as a modern development from the custom of heavy black-letter, was reflected elsewhere with a search for a sans face of the era, rather

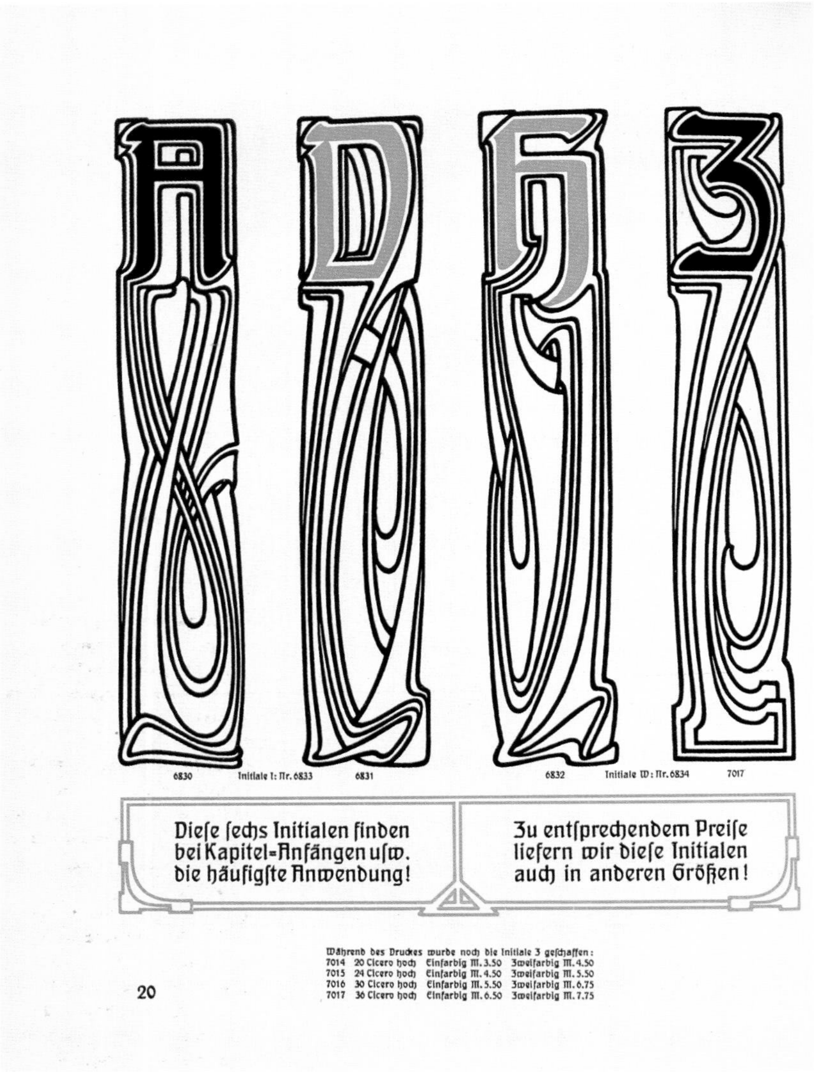

AEG
AEG

Left: Peter Behrens' contribution to the Jugendstil movement is marked by the initial letters he designed in 1900. However, it is the work that he did for the Allgemeine Elektrizitäts Gesellschaft, better known as the company AEG, that he is remembered for. As the architect overseeing everything from the design of the factory to the application of the logo (development above), he was a pioneer who influenced leading Modernists, including Gropius.

Above: the Wiener Werkstätte logo, which was probably designed by Koloman Moser, 1903, inverts a typographic mark Moser originally used to denote the two Ms in a title on a bookbinding he made in 1896.
Left: in 1905 a booklet was published carrying the marks of WW artists and craftsmen. Here, from top: Friedrich König, Adolf Böhm and Gustav Klimt.
Far left: design by Adalb Carl Fischl, 1900, rationalizes the alphabet forms within a set of angles and curves, but in the process loses legibility as the distinction between characters becomes seriously eroded.

than the numerous and largely undistinguished cuts amassed during the nineteenth century. The American Type Founders' (ATF) amalgamation of firms had about fifty "gothics" in its early specimen book, covering everything from extra-condensed to extra-extended. Yet one of the first faces Morris Fuller Benton (1872–1948) was asked to develop as their chief designer was a new sans. This drew on tradition, and on new market demand, as the face was targeted at the burgeoning requirements of advertising. Benton's drawings in 1902 amalgamated the qualities of the early nineteenth-century models: the resulting Franklin Gothic stands out in contrast to Stempel's Akzidenz Gothic of 1896 (another gothic destined to last throughout the twentieth century) by breaking from any regular line. Details such as the thinning of strokes where rounds join stems give a life to the face that distinguishes it from other heavy sans. It was released in 1905 and proved popular, with Benton cutting further weights besides the initial extra bold. Pushing out the whole family of ATF gothic faces (Alternate Gothic and News Gothic being just two other weight variants) was an early example of the type foundries' latching on to the printer's requirement for a full range of weights and sizes in one face, rather than odd sizes and weights of dramatically different cuts.

A different gothic was being drawn by the other prolific type designer of the period – Copperplate Gothic by Frederic Goudy (1865–1947), also for ATF. This, in fact, is not a gothic at all, in the sense of being either a bold sans face or a black-letter face (the word "gothic" in type description is

F

Franklin Gothic *24pt*

A B C D E F G H I J K L M N
O P Q R S T U V W X Y Z
a b c d e f g h i j k l m n
o p q r s t u v w x y z

g

News Gothic *24pt*

A B C D E F G H I J K L M N O P Q R S T U V W X Y Z
a b c d e f g h i j k l m n o p q r s t u v w x y z

applied to so many kinds of faces that it is all but useless). Instead it is a face that owes its reference to the forms of letters chiselled in stone, which are described as glyphic. Copperplate Gothic crosses boundaries: the serifs are so tiny as to be almost invisible in small sizes, merely helping hold the definition of character and converting the appearance to that of a sharp sans. The appearance is stylized, and the face was intended – and is still used – for titling and cards. It has found use in packaging, combining a crisp legibility with character. There is a subtle inflection of stroke weight – note the capital "C" – giving a dynamic that is missing with constant line sans serifs.

The type design and typographic development of this period took place against the gradual acceptance of the crucial role

KING
OF ALL TYPE
The Cheltenham Family
The sovereignty of the Cheltenhams in the big world of advertising has been thoroughly established. The growing popularity of the new members which have recently been added is an indication that this most pleasing type family will remain in favor for many years to come. When we consider the versatility and dignity of this monarch of display, we readily appreciate the reason for its phenomenal success. The progressive printers and publishers buying liberal weight fonts are certain to give the Cheltenhams first place in their composing rooms. Never in the history of type casting has the printing trade been presented with such variety and harmony in a single series of type faces. Its intrinsic worth and great adaptability is acknowledged by all. Sold in weight fonts at our regular body type prices

Opposite: Morris Fuller Benton's Franklin Gothic (drawings from 1902, released 1905) and News Gothic (1908) were among many faces he designed for American Type Founders. These aimed to serve the fast-growing demand for display advertising type. They draw on the handcut character of nineteenth-century wood letter, retaining a sense of individual, lively calligraphic form at the expense of geometric unity.
Right: Cheltenham, created by Bertram Goodhue in 1896, was a popular display type, remarkable not for any beauty, but for robustness and flexibility, being cut in many weights and sizes.

that hot-metal setting would come to play. At the end of the nineteenth century the launching of mechanized typesetting with the hot-metal machines of Linotype (1886) and Monotype in the 1890s formed the basis for the massive expansion in printed production, enabling much greater productivity in setting. These machines required their own proprietary faces to be cut for the matrices from which the hot-metal letters would be formed (as lines of type with Linotype, or as individual characters with Monotype; hence the names). While the Linotype had been enthusiastically received for the mass printing of newspapers and magazines (six thousand machines in place by 1900), the Monotype machine was now emerging as a genuine rival, offering qualities that could compare with cold-metal handcrafted

typesetting. In 1905 the Monotype caster was improved to cope with larger sizes – casting up to 24 point, albeit only able to compose up to 12 point. In 1907 Monotype developed with a faster keyboard, copying the typewriter layout, with extra keys.

Alongside this technology push, there were moves to make consistent standards in measurement. In America and Britain agreement was reached on the point system, though continental Europe still worked to a different measure, which made for some difficulties in the compatibility of faces and equipment. Although the points system was first proposed by Fournier in Paris in 1737, and later amended by Didot to a measurement of one point equalling 0.3759mm, it was only in 1886 that American foundries settled on a point size of 0.3515mm.

Despite its lack of decimal logic, the system often still applies, overlapping with metric and imperial measurements, and is a testament to industrial inertia. And that is a force at times as powerful as the revolutionary urges more typically covered in these pages.

Copperplate *24pt*

A B C D E F G H I J K L M N
O P Q R S T U V W X Y Z

Opposite: the American Type Founders Company, formed in 1892 from the merger of many type foundries, came to dominate the American type market with its breadth of choice, supported by strong marketing. Its substantial and durable catalogues not only demonstrated the fonts in the graphic styles of the day, but did so in a way that showed the variety of expression possible with a large family of cuts. This encouraged printers to consider buying different weights and sizes. Here News Gothic is put through its paces.
Left: Copperplate Gothic, designed in 1901 by Frederic Goudy and released by ATF, was not rated by its designer and indeed is a curious amalgam of traditions. It draws on stone-cut lettering in its technique of minute serifs, but lacks the appeal of glyphic precedents. However, the face is seen the world over in titles and cards because of the illusion of crisp form it delivers in small sizes through the near-invisible serifs.

1910

All a poet can do today is warn.

Wilfred Owen 1893-1918

"...we have entered upon a period of revolution which may last fifty years before the revolution is at last victorious in all Europe and finally all the world."

So the Russian Communist theoretician and economist Nikolai Bukharin commented in 1919 to the English writer Arthur Ransome. He was to be executed in 1938 as part of Stalin's purges of likely opposition. Ransome became a great author of children's books. And the political revolution they discussed? Perhaps that ended at various points: with the death of Lenin, the rise of Stalin, or gradually with each of the party bosses who stretched from the 1950s until Gorbachov and Yeltsin finally pulled the plug on Communist Russia in the 1980s and 1990s. But the age of revolution and its results remains.

By the time of the Great War and the Russian Revolution, the notion of revolution could no longer be an isolated explosion, as in the late eighteenth and nineteenth centuries. Communications of telegraph and press and (soon) radio, along with growing mass literacy, saw to the rapid and popular dissemination of dramatic news. The revolution in society brought about by the Great War, 1914–18, its reshaping and fracturing of countries and their societies, left marks that have never disappeared. We only have to look to Sarajevo: 1914 remixed in 1992–6.

But Bukharin's comment does not have to be read with any sense of irony about the subsequent tragic turns of history if matched against the revolution of the graphic arts that came to prominence in this decade.

Cubism and Futurism sprang to prominence, Suprematism and Constructivism extended the aesthetic revolution into pure abstractions, and in general "the isms of art" clocked up at a rapid rate. These idealist expressions of the changing times have continued to live with us since. Their effect was to challenge the ground rules of graphic production and design thinking, and whether embraced or reacted against they have helped define not just Modernism but the quest for a sense of what it is to be modern, working in art or communication in the twentieth century. That revolution took fifty years or less to impact on every city in the world. Bukharin, editor of both key Communist newspapers *Pravda* and *Izvestia* at various times, may have accepted his prediction as being accurate at least in its recognition of the internationalism and power of media.

By 1910 there were profound challenges across Europe to the assumptions about vision and language. This is most famously recognized in fine art with Cubism's violent fracturing of realism. The Cubism of Braque and Picasso compressed and analysed the planes involved in presenting three-dimensional forms, bringing in the fourth dimension of time to add to space. Objects could be viewed from more than one perspective in a single image. In their experiments with *papiers collés* montage constructions in 1911 and 1912 they introduced the sense of popular print and the abstraction of typographic communication into their work. The Italian Futurist painters Balla, Carra and Severini responded to this by also drawing on typographic materials, incorporating newspapers and other print into their work. The Futurist manifesto called for the expression of the dynamic forces at work in society, and the populism and ephemeral nature of mass-print was a daily manifestation of this energy.

The Futurist mission to question and shock was led by the writings and work of Filippo Tommaso Marinetti (1876–1944). Marinetti advocated the principle of "words-in-freedom". He challenged the need for orthodox language, both in its verbal and visual contexts. In his 1914 book *Zang Tumb Tumb* the idea found fresh typographic form, with stories/poems as visual/verbal exercises, doing with type what the Futurist artists were attempting in paint, collage and sculpture.

The basis for this work can be read in Marinetti's 1913 manifesto *Destruction of Syntax – Imagination without Strings – Words – Freedom*. Here he fires a verbal flame-thrower at Italian cultural history and then promises to set off his own fireworks to give a new force to the word:

"I initiate a typographic revolution aimed at the bestial nauseating idea of the book of passéist and D'Annunzian verse, on seventeenth-century handmade paper bordered with helmets, Minervas, Apollos, elaborate red initials, vegetables, mythological missal ribbons, epigraphs and Roman numerals. The book must be the Futurist expression of our Futurist thought. Not only that. My revolution is aimed at the so-called typographical harmony of the page, which is contrary to the ebb and flow, the leaps and bursts of style that run through the page. On the same page, therefore, we will use three or four colours of ink, or even twenty different typefaces if necessary. For example: italics for a series of similar or swift sensations, bold face for the violent onomatopoeias, and so on. With this typographical revolution and this multicoloured variety in the letters I mean to redouble the expressive force of words."[1]

Elsewhere Marinetti set down his notion of typography for the emerging medium of cinema.

"Filmed words-in-freedom in movement (synoptic tables of lyric values – dramas of humanised or animated letters – orthographic dramas – typographical dramas – geometric dramas – numeric sensibility, etc.)."[2]

Such clattering of words together is the equivalent of the conflicting, disintegrated elements within Futurist paintings, and of the discordant "music" performed by Marinetti, Soffici and Carlo Carra (1881–1966). The magazine *Lacerba* published a series of Carra's free-word experiments in 1914, "Tipografia in liberta", propagandizing a sense of purely expressive, unstructured typography that perhaps had to wait until the digital age for its full realization. The "dynamism" it sought to represent was that of the new industrial age, but it was not a dynamism that found easy accommodation in the fledgling mechanized type technology of the era. Instead, the long-standing craft of handsetting was still required to realize such free-word pieces: the machine-age aesthetic only found its individual form through handcrafting.

forme
geometriche
città moderne
STRADA
ORCHESTRA
RUMORI
traaak tatatraak
echi echi echi echi echi
LA ROSA
EVVIVAAA
MUSIC
cervellinmelma
ECHI
(Tokio)
ways biciclette
pedoni
Piazza
folle
TOT
EVVIVAAA
L'ESERCITO
COSTELLAZIONE per nuovi più acuti astronomi
siamo la PRIMA
NOI
viatore
battere il record
SPORTS
suoni ru- flatulenze
mori odori pesi calore
buttARE
Richiami
canzoni
calma
cose granitiche deserte
Amiciparenti
TRrrrrrrrrrrrr
TRBBBBBB
leggiero CARRÀ

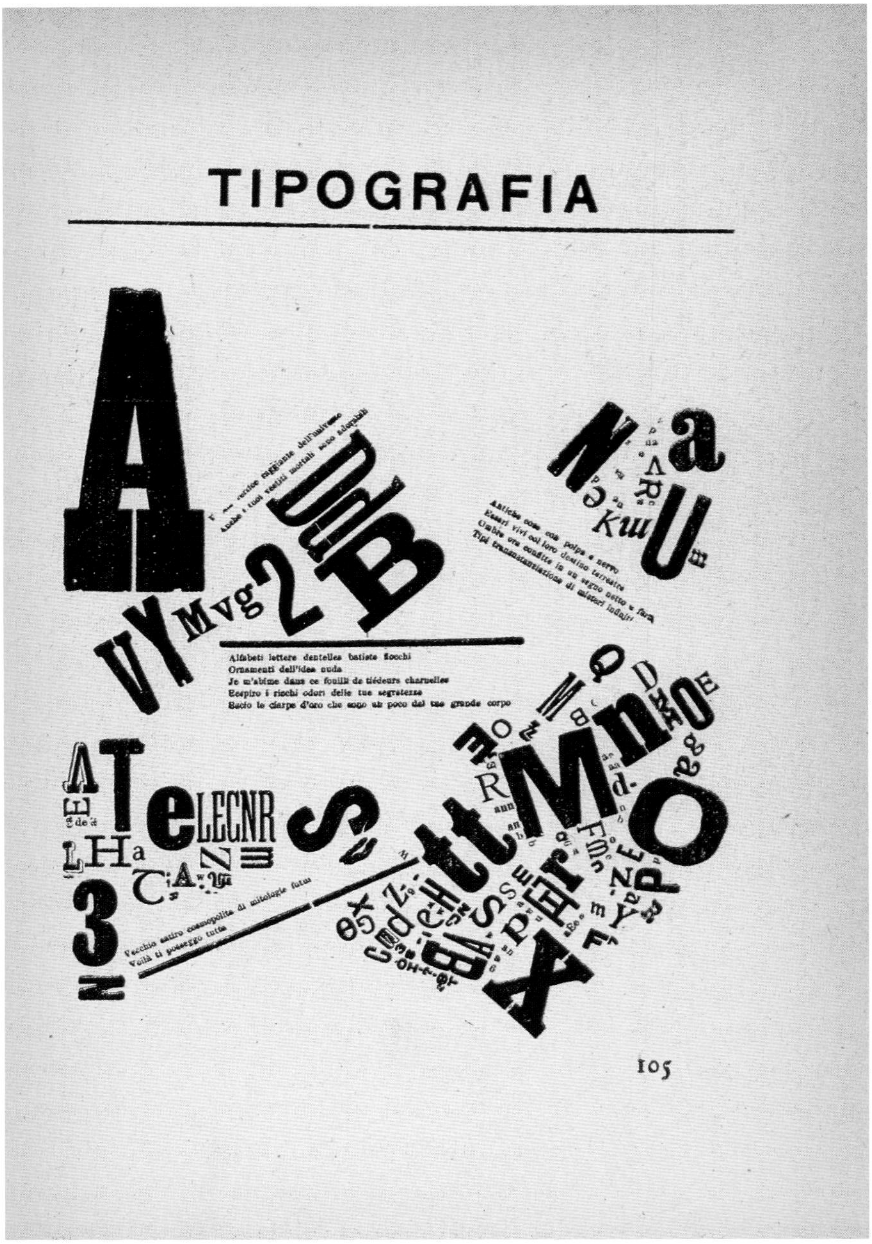

Previous page: *Manifestazione interventista* by Carlo Carra, 1914, a collage of paper and paint on board. The Italian Futurist painter explores the Futurist principles of dynamism, speed and conflict with techniques that put words into motion by using layers, rotation, and violent juxtaposition of elements to break free of both pictorial and text conventions. Above: war loans poster by Lucien Bernhard, 1915. This exemplifies the brutal simplicity of the German Plakatstil. Strong colours, one image, the advertiser's name, and a call-to-action copyline – ad rules that would become commonplace later.

Opposite right: page from *BIF & ZF + 18* by Ardengo Soffici, 1915, a book of typographical experiments using found and constructed imagery that aimed to reinvent literary communication. Soffici (1879–1964) was a painter and writer who had broken with the Italian Futurist group by this point. Below: cover and inside page of the novel *Zang Tumb Tumb*, 1914, by Filippo Marinetti. The Futurist leader explores his idea of "words-in-freedom" by taking a true story of an incident in the Balkan war of 1912 and telling it through free-form layouts that are full of typographic puns and word-plays, and challenge the linearity of reading.

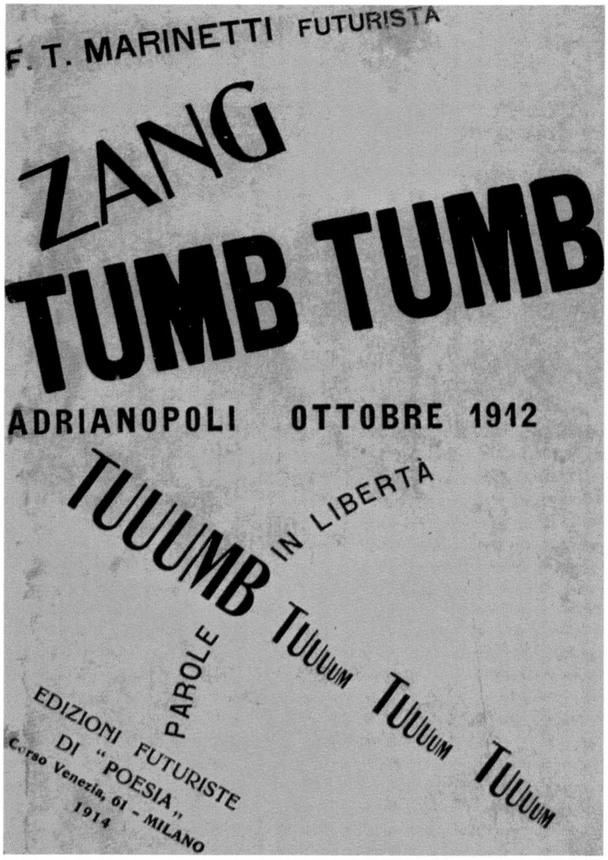

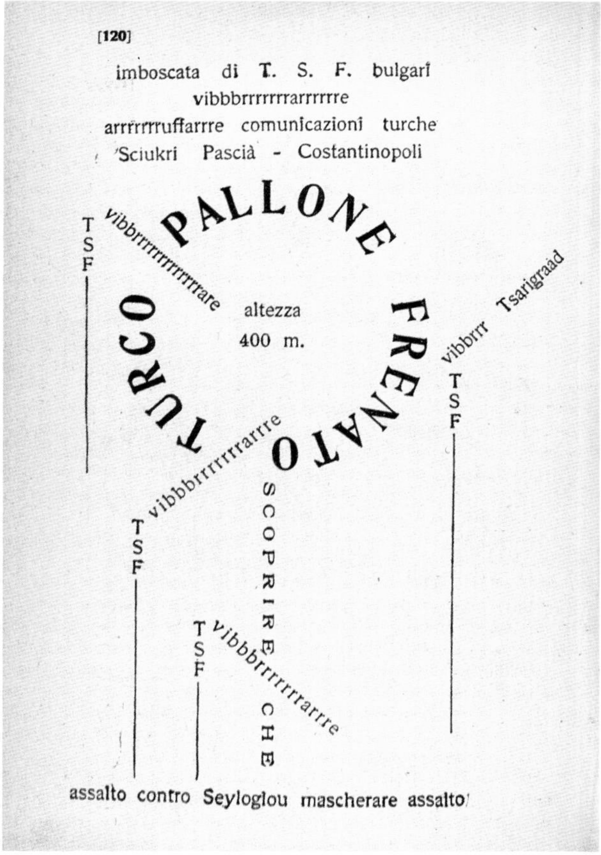

The Russian Futurists were substantially different from the Italian Futurists, having different roots and different results, but they were no less influential. They took inspiration from the Cubist break with representational traditions, but were unconnected with the Italian manifestos. Instead, their reaction was against Russian symbolist art and sought to revive some primitive forms as a rejection of Czarist culture. Between 1912 and 1916 the various artists loosely grouped under this banner combined to produce work that included several innovative books and other printed artefacts.

In what might seem a conundrum given our subject, these books are often distinguished by an absence of typography. Lithographic, with the artist's calligraphy as well as images, in effect they "painted" the page of the book, removing the need for typographical input and its restrictions. The adventures of design discovered in the free form given to the poster by lithography were extended into book form. The 1912 *Worldbackwards* and 1913 *Explodity* by Alexei Kruchenykh also used techniques such as rubber stamp blocks to print poems, accompanied by stencilling or potato-printing of key letters. Such Futurism seemed to be going in the opposite direction to the Italian movement, rejecting rather than embracing modern processes.

The most influential of Russian Futurist books did feature type. Vladimir Mayakovsky's *A Tragedy* varies type weight, has incongruous upper case and displays a dramatic use of white space to construct a visual metaphor for the emotive response sought from Mayakovksy's play. It was designed by Vladimir and David Burliuk, and includes their drawings. Thought to have been admired by Alexander Rodchenko (1891–1956) and El Lissitsky (1890–1941), the book can be seen as an antecedent of postwar, post-Revolution graphics.

Out of the Russian Futurists evolved other significant movements which were to probe the boundaries of typography further. Kasimir Malevich's Suprematist paintings from 1916, boldly non-figurative and geometric, provoked thought about the two-dimensional plane and its formal arrangements. This had a direct impact on El Lissitsky who found a link with typographic communication: his early Constructivist painting of 1919, *Beat the whites with the red wedge*, can be seen in direct connection with his children's story book *Of Two Squares* (conceived in 1920, published 1922), which explores typographic construction and its notions of narrative largely without conventional typographic elements.

Another passing influence on El Lissitsky (a nodal point in typography, whose own work and thought was to be so influential in the 1920s), was that of the English Vorticist movement, another Cubist/Futurist group. The propagandist periodical *Blast*, launched and designed in 1914 by the Vorticist leader Percy Wyndham Lewis (1882–1957), was seen as a direct precedent for Burliuk and Mayakovsky's 1915 publication *Vzyal: baraban futuristov* [*Took: a futurist's drum*], which like *Blast* featured a single declamatory word coarsely printed on the cover.

Following a separate path of typographic exploration were the Dadaists, who first appeared around the middle of the First World War in Zurich and then spread to German cities, and to Moscow and Paris. The poetry of Hugo Ball mixed typefaces in a deliberately illogical, nonsensical manner that parodied poetic form. His statement that "the word and the image are one" expresses this desire for a medium free of the mechanical and cultural constraints that beset print. Another key Dadaist, Kurt Schwitters (1887–1948), explored the textural and ironic implications of using printed ephemera. As early as 1919, in his series of works entitled *Merz*, he presented art culled from assorted, perhaps random, typographic communications. In 1919 Raoul Hausmann edited the first issue of the periodical *Der Dada*, with an expressive type cover that extended Futurist experiments. Hausmann, Hannah Hoech and (most notably) John Heartfield pioneered photomontage from 1917, a distinctive Dadaist questioning of the relationship between the representation of surface and space, two and three dimensions.

In Holland this decade saw the birth of the De Stijl movement, formed around the publication of the magazine *De Stijl* in 1917 by the painter, designer and writer Theo van Doesburg (1883–1931). The first cover sported a logotype based on a painting by Vilmos Huszár (1884–1960), which drew the characters in combinations of rectangles – an intimation of the mechanized and electronic signage typefaces used later in the century, as well as a theoretical statement about purity and reduction in form.

While the pioneers of Cubism, Picasso and Braque, did not directly link their art to communication art and typography, the French poet and critic and champion of the Cubists, Guillaume Apollinaire (1880–1918), made an influential connection between the new approach to art and the visual potential of words. He wrote calligrams – poems that used the type and layout of the page as an expressive element of the piece. There are precedents for this, notably Lewis Carroll's dwindling mouse tale/tail sentence and typographic pun in *Alice's Adventures In Wonderland* (1865) or Stéphane Mallarmé's layouts in *Un Coup de Des* (1897). They are part of an ongoing stream of literary self-consciousness with visual play that can be traced back at least as far as Laurence Sterne's wit-laden *Tristram Shandy* (1760). Another French writer experimenting with form around the time of Apollinaire was Blaise Cendrars; his 1913 "simultaneous" book *La Prose du Transsiberien et de la petite Jehanne de France* was a two-metre long poem, printed in different colours and type sizes. He dispensed with the neutral page background by having the poem printed over an abstract painting specially designed by Sonia Delaunay.

The various movements outlined above had no direct effect on mainstream communications – they were creating art pieces. However, the questions they raised can be seen to feed through to commercial activity within a decade. Their questioning of conservative typographic form, where words on a page were presented either formulaically or in a manner aimed to smooth and please the eye, led them to devise methods that would serve the fast-expanding needs of advertising where the ability to arrest and provoke the eye was vital.

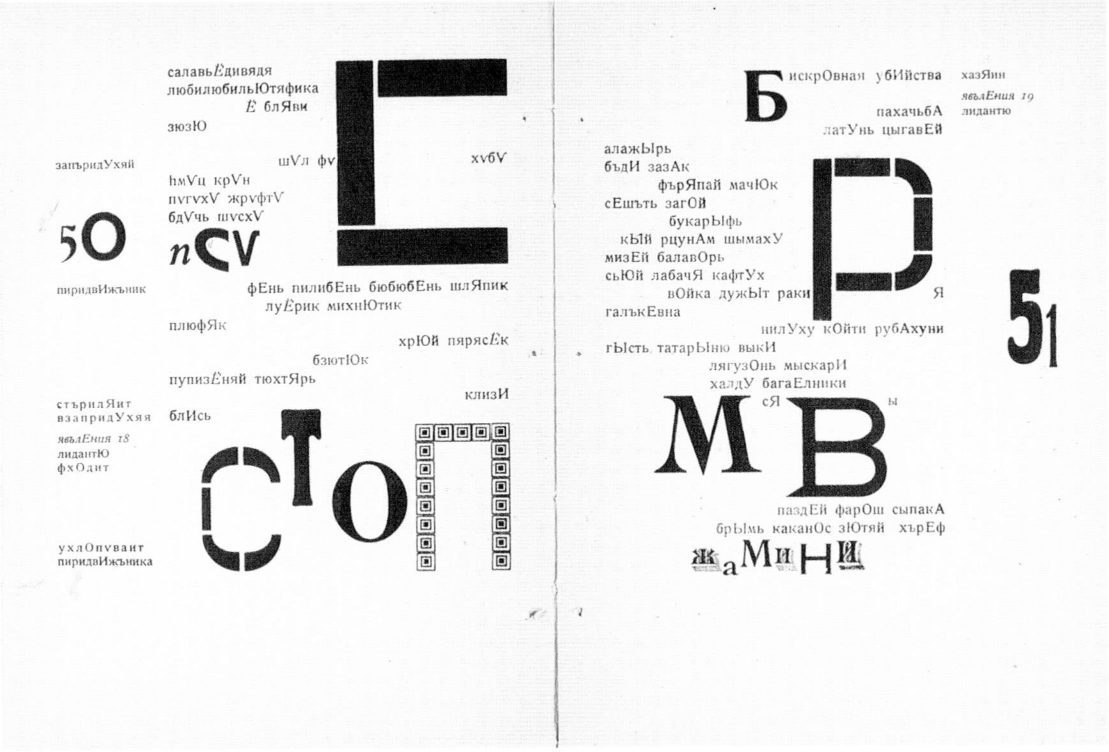

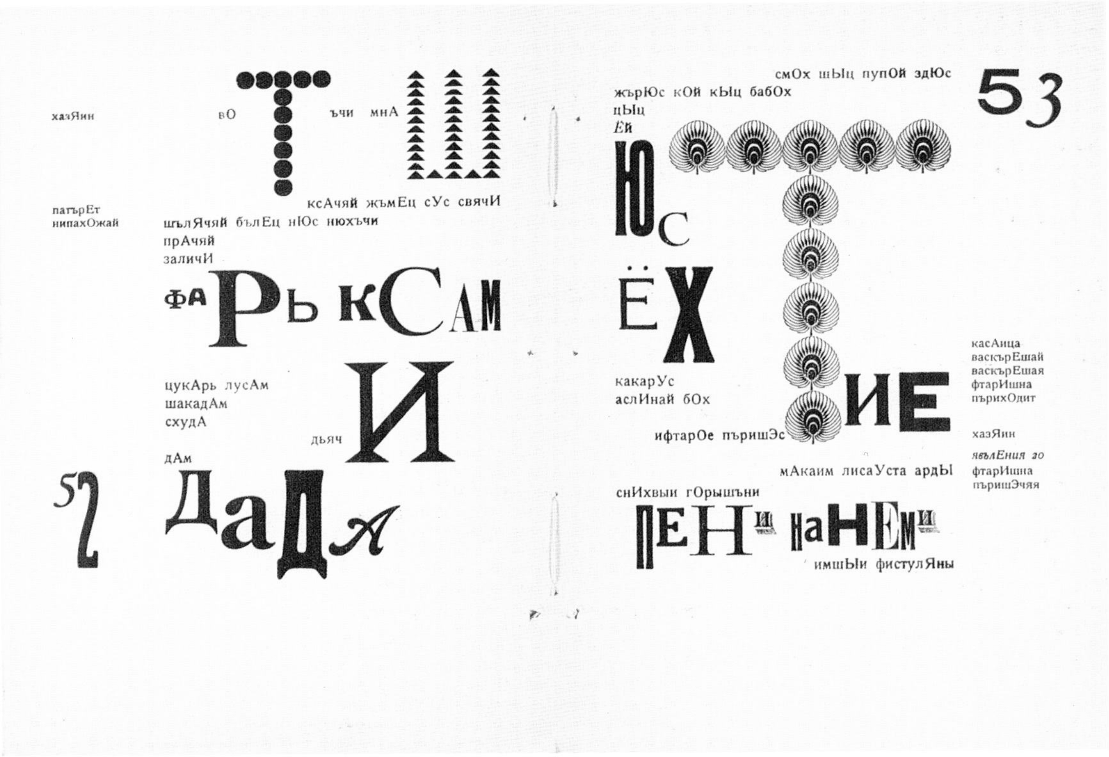

Left: two consecutive spreads from *Le-Dantyu as a Beacon* by Ilya Zdanevich, a drama about art involving two painters and offering multiple readings. It included obscene double meanings. Zdanevich (1894-1975) was a Russian Futurist who from 1910 onwards helped to develop the idea of "zaum" – a theory of "transrational language" that took words and other forms of expression beyond their conventional use. In the play, each spread can have several possible readings. Although Zdanevich began his dramatic works in Tbilisi, Georgia, this volume was not produced in Paris until 1923.

While these revolutionary ideas were filtering through, the world of commercial typography was seeing a concerted effort to improve standards by reviving classic faces or forms. This revivalism is a key theme of the century's typography, with waves of rediscovery adding layers of historical reference to the typographic culture.

The pace of technological change was quickening, particularly with the refinement of typesetting machines. In 1911 the Linotype was developed to carry three magazines of matrices at once, the different fonts interchangeable at the press of a lever. In the same year this was increased to four magazines, and almost annual announcements pushed the technology forward (a forerunner of the technology upgrades familiar with software and hardware today). Linotype's developments were not a result of curiosity but competition. And Monotype was not the only competitor; in 1912 Intertype launched a rival linecasting system following the expiry of the Mergenthaler patent on the basic system. In 1918 the *New York Times* ordered Intertype casters, firmly establishing the company. Headline setting was outside the capabilities of the Linotype and Monotype, still requiring wood-letter. But the launch of the Ludlow machine for casting from hand-assembled large-character matrices pointed the way forward and heralded the decline of the wood-letter industry and its skills in hand-cut letters.

Meanwhile, Monotype was strengthening its grip on fine machine typesetting, with developments including the increase of point size capability to 24 point in 1914. But

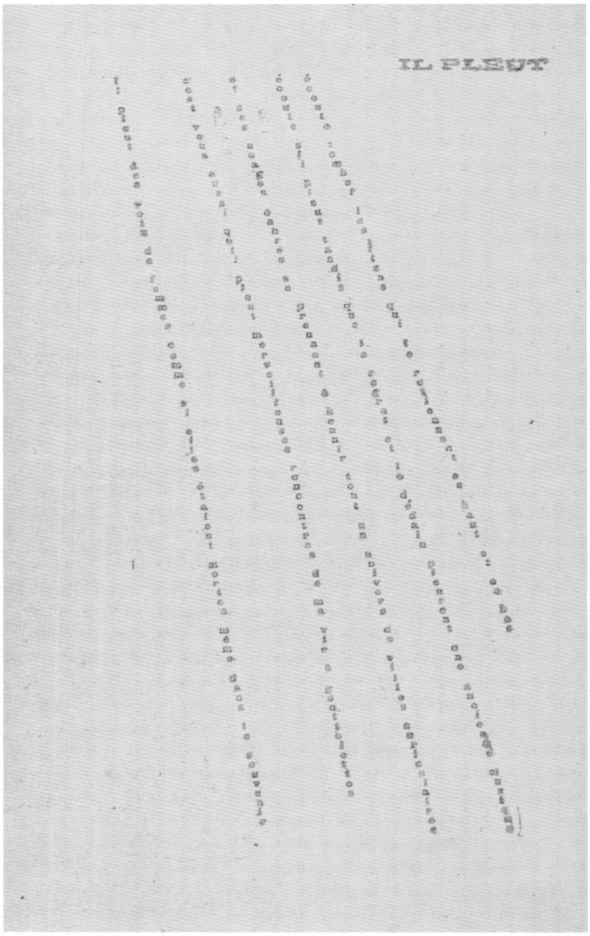

1

BLAST First (from politeness) ENGLAND

CURSE ITS CLIMATE FOR ITS SINS AND INFECTIONS

DISMAL SYMBOL, SET round our bodies,
of effeminate lout within.

VICTORIAN VAMPIRE, the LONDON cloud sucks
the TOWN'S heart.

A 1000 MILE LONG, 2 KILOMETER Deep

BODY OF WATER even, is pushed against us
from the Floridas, TO MAKE US MILD.

OFFICIOUS MOUNTAINS keep back DRASTIC WINDS

SO MUCH VAST MACHINERY TO PRODUCE

THE CURATE of "Eltham"
BRITANNIC ÆSTHETE
WILD NATURE CRANK
DOMESTICATED
POLICEMAN
LONDON COLISEUM
SOCIALIST-PLAYWRIGHT
DALY'S MUSICAL COMEDY
GAIETY CHORUS GIRL
TONKS

Van Doesburg *40pt*

ABBCDEFGH
IJKLMNOPQ
RSTUVWXYZ

From opposite left: "Il Pleut", a calligram by the poet Guillaume Apollinaire, 1918, drew on ancient texts as well as contemporary experiments. The first issue of *Blast*, 1914, edited and designed by Percy Wyndham Lewis. This was the Vorticist bid to free words (with nineteenth-century wood letter). Above is a 1919 alphabet by Theo van Doesburg based on a square of 25 equal parts. Drawn as a font by The Foundry, 1990s.

perhaps the most significant creative development was Monotype's cutting of Imprint in 1913, the first face specifically developed for machine setting. It was named after a new magazine dedicated to typography, and the type design was by the magazine's editors and founders, Gerard Meynell and J.H. Mason, working with F. Ernest Jackson and Edward Johnston. The face had a large x-height, and a thickened and very regular italic, features designed for the robust requirements of machine setting and printing.

The short-lived *Imprint* magazine and the setting up of the American Institute of Graphic Arts in 1914 signified a new awareness of the role of the graphic designer, as separate from the skills of the type compositor and printer. It was also in this period that the likes of Frederic Goudy and Bruce Rogers (1870–1957) emerged as eminent figures in their field in America, with Rudolf Koch (1876–1934) and Edward Johnston (1872–1934) in Europe. The type designer could now separate from the printer/foundry, albeit needing a commission or outlet for the manufacture of a typeface. Goudy's prolific work for ATF involved a range of loose revivals, remixing various historical sources through his eye and craft, with occasional commercial pressures brought to bear by the manufacturer (for example, the short ascenders in Goudy Old Style of 1914, a compromise sought by ATF).

The combination of immense calligraphic skill and a new typographic sensibility was apparent in the work of Koch

Right: Centaur, designed in 1914 by Bruce Rogers for publications of the Metropolitan Museum in New York, took its name from being the face for Maurice de Guérin's *The Centaur*, published by Montague Press in 1915. A revival of the fifteenth-century Jenson, it has been widely admired but rarely used – perhaps because its prettiness only bears up under fine printing and then impedes easy reading. It was finally fully released by Monotype in 1929, with an italic. Below right: Imprint was described as the first original face for mechanized typesetting. This Monotype face draws on the eighteenth-century Caslon, but has a larger x-height and thickened strokes for durability. Opposite top: Plantin, a 1913 revival from Monotype based on a sixteenth century Dutch master. Opposite: Underground type by Edward Johnston, 1916, still in use (in its New Johnston digital form) on the London underground system. The first Modern sans serif? Consistent line is relieved by varied characteristics such as a diamond over the "i" and "j", and the uneven "t" bar.

Centaur *24pt*

ABCDEFGHIJKL
MNOPQRSTUVWXYZ
abcdefghijklmnop
qrstuvwxyz

K

Z

Imprint *18pt*

ABCDEFGHIJKLMNOPQRSTUVWXYZ
abcdefghijklmnopqrstuvwxyz

(designer of Frühling and Maximilian in this decade, among others) and Johnston, whose key typographic achievement is the remarkable sans serif he designed for the London Underground in 1916. This broke with Victorian sans serif precedents by applying a strict classical awareness of forms to the letters, involving an integration of geometric thinking that anticipated the work to be produced in the 1920s. In its new digital form, it still exists in use as the identity typeface of the London underground system. While it has never been openly available, it soon had an influence on other seminal faces, such as Futura and Gill, while Johnston's knowledge of calligraphy was an inspiration to the young Jan Tschichold.

There was a growing awareness of the need to revive the typographic heritage for the new technology. From 1912 the extensive culture of re-making Garamond began, first at the Parisian foundry Deberny & Peignot, and in the years after at all other major foundries. Put together, the faces show cultural similarities, but also remarkable variations. In effect, Garamond was a reference point and aspiration for a range of new cuts, an ideal to be expressed or a label to be exploited rather than a simple act of faithful copying. Such are remixes.

Plantin *18pt*

ABCDEFGHIJKL
MNOPQRSTUVWXYZ
abcdefghijklmnop
qrstuvwxyz

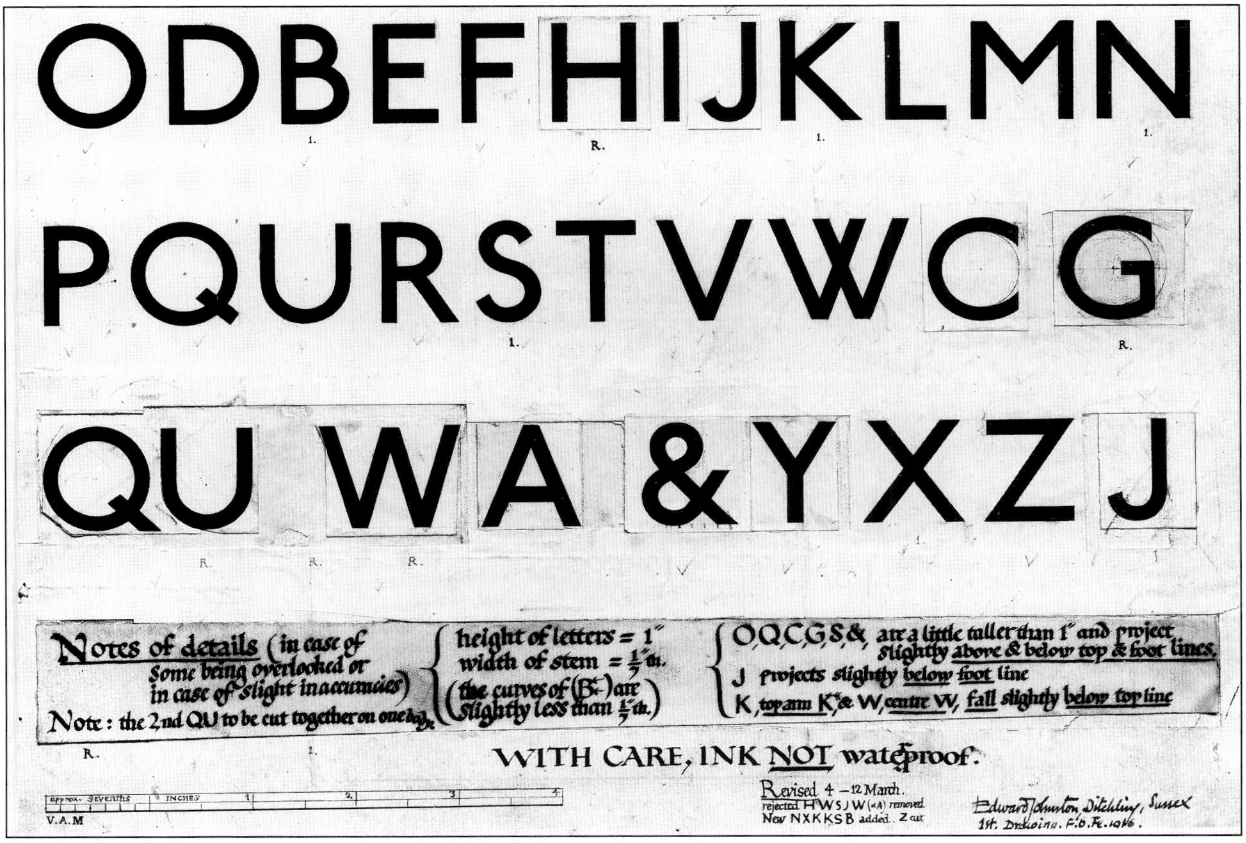

FUT

URE

The manifestos for much that has happened in graphic design this century were written and visualized in the 1920s. The decade saw a ferment of both radical and conservative typographic ideas. From the experimental came a sense of the Modern, that would soon filter into advertising and other commercial usage; meanwhile, the peaks of typographic history were revived by traditionalists as representing values that needed to be restored. The ideas and activities of these years reveal the emerging significance of typography, its position in the flux of creativity between fine art and architecture, and its value as a crucial political and commercial tool.

At the centre of the emergence of a new typography was the Bauhaus. The work produced by its teachers and students, and by others associated with them or influenced by them, came through a synthesis of the new ideas in art. This radically new school, which taught architecture and the applied arts as interdisciplinary subjects, was founded in Weimar in 1919. Das Staatliches Bauhaus emerged from an earlier, prewar school that had been run by the Belgian architect and designer Henry Van de Velde, renowned for his influential contribution to Art Nouveau. But the agenda of the new school's director, the architect Walter Gropius, a former assistant of Peter Behrens, projected a philosophy that expressed and expanded the emerging Modernist sensibility, in which the integration of art and technology and the development of a mass-production aesthetic were vital. The school's lifespan of 1919 to 1933 mirrored that of the Weimar Republic, and its struggles reflected those of the years – it fought for funds, moved three times in fourteen years and was regularly attacked for its socialist politics.

Typography was not fully a part of the initial Bauhaus programme. The first leader of the Bauhaus's preliminary course, Johannes Itten, included lettering skills and produced some Dada-influenced typographic art of his own, but it was with the arrival in 1923 of László Moholy-Nagy (1895–1946) to run the preliminary course that the Bauhaus began to make a significant statement in graphics; indeed, it helped forge the idea of graphic design studies. His five years at the college produced a body of work and publications that set down ideas that were to spread around the world. This period saw graphic design, photography and film take a more prominent role in the output of the Bauhaus than they had before or would afterwards, a direct result of Moholy-Nagy's teaching. Gropius had set up the school's teaching structure from the viewpoint that architecture was the ultimate objective and thus building was the final course of study, following on from the other applied arts. His successors in the role of director – first Hannes Meyer, in 1928, and then Mies van der Rohe, in 1930 – further emphasized the architectural content of the school programme. However, Gropius reached out from his own architectural background to create a school that made a major contribution to the development of graphics, products, furniture and fine art as well as architecture. Teachers such as Paul Klee, Wassily Kandinsky and Lyonel Feininger in painting, and the outside influences of other artists such as van Doesburg and El Lissitsky, ensured a dramatic and eclectic contribution to new ideas in two-dimensional communication.

In 1923 Moholy-Nagy called for "absolute clarity in all typographical work". He argued that:

"Communication ought not to labour under preconceived aesthetic notions. Letters should never be squeezed into an arbitrary shape – like a square.... A new typographic language must be created, combining elasticity, variety and a fresh approach to the materials of printing, a language whose logic depends on the appropriate application of the processes of printing."[1]

At the forefront of Moholy-Nagy's graphics output was the Bauhaus books series from 1923. His advertising for the books incorporated Constructivist and De Stijl ideas – the elements of the page such as rules, full points and blocks of text, colour and white space are organized asymmetrically on modular grids (as opposed to traditional centring on linear grids) and are suggestive of the paintings of van Doesburg and Mondrian. The covers, which worked as a series but had different arrangements, stripped down the design to elements that were purely typographic and arranged these so boldly as to be a statement at least as strong as the meaning of the words displayed.

For all its self-consciousness and relationship with ideas in related art movements, this work is among the first examples of a commercially relevant new typography, showing a move from the more strident art statements of Futurist, then Dada, De Stijl and Constructivist typography. More than being idealistic manifestos, the Bauhaus books, and following work from the printshop and advertising course, were a stepping stone into relating these ideas to mass communication.

In his 1925 essay on "Contemporary Typography – Aims, Practice, Criticism", Moholy-Nagy anticipated the replacement of much typographic communication by sound recordings and film images. In response, typography needed to raise itself to a new level of expressive power and effectiveness. This involved embracing and developing the machine age in print production, and moving on from the period of experimental typography that used old technology to express new ideas (which would seem to criticize the Futurists and De Stijl artists) to a more serious grasping of new technology and the new visual experiences of the age. He looked forward to the pages of grey text being transformed into colourful narratives, and being conceived of as a dramatic whole so that individual pages were part of a sequence much like film frames. In this he was a prophet of debates surrounding new media in the 1990s.

In the essay Moholy-Nagy went on to outline principles of new typographic practice. Tension was to be introduced into layouts by contrasting visual elements – such as empty/full, light/dark, multicoloured/grey, vertical/horizontal, upright/oblique – and these were to be achieved chiefly through the disposition of type. Typographic signs were also an element, but not as ornamental borders and the like so

DER OFFSET-VERLAG.G.M.B.H.LEIPZIG
OFFSET
BUCH UND WERBEKUNST
HEFT 7
1926
ENTWURF: JOOST SCHMIDT. BAUHAUS IN DESSAU
BAUHAUS-HEFT
HOFBUCHDRUCKEREI VON C. DÜNNHAUPT G.M.B.H. DESSAU

Left: cover of issue number seven of *Offset Buch und Werbekunst*, 1926, designed by Herbert Bayer. The rapid growth of interest in the work of the Bauhaus was confirmed by this printing industry magazine devoting a special number to it.

beloved of the traditional printshop and typical of the vernacular ephemera.

Moholy-Nagy said there was a need for a standard form of writing, a single design without the two sets of letters involved in lower case and capitals. He lamented the lack of a typeface that had correct proportions, was purely functional and without individual flourish. Attempts at such faces were drawn by Bauhaus students – notably in 1925 by a Bauhaus colleague and former student, Herbert Bayer (1900–85).

Bayer was the first head of a new typography workshop at the Bauhaus, which was established in 1925 when the school moved to Dessau. He held the post until 1928, when he resigned along with Gropius and Moholy-Nagy. As a student he displayed a bold clarity in his work and an integration of the ideas of De Stijl and Constructivist thought. His banknotes for the State of Thuringia, produced in 1923, can be seen as an early signpost of the distinctive Bauhaus look that emerged in graphics. Such a notion of a style dismayed Gropius, who was against the superficial thought implied by the concept of style. But being seen to have a style was inevitable due to the contrast between the new Bauhaus notions of typographic form and those of tradition, particularly the conservatism of German printing with its emphasis on dense black-letter.

Bayer's minimalist sans serif face was one of a number of proposals for such a reductive typeface – others included van Doesburg's alphabet of 1919 and Tschichold's universal

Albers *24pt*

ABCDEFGHIJKLMNOPQRSTUVWXYZ
abcdefghijklmnopqrstuvwxyz

lettering a few years later – but it had the benefit of being preached through the Bauhaus course. The argument for a single alphabet was based on the fact that the upper case is not heard, but is only seen. It made written language and its presentation more complex and expensive, demanded more effort in the learning and then in the setting as well as the typesetter's carrying of more characters. Bauhaus publications began dropping the use of capitals from this time. Bayer's single alphabet proposal is distinctive for generating its forms from a declared reductive range of a few angles, arcs and selected lines. This results in a simplicity in which the "m" and "w" are the same inverted, and the "x" is little more than an "o" cut in half and turned inside-out. Bayer developed a number of experimental typefaces in the period 1925–27, mostly of interest only for display purposes, such as a semi-abstract shadow typeface in which the shadow was all that was left, all the initial outline being removed as unnecessary to the suggestion of the form. His type design ideas finally emerged into the harsh light of commercial availability as Bayer-type for Berthold in 1935, but it was notably conservative, a condensed didone with short descenders and a rather fussy character, a long way from the ideas pioneered at the Bauhaus.

For all the Bauhaus' aspirations to a machine-age aesthetic, the printing workshop under Bayer was restricted pretty much to the old technology of hand-setting. (This provides a neat paradigm for the work of Modernist architects of the period who sometimes simulated the plasticity of concrete, steel and glass forms by rendering over brick or stone.) A

Bayer *48pt*

abcdefghijk
lmnopqrstu
vwxyz

Opposite: 1925 design for stencil lettering by Josef Albers (1888-1976), who taught at the Bauhaus from 1923 until it closed in 1933. Albers reduced his alphabet to geometric shapes drawn out of a grid, with the square, the triangle and the circle as the elements (plus the double line for a crossbar). Below the original drawing is a 1990s digital version from The Foundry.
Left: design for a single alphabet by Herbert Bayer, 1925. The geometric reduction of form here sees a consistent arc become a dominant element of characters. Only the "T" is retained from distinct upper-case letterforms.

sans serif face existed in a number of sizes for hand-setting, which could be printed on a platen (flat-bed) press or a rotary proof press. All the printed materials needed by the college – forms, brochures and posters – came from the print department, produced to designs by Bayer or students.

Bayer's teaching was not formal; instead he directed the work of students on real commissions that were pulled into the department. Advertising was of particular interest to Bayer and he promoted ideas on the psychology of advertising and its relationship to the consciousness. The importance of placing arresting and symbolic elements into typographic form was made apparent. The primacy of red and black in two-colour printing, the power of dynamic white space (rather than static borders), highly contrasted type

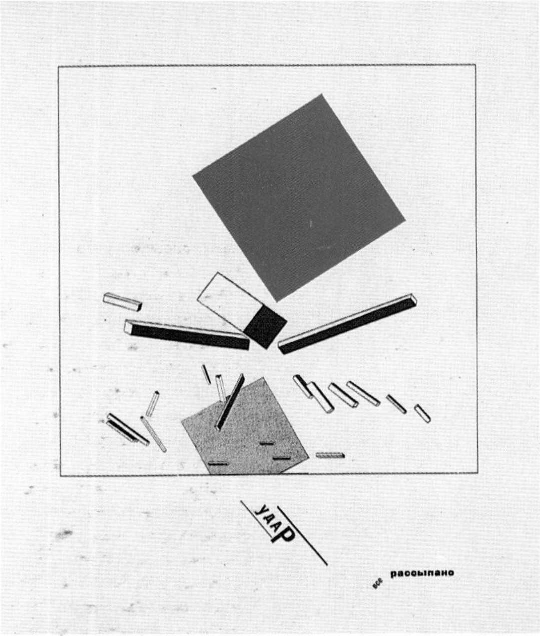

sizes used to express relative values of information and the growing use of photomontage and collage elements were all recognized as key concepts. Bayer's determination that work should contribute to a mass-production age meant that he had all work carried out to standard DIN (German standards authority) sizes of paper.

Bayer was succeeded in 1928 by Joost Schmidt (1893–1948), under whom the printing workshop changed its name to the advertising workshop, revealing how significant this new discipline was to the Bauhaus – it was not possible to train elsewhere in advertising. There was even more emphasis on bringing in outside projects, and Schmidt pushed the Bayer/Moholy-Nagy line – investigating ideas of incorporating photography and the power of high contrast elements in form and colour. Schmidt encouraged a slightly wider range of typefaces and evolved grids that moved away from the strictly modular, experimenting more with overlaying one simple pattern on another to create dynamic complexities. In Schmidt's time typography became more strongly a part of the Bauhaus core curriculum, being taught over two terms of the preliminary course.

Prior to the Bauhaus becoming typographically energetic, and during its main period of activity in this area (1923–30), there were significant contributions to Modernist graphic communication in the Soviet Union, Holland, elsewhere in Germany, in Poland, Czechoslovakia and Hungary. In the recently established Soviet Union, a whole cluster of artists were exploring new ideas about photomontage and type

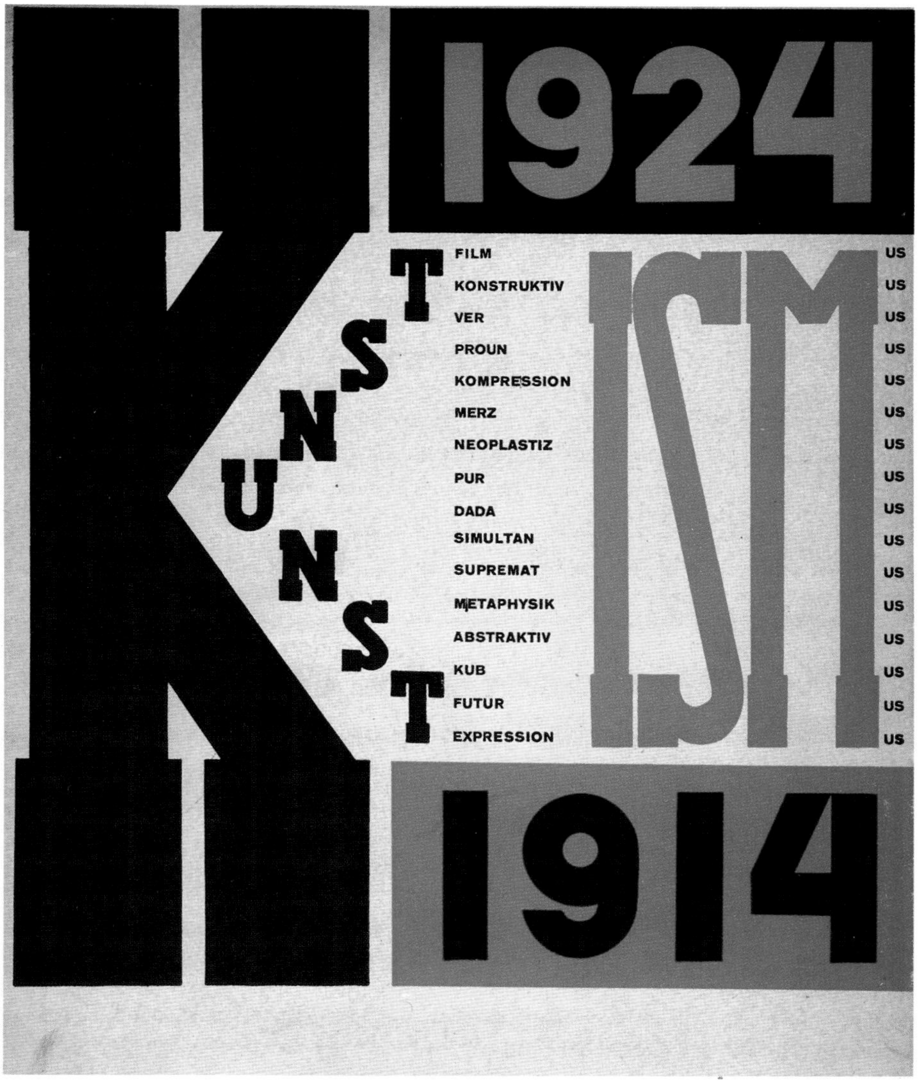

Opposite: cover and sample spread from *Of Two Squares* by El Lissitsky, typographical "paintings" constructed in 1920 and printed as a 24-page book in 1922. These Suprematist works, Prouns, were produced in a period in which Lissitsky taught with Kazimir Malevich at the Vitebsk art school, where they launched a radical programme in 1919, renaming the institution Unovis as they propounded Suprematist ideals that unified Cubist and Futurist thinking. The book takes Malevich's idea of the square as the generator of form, presenting a child's story of two squares coming to earth and colliding with black shapes. The red, of course, is triumphant.
Left: cover of *Die Kunstismus [The Isms Of Art]* by El Lissitsky and Hans Arp, 1925. An attempt to summarize the art movements of 1914-24, the book is an interesting artwork in its own right. Lissitsky's layout is locked to a reductive grid of three columns per page, one for each of the three languages used. Akzidenz Grotesk bold, with minimal size variation, is used.

p.47

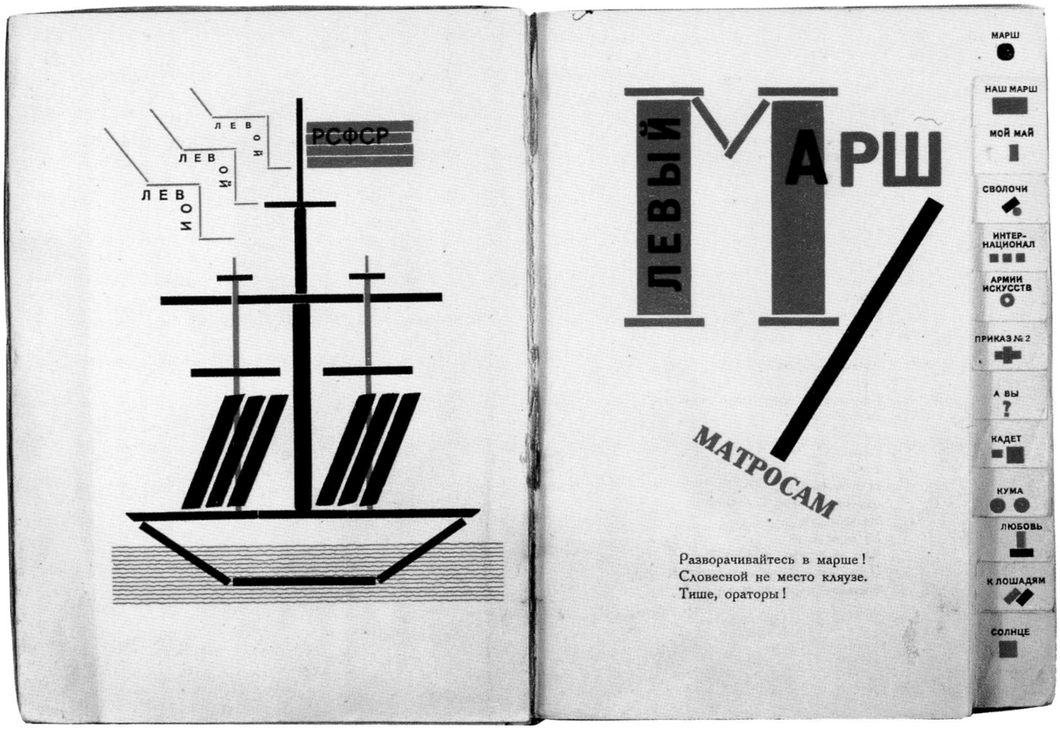
ЛЕВ ОЙ
ЛЕВ ОЙ
ЛЕВ ОЙ
РСФСР
ЛЕВЫЙ МАРШ
МАТРОСАМ
Разворачивайтесь в марше!
Словесной не место кляузе.
Тише, ораторы!
МАРШ
НАШ МАРШ
МОЙ МАЙ
СВОЛОЧИ
ИНТЕР-НАЦИОНАЛ
АРМИИ ИСКУССТВ
ПРИКАЗ № 2
А ВЫ
КАДЕТ
КУМА
ЛЮБОВЬ
К ЛОШАДЯМ
СОЛНЦЕ

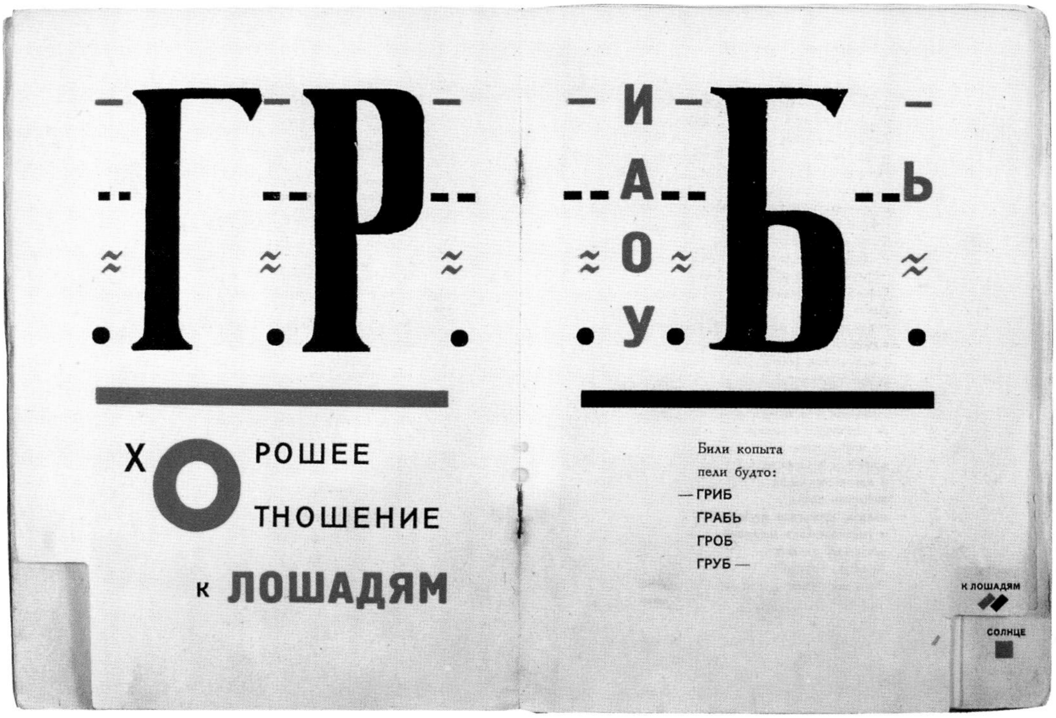
Г Р
И А О У Б Ь
ХОРОШЕЕ ОТНОШЕНИЕ к ЛОШАДЯМ
Били копыта
пели будто:
— ГРИБ
ГРАБЬ
ГРОБ
ГРУБ —
К ЛОШАДЯМ
СОЛНЦЕ

elements in the development of political and commercial design in the 1920s. Chief among them were Lissitsky and Rodchenko.

Lissitsky influenced Moholy-Nagy and van Doesburg, whom he met regularly in the early 1920s. His work varies between the locked-up elements packed into the pages of *The Isms of Art* of 1925 and the light, spare statements involved in his design for Mayakovsky's poems *For Reading Out Loud* in 1923 or Lissitsky's own *Of Two Squares*, his 1920 Suprematist children's story book that explores the relationship between the fourth dimension – time – the three dimensions of the book and the two dimensions of the page. Lissitsky's ideas partly evolved and were propagated through innovative Soviet art schools (Vkhutemas and Vitebsk) where he was brought in by Kandinsky and Chagall. Here the crossover of innovative ideas in graphic design and the fine art world was at its most fluid, with questions relating to colour, abstraction, form and space being applicable to both, as was the discussion of the social relevance of such debate. The new typographic and illustrative forms that were derived from this teaching can be seen in the poster culture of Moscow in the 1920s.

Rodchenko pushed the integration of photography and type: his mastery of both elements gives his posters a powerful, direct quality. His originality in photography was combined with a sensitivity to the point of focus on type: confrontational slabs of type, with colour integrating word and image, challenge the viewer to find connections and interpret

Opposite: two spreads from *For Reading Out Loud*, a collection of poems by Vladimir Mayakovsky, designed by El Lissitsky and published in Berlin in 1923. Each spread is a poem, and the die-cut tabs help the reader recognize where each one is located, being in alphabetical order with a symbol linking to the page content. Only materials readily available at the typesetter were used, thus illustrations such as the ship and even the inclusion of large characters required rules and bars and other devices to be employed. Besides the constructions, the dynamic white space also stood out. Right: advertisement for GUM, Moscow's state department store, designed by Aleksandr Rodchenko with text by Mayakovsky, 1923. This Constructivist image is built from blocks of type and product shots to make a figure that says Mozer are the only watches worth having, to be found at GUM.

documentary stories between pictures or typographic elements.

De Stijl and Dada continued to evolve in the 1920s. Theo van Doesburg, a seminal figure in both movements, lived in Weimar between 1921 and 1923 and conducted lectures attended mostly by Bauhaus students. He saw his lectures as a directly subversive element to be spread among the students and to take root within Gropius's system. In 1922 he published the first issue of *Mecano*, a Dadaist journal. Its eclectic mix of elements contrasts with the purer form of the De Stijl magazine that he brought out and which can be seen, along with Lissitsky's work, as the clearest influence on Moholy-Nagy's ideas at the Bauhaus. Like Lissitsky and then Moholy-Nagy, van Doesburg was among the first to be concerned with creating a new plasticity in print. They all sensed the potential of new technology and the significance of film and broadcast communication.

Kurt Schwitters was close to Lissitsky and van Doesburg in the early 1920s, his work presenting a different synthesis of Dada, De Stijl and Constructivism. His *Merz* assemblages from 1919 evolved into a journal of the same name that ran from 1923 until 1932. Issues featured contributions from influential figures from these movements, including an edition in 1924 that was jointly edited with Lissitsky and a later edition devoted to advertising typography. There is more humour in Schwitters's work than in that of his contemporaries; form and spatial ideas drawn from Lissitsky are mixed with the Dadaist sense of experimentation for

disruption's sake. Underlying Schwitters's designs there seems to be a sense of the dislocation required in effective poster and cover art, akin to the "defamiliarization" espoused by Russian Formalist literary theoretician Viktor Shklovsky as a central element of the emerging Modernist consciousness of art. Schwitters's methods, such as laying type over the bold rules that establish the grid, interrupting blocks with other lines or inserting pictures in seemingly unbalanced asymmetrical layouts pick up the ideas of a new typography and begin to disrupt them in a way similar to what had been done with the traditional forms.

Another innovator, working largely in isolation from the seed beds of change, was the printer-typographer Hendrik Werkman (1882–1945). After becoming aware of the new art

Opposite: *Small Dada Evening*, a poster by Theo van Doesburg and Kurt Schwitters, 1922. Hand-lettering with dramatic contrasts of size and weight, mixed with type, and with printer's marks (the hand, the border), may seem anarchistic, but involves the origin of new rules – the diagonal is used as a dynamic, tension-making device, the lettering blocks against the headlines and the red DADA provide a clear hierarchy of typographic communication. Left: Kurt Schwitters' single alphabet of 1927 tried to link sounds closer to forms. He played with heavier forms for vowels, and different versions. The full alphabet here is a 1990s digital recut produced by The Foundry, with variants. Bottom: *Merz 8/9* magazine cover by Schwitters, 1924.

Schwitters *28pt*

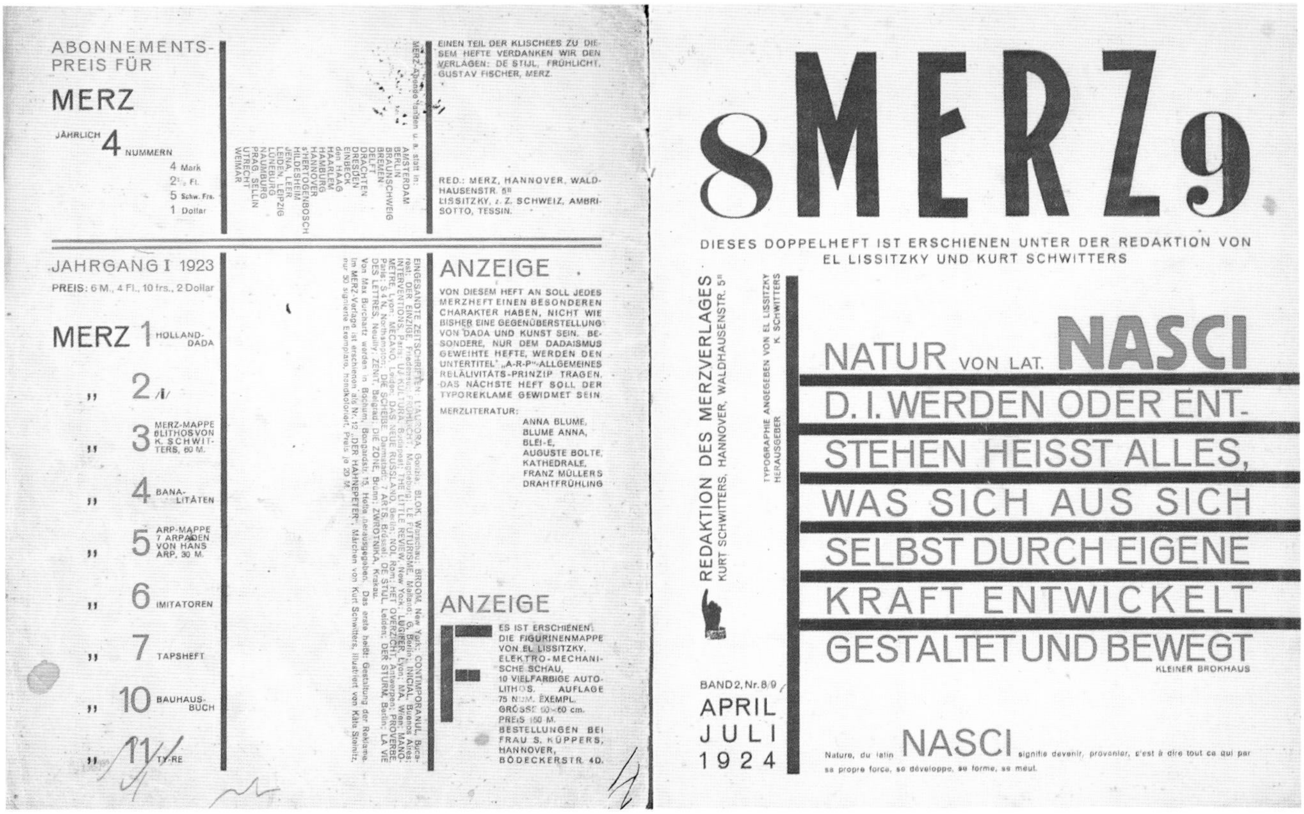
ABONNEMENTS-PREIS FÜR

MERZ

JÄHRLICH 4 NUMMERN

4 Mark
2½ Fl.
5 Schw. Frs.
1 Dollar

MERZ-Abende fanden u. a. statt in:
AMSTERDAM
BERLIN
BRAUNSCHWEIG
BREMEN
DELFT
DRACHTEN
DRESDEN
EINBECK
den HAAG
HAARLEM
HAMBURG
HANNOVER
s'HERTOGENBOSCH
HILDESHEIM
JENA, LEER
LEIDEN, LEIPZIG
LÜNEBURG
NAUMBURG
PRAG, SELLIN
UTRECHT
WEIMAR

EINEN TEIL DER KLISCHEES ZU DIESEM HEFTE VERDANKEN WIR DEN VERLAGEN: DE STIJL, FRÜHLICHT, GUSTAV FISCHER, MERZ.

RED.: MERZ, HANNOVER, WALDHAUSENSTR. 5II
LISSITZKY, z. Z. SCHWEIZ, AMBRI-SOTTO, TESSIN.

JAHRGANG I 1923

PREIS: 6 M., 4 Fl., 10 frs., 2 Dollar

MERZ 1 HOLLAND-DADA
„ 2 /i/
„ 3 MERZ-MAPPE 6LITHOS VON K. SCHWITTERS, 60 M.
„ 4 BANALITÄTEN
„ 5 ARP-MAPPE 7 ARPADEN VON HANS ARP, 30 M.
„ 6 IMITATOREN
„ 7 TAPSHEFT
„ 10 BAUHAUSBUCH
„ 11 TY-RE

EINGESANDTE ZEITSCHRIFTEN: L'ALBORA, Gorizia; BLOK, Warschau; BROOM, New York; CONTIMPORANUL, Bucarest; DER EINZIGE, Friedenau; FRÜHLICHT, Magdeburg; LE FUTURISME, Mailand; G, Berlin; INICIAL, Buenos Aires; INTERVENTIONS, Paris; UJ KULTURA, Budapest; THE LITTLE REVIEW, New York; LUCIFER, Lyon; MA, Wien; MANOMETRE, Lyon; MECANO, Leiden; DAS NEUE RUSSLAND, Berlin; NOI, Rom; HET OVERZICHT, Antwerpen; PROVERBE, Paris; S 4 N, Northampton; DIE SCHEIBE, Darmstadt; 7 ARTS, Brüssel; DE STIJL, Leiden; DER STURM, Berlin; LA VIE DES LETTRES, Neuilly; ZENIT, Belgrad; DIE ZONE, Brünn; ZWROTNICA, Krakau.
Von Max Burchartz werden in Bochum, Bongardstr. 15, Hefte herausgegeben. Das erste heißt: Gestaltung der Reklame.
Im MERZ-Verlage ist erschienen als Nr. 12 „DER HAHNEPETER", Märchen von Kurt Schwitters, illustriert von Käte Steinitz, nur 50 signierte Exemplare, handkoloriert. Preis je 20 M.

ANZEIGE

VON DIESEM HEFT AN SOLL JEDES MERZHEFT EINEN BESONDEREN CHARAKTER HABEN, NICHT WIE BISHER EINE GEGENÜBERSTELLUNG VON DADA UND KUNST SEIN. BESONDERE, NUR DEM DADAISMUS GEWEIHTE HEFTE, WERDEN DEN UNTERTITEL „A-R-P"-ALLGEMEINES RELÄLIVITÄTS-PRINZIP TRAGEN. DAS NÄCHSTE HEFT SOLL DER TYPOREKLAME GEWIDMET SEIN.

MERZLITERATUR:
ANNA BLUME,
BLUME ANNA,
BLEI-E,
AUGUSTE BOLTE,
KATHEDRALE,
FRANZ MÜLLERS DRAHTFRÜHLING

ANZEIGE

ES IST ERSCHIENEN: DIE FIGURINENMAPPE VON EL LISSITZKY. ELEKTRO-MECHANISCHE SCHAU, 10 VIELFARBIGE AUTOLITHOS. AUFLAGE 75 NUM. EXEMPL. GRÖSSE 50×60 cm. PREIS 150 M. BESTELLUNGEN BEI FRAU S. KÜPPERS, HANNOVER, BÖDECKERSTR. 4D.

8 MERZ 9

DIESES DOPPELHEFT IST ERSCHIENEN UNTER DER REDAKTION VON EL LISSITZKY UND KURT SCHWITTERS

REDAKTION DES MERZVERLAGES
KURT SCHWITTERS, HANNOVER, WALDHAUSENSTR. 5II

TYPOGRAPHIE ANGEGEBEN VON EL LISSITZKY
HERAUSGEBER K. SCHWITTERS

NATUR VON LAT. NASCI
D. I. WERDEN ODER ENT-
STEHEN HEISST ALLES,
WAS SICH AUS SICH
SELBST DURCH EIGENE
KRAFT ENTWICKELT
GESTALTET UND BEWEGT
KLEINER BROKHAUS

BAND 2, Nr. 8/9
APRIL
JULI
1924

Nature, du latin NASCI signifie devenir, provenier, c'est à dire tout ce qui par sa propre force, se développe, se forme, se meut.

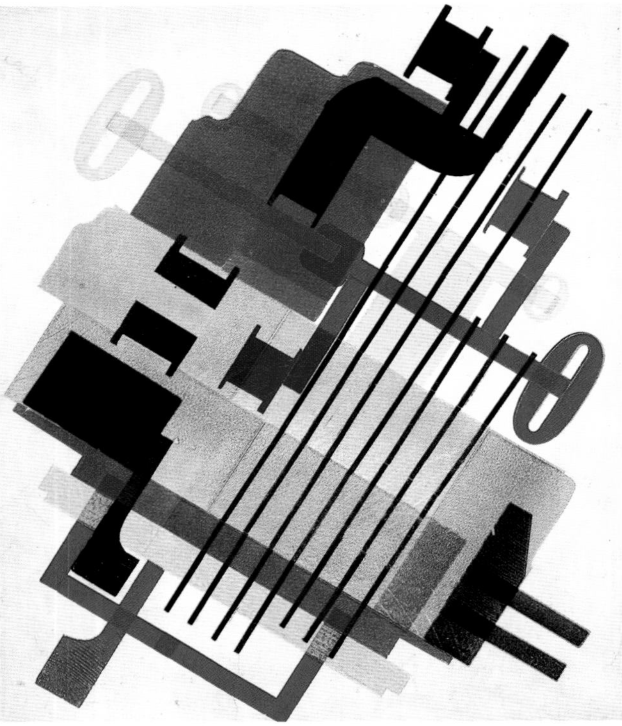

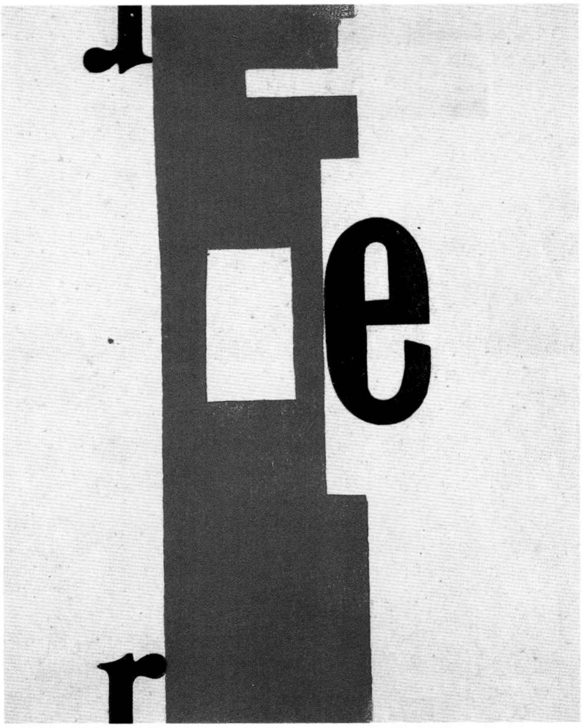

HOW CABLE-HAVOC BEGINS
AT LAST: HOT SPOTS
HOT SPOTS
50
AND BREAK DOWN
WHY RISK BREAK DOWN
WHILST THERE ARE
N.C.W.-CABLES
WITH HIGH
IONISATION
VOLTAGE
?

if you like to make money
by saving it
buy N.C.W. products
51
power cables
telephone cables
copper wire
solid and stranded
compounds

of the early 1920s, he produced, from 1923, his own magazine, *The Next Call.* By 1926 there were nine issues of the magazine, which became increasingly experimental in its investigation of the nature of the printing task. Elements of the printing process – the ink, the paper, the pressure, the wooden or metal types and the pieces of page furniture inserted to hold a chase together, along with colour and form – were all revealed in different ways. Random elements crept into the designs that reflected aspects of the materials and construction of the page. The first issue, for example, included an apparently abstract image that was part of a lock incorporated into the design.

Piet Zwart (1885–1977) was another Dutchman who contributed to the emerging Modernist typography. From an architectural background, his first typographic exercises, around 1920 and 1921, were influenced by the De Stijl group, but by 1925 typography was his main occupation and he developed a strong individual approach. He was prolific in producing advertising and other promotional literature, his designs displaying the most dramatic contrasts in type size possible within the confines of the poster sizes. Characters were used so large as to become abstract forms on the page, as well as existing within words. He often wrote his own copy, which helped with the clever play of words and image. The primary colours red, blue and yellow (also beloved by the Bauhaus) were often used, and in the late 1920s he incorporated more photography, exploring negative images, overprinting and sharp cropping in highly formalized shapes (often a circle, as if a telescopic image). He said that

Tschichold *44pt*

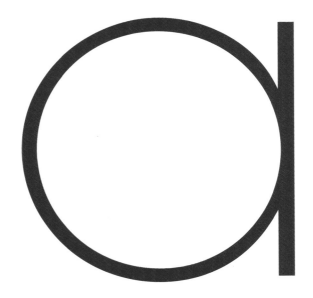

abcdεEfghijklmn
opqrsTUVWXYZ

a

Opposite top: on the left, "The Cylinder Press", 1925, and on the right, cover of the first issue of *The Next Call*, 1923, both by Hendrik Werkman, the Dutch printer whose typographic compositions used letterpress elements and other materials – the unusual shape on *The Next Call* is part of a lock. Werkman's pieces deconstructed print, placing the paper on the bed of the press and pressing type and other objects on to it, rather than running paper through a press. Opposite below: spread from a catalogue for the Netherlands Cable Works, designed by Piet Zwart, 1927-8. From 1925 Zwart worked for the client, producing hundreds of pieces that brought the new typography into commercial practice: the dramatic diagonal, the white space, the abstract forms and extreme contrast of type size are typical of this breakthrough work. Left: the universal alphabet was a regular subject of discussion, and Jan Tschichold made his attempt with a 1929 proposal that drew on Bayer's earlier work. A 1990s cut by The Foundry gives the full character set here.

the simpler and more geometric the character, the more useful he found it.

These various experiments and implementations of a new sensibility in graphic communication found their chronicler and apostle in the seminal book *Die Neue Typographie* ("The New Typography"). Its author, Jan Tschichold (1902–74), was a young Austrian teaching typography and lettering in Munich who had been a close observer of the work of Lissitsky and those at the Bauhaus, among others. He was also an uncompromising modern designer in his own right. In 1925 he published his first writings on the subject in a special issue of the journal *Typographische Mitteilungen*, which was given over to his essay, "Elementare Typographie". In this precocious piece Tschichold introduced Lissitsky's work to the readership of practising printers for the first time. The ideas behind asymmetric typography, sans serif typefaces and a limited choice of faces, plus the relationship of type and white space, were put into terms aimed at providing new rules for the printer. His was a familiar attack on the supposedly debased standards of nineteenth-century printing, and it expressed contempt for the grey nature of blocks of text locked up with little for the eye to be excited by, as well as berating the clutter of advertising typography. While he was partly criticizing the traditions, he was also against some of the variation in print forms derived from more exotic choices in typefaces and typographic arrangements used by printers in the 1920s trying to produce new decorative qualities.

FUTURA Figuren-Verzeichnis

A B C D E F G H I J K L M N O
P Q R S T U V W X Y Z Ä Ö Ü
a b c d e f g h i j k l m n o p q r ſ s t
u v w x y z ä ö ü ch ck ff fi fl ft ſſ ſi ſt ß
mager 1 2 3 4 5 6 7 8 9 0 & . , - : ; · ! ? ' (* † « » §
Auf Wunsch liefern wir Mediäval-Ziffern 1 2 3 4 5 6 7 8 9 0

A B C D E F G H I J K L M N O
P Q R S T U V W X Y Z Ä Ö Ü
a b c d e f g h i j k l m n o p q r ſ s t
u v w x y z ä ö ü ch ck ff fi fl ft ſſ ſi ſt ß
halbfett 1 2 3 4 5 6 7 8 9 0 & . , - : ; · ! ? ' (* † « » §
Auf Wunsch liefern wir Mediäval-Ziffern 1 2 3 4 5 6 7 8 9 0

A B C D E F G H I J K L M N O
P Q R S T U V W X Y Z Ä Ö Ü
a b c d e f g h i j k l m n o p q
r ſ s t u v w x y z ä ö ü ch ck
ff fi fl ft ſſ ſi ſt ß
1 2 3 4 5 6 7 8 9 0
fett & . , - : ; · ! ? ' (* † « » §

Tschichold's key points were all directed at creating a purer, elementary functionalism in typography. The thesis could be crudely summarized as: asymmetry, sans serif. A few more words and you would tend to get into the more naïve aspects of the book, which would as a whole be later renounced by Tschichold. But in that it clarified coherent themes in the work of the Modernist typographers, this publication was immensely significant. It presented typography as the graphic arrangement of type and choice of type, rather than a broad descriptive term for other more practical aspects of printing.

It was the man who gave Tschichold his teaching job in Munich who created the most emblematic face of the 1920s: Futura, designed by Paul Renner. Designed for Bauer and issued from 1927, the face can be seen to have antecedents in the Erbar sans, which was released only a few years before and was also highly popular. Futura (its name was an inspired piece of identity) is distinguished from Erbar by characteristics such as the upper-case "Q" with its tail beginning inside the bowl, and the lack of a tail on the lower-case "j". Renner first designed an even more elemental face, almost abstract in parts (an "r" consisted of just a stem and an unattached point floating where the spur should be). In comparison with other earlier sans, distinguishing features are the clear geometric forms, the single storey "a" and open-tail "g". For twenty-five years Futura would be the leading sans serif face, taking a

Promotional material for Futura, which was issued by the Bauer foundry in 1927. This design by Paul Renner drew on the search for a geometric sans that captured the spirit of the new principles, and coming from a commercial foundry it spread rapidly. A set of ornaments, left, were also made available, that encouraged designers and printers to use imaginatively a set of geometric page furniture that was in keeping with the character of the font. Renner's earlier experimental drawings for such a font were revived in the 1990s as Architype Renner by The Foundry. The "g" and the "r" stand out with quirky features that were ironed out by the time Renner came to draw Futura.

Renner *28pt*

ABCDEFGHIJKLMNOPQRSTUVWXYZ
abcdefghijklmnopqrstuvwxyz

prominent role in advertising in its many variations.

Outside Germany and Holland, one of the first implementations of the new typography in commercial practice was seen in Czechoslovakia, where the artists and designers who went under the Devetsil group banner included two influential typographers, Karel Teige and Ladislav Sutnar. The poet and artist Teige wrote his own version of the new principles in an essay, "Modern Type". Its call for dynamic forms that rejected the traditional was embraced by Sutnar (1897–1976), who was a design teacher as well as a publisher's art director. His work in the late 1920s and early 1930s represented another mixture of the ideas of De Stijl, Constructivism and the Bauhaus teachers. Bold photomontage is placed with pared down type, alongside demonstrations of the play possible with perspective and the use of colour for depth and foregrounding. Sutnar emigrated to the United States in 1939, giving a second lease of life to his influence.

In Poland, the work of Henryk Berlewi (1894–1967) took a different route forward from the Constructivist ideas spread by Lissitsky. His approach to functional communication was to create a "mechanical art" (*Mechano Faktur*), a systemized idea of creativity that reduced typographic work (amongst other things) to a range of functional elements that could be combined together as building elements. It was a rejection of individualism as well as of the traditional forms associated

Ballmer *28pt*

abcdefghijklmnopqrstuvvwwxyzz
0123456789

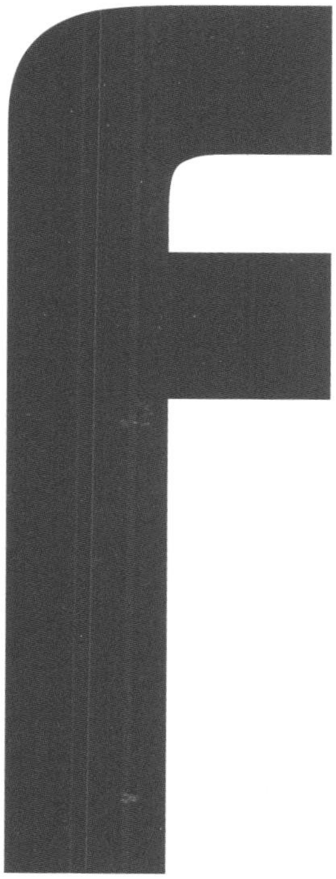

Left: poster from 1928 by the Swiss designer Theo Ballmer (1902-65), which is for an exhibition of industrial standards. Elements of De Stijl are put through a Bauhaus training, and the commitment to a visible grid prefigures the post-war Swiss Style. Note that just two weights of type are used, one for the headline, one for text, all text ranged to a line. The alphabet developed by Ballmer for this and other posters of the period takes the grid also, with forms tending towards the square. Architype Ballmer, top, is a 1990s digitized version by The Foundry. Opposite: poster by Vilmos Huszár (1884-1960), for an exhibition of industrial arts, 1929. This Hungarian, who lived in The Netherlands, contributed to the first issue of *De Stijl* but left the group in 1923. The poster shows his merging of typographic and abstract shapes so that original letterforms, blocks of colour and geometric pattern project a dynamic image that suggests the three-dimensional and figurative without ever being explicit. It straddles a border between the experimental origins of the new typography, and the stylized outcome of the work, Art Deco.

HET
BNA
KVB
VANK
25 JAAR
1929
TENTOONSTELLING
VAN HEDENDAAGSCHE
KUNSTNYVERHEID
KLEINPLASTIEK
ARCHITECTUUR
STEDELYK MUSEUM
AMSTERDAM
29·JUNI—28·JULI
GEOPEND VAN 10-5
INGERICHT DOOR DEN TENTOONSTELLINGS
RAAD VOOR BOUWKUNST EN VERWANTE KUNSTEN
V. HUSZAR

with a past age. Berlewi went on to apply his ideas by establishing an advertising agency as well as promoting them in other areas of the applied arts.

For all this revolution in the creation of a typography that reflected the Modernist sensibility, the mass of printed communication continued to conform to traditional values, for good or bad. And it was dismay at the latter that drove the traditionalists to argue for the restoration of values they felt had been debased in the move to greater mass communication.

Publication of the seventh and final issue of the typographic journal *The Fleuron*, in 1930, is a crucial point in the recording and exploration of traditional typographic values. Over its seven issues, 1500 pages and eight years during the 1920s, *The Fleuron* set out to cover the quest for the highest typographic standards in Europe and the USA. Despite a prestigious list of contributors there was no place in the index for any designer who might have fallen under the description "Modernist".

In the final issue, Stanley Morison, the editor, set out the principles behind the tradition explored in *The Fleuron*. His "First Principles of Typography" addressed the craft of book design in particular, but he commented on innovations in other areas. In his postscript to the final issue he attacked those who sought to work outside his rules:

This page: Fournier ligature. Opposite: Bembo, Baskerville, Fournier and Bodoni were in a wave of refined revivals by the Monotype drawing office in England during the 1920s, guided from 1922 by the advice of arch-traditionalist Stanley Morison. Bembo (1929), like Monotype's Poliphilus (1923) before it, was based on the designs of punchcutter Francesco Griffo, working for the Venetian printer Aldus Manutius (1450-1515). Its sharp serifs are seen as delivering "brightness"; the face remains popular in editorial work. Baskerville (1924) revived the work of eighteenth-century English printer John Baskerville. Bodoni (1921) cleaned up and revived the "modern" face associated with Giambattista Bodoni (1740-1813) of Parma, which had already been recut by the Italian foundry Nebiolo in 1901 and ATF in 1911 – but the most admired revivals were to be those cuts created by Giovanni Mardersteig (1892-1977) for his private press Officina Bodoni from the mid-1920s. Fournier (1925) was a result of Morison's enthusiasm for the light roman of the eighteenth-century French printer Pierre Simon Fournier.

"The apostles of the 'machine age' will be wise to address their disciples in a standard old face – they can flourish their concrete banner in sans serif on title pages and perhaps in a running headline. For the rest, deliberate experiments aside, we are all, whether we like it or not, in absolute dependence upon ocular law and national custom."

In a sense, Morison comes quite close to the Bauhaus search for simple, non-decorative, clear forms of typography in which every element is significant to the communication. But he was a long way away in how he saw such principles being implemented.

"No printer should say 'I am an artist therefore I am not to be dictated to, I will create my own letter forms,' for, in this humble job, individualism is not very helpful. It is no longer possible, as it was in the infancy of the craft, to persuade society into the acceptance of strongly marked and highly individualistic types – because literate society is so much greater in mass and correspondingly slow in movement. The good type designer knows that, for a new fount to be successful, it has to be so good that only very few recognise its novelty." (*From* "First Principles of Typography")

Morison's words set in print what had existed as good practice and what underlay the finest achievements of the print revival projected by the private presses. For the young typographer-compositor in a printworks, and as a text for

Bembo *24pt*

ABCDEFGHIJKLMNOPQRSTUVWXYZ
abcdefghijklmnopqrstuvwxyz

Baskerville *24pt*

ABCDEFGHIJKLMNOPQRSTUVWXYZ
abcdefghijklmnopqrstuvwxyz

Fournier *24pt*

ABCDEFGHIJKLMNOPQRSTUVWXYZ
abcdefghijklmnopqrstuvwxyz

Bodoni *24pt*

ABCDEFGHIJKLMNOPQRSTUVWXYZ
abcdefghijklmnopqrstuvwxyz

evening classes to call on, this essay was a valuable marker. Morison addressed his text to the "amateur", even though by being published in *The Fleuron* it was going to the elite (there was a very small, specialized print run – 1000 copies printed on English-made wove, and 210 on English handmade wove paper). In 1936, though, the essay was reprinted in British, American and Dutch editions, and after the Second World War it was translated into German, Danish, Dutch and Spanish, and reprinted again.

A glance through the index of *The Fleuron* shows that there was no room for Bauhaus artists or other Modernists, but the eclectic English craftsmen Edward Johnston and Eric Gill (1882–1940) made it, with a lengthy essay on Gill appearing in the final issue. Gill Sans was Eric Gill's first face to be issued for Monotype, and it quickly became popular, embracing the simple, geometric qualities advocated by the new typography while having a liveliness that displays a sense of the hand behind it and gives some fluidity to the face when seen in continuous text. The face was initially seen as a titling alphabet (it was derived from a bookshop sign painted by Gill), and was in many ways a publicly available variation on Johnston's sans designed for use on the London Underground, from which it was partly derived (Gill had worked with Johnston a little on the earlier face). But it came to be used more than its antecedent thanks to its distribution and to its distinctive character, which also distinguishes it from being just a rolling out of Johnston. Differences to note are the subtle down-curve of the "R", the half-height middle strokes of the "M" that avoid the optical shading noticeable in

Broadway *24pt*

ABCDEFGHI
JKLMNOPQ
RSTUVWXYZ
abcdefghij
klmnopqrst
uvwxyz

some heavy "M"s, and the dropping of the strictly monotone weight of stroke in the lower case.

Work that is often classified under the tag of Art Deco features certain typefaces and a typographic or calligraphic practice that gave a strong flavour to some print of the interwar period, particularly in stylish advertising on posters and in magazines. The Deco style formally centres around the Paris Exposition Internationale des Arts Décoratifs et Industriels Modernes of 1925 and its advocacy of a revival of decorative craft in modern production. However the Deco label is applied to a range of Moderne trends (distinct from Modernist) apparent in all creative areas from architecture to advertising. It had different inflections in different countries, being particularly strong in France, initially, and in America

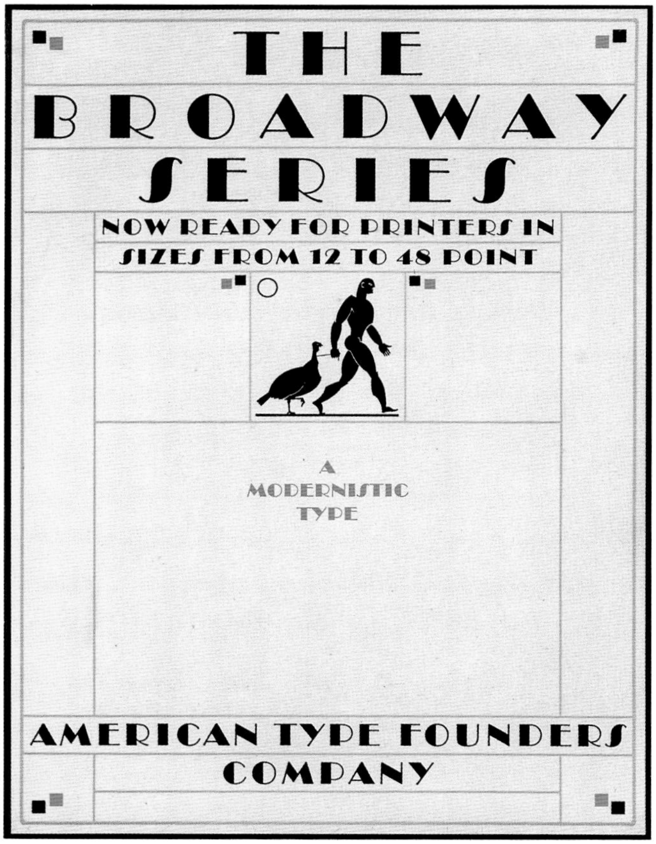

Opposite: front page of *The New Yorker*, 1925, after its redesign with Irvin as a special headline face, styled around the logo, which has remained essentially unchanged since. In 1991 Gert Wiescher designed FF New Yorker Type, a complete alphabet, which with its slightly imbalanced angularity and contrasting strokes is typical of the Deco styling. This period effect is almost instant with Broadway, shown opposite and with original brochure this page. Designed by Morris Fuller Benton, 1929, for American Type Founders, it merges fat face and lineale type characteristics and has probably appeared on thousands of restaurant and bar promotions since.

later on, and continued into the late 1930s, passing through Jazz Age style to the streamlined look. Graphic artists working in this vein mixed the new approaches of Cubism and post-Cubism with the bold illustrative traditions that had been worked into Art Nouveau and the Plakatstil's development of advertising language. The most noted of the poster artists of this period was A. M. Cassandre (the pseudonym of Adolphe Jean-Marie Mouron, 1901–68). His posters pared down the language of pictorial image and typographic form and then applied the warp of perspectives drawn from the Modernist artists of Cubism and post-Cubism. Out of this approach came his first face, the semi-abstract, highly stylized Bifur, issued in 1929 by Deberny & Peignot. He explained that it was "designed for advertising...designed for a word, a single word, a poster word". It was not ornamental, he stressed, but an attempt to get back to the essential characteristic of individual letters. "If Bifur looks unfamiliar and strange", he argued, "it is not because I have dressed it up eccentrically but because, in the midst of a fully clothed crowd, it is naked." The type specimen book had Cassandre demonstrating how the face could be used in different ways, such as having colour dropped in on the shadow part of the letter.

The Art Deco look spread rapidly in advertising communication, and in the late 1920s and into the 1930s a magazine page of small ads would often contain a variety of fancy Deco faces that are now mostly long disused. One that was widely employed was Broadway, which was designed by Morris Benton, issued by both American Type Founders and

A.M. Cassandre took the ideas of Modernist pioneers into powerful commercial works, which have become among the most treasured commercial graphics of all time (double copyright paid on these images). His ability to merge image and lettering in one powerful pictorial work made Cassandre's posters highly influential. Left: Nord Express (1927) typifies his combination of reductive elements, vignette colour, and visual puns (here the cities lettered on the track map, and the association between the train and the telegraph speed). Cassandre's unique lettering in his posters occasionally spawned extreme typefaces, the first being Bifur for foundry Deberny & Peignot in 1929, its original promotional brochure shown opposite. Bifur reduces characters to the distinguishing core features, and then suggests the rest by shadow lines.

Monotype at the end of the 1920s. The heavy contrast of thick and thin strokes, made even more extreme in an inlined version, may be highly impractical for widespread use, but this made it all the more suitable as an emblematic face for the Deco style.

Much of what is interesting typographically in Art Deco lettering and layouts was not formalized as a foundry face or under any clear rules, such as those set out by Tschichold or Morison. But one influential Art Deco-related publication was A. Tolmer's *Mise en Page*, published in Paris, which set down principles for the advertising designer and printer and had a practical, commercial application that made it more successful than the more substantial theoretical positions of Tschichold and the Bauhaus designers. It emphasized the need for a clarity and boldness in execution that could give maximum impact to an advertisement. In this it offered a synthesis of the new typography and the old. In a decade, work from pioneers of art theory had become – if not mainstream – certainly widely practised and discussed.

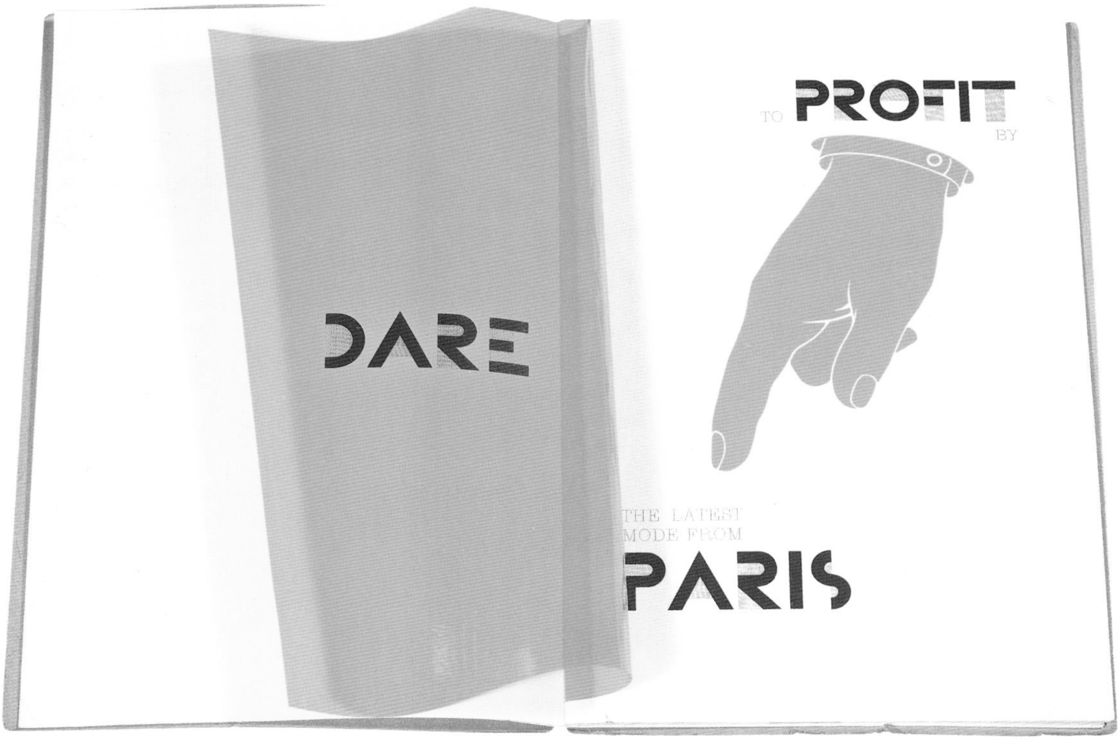

CREAZIONI
TIPOGRAFICHE
DEPERO
1927

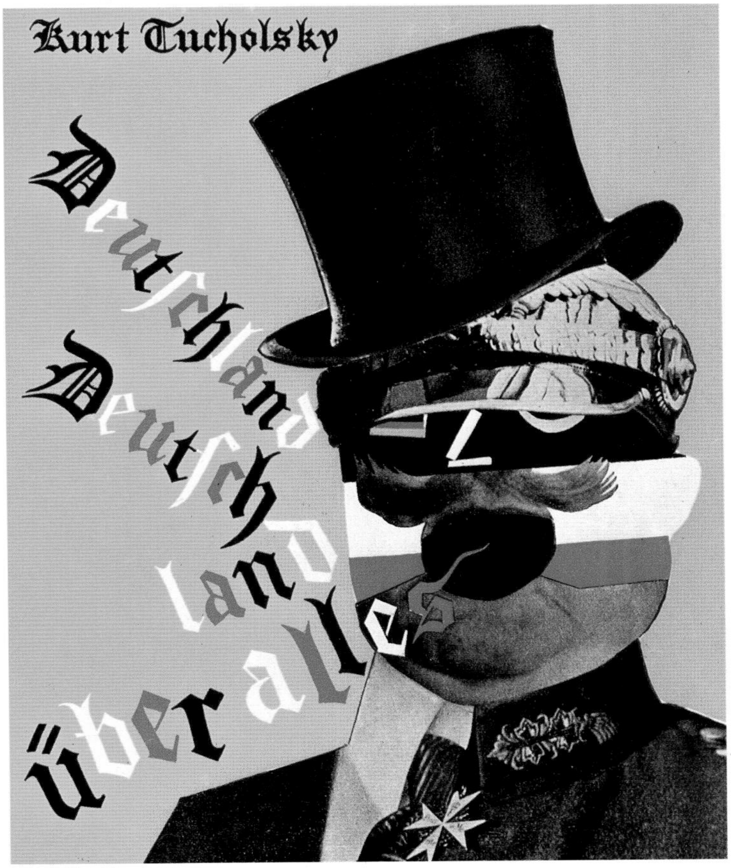

Opposite: design for a visiting card in 1927 by Fortunato Depero (1892-1960). The anarchism and explosiveness of Italian Futurism dissipated in the 1920s, but Depero's application of the ideas in commercial work stands out through his pioneering Campari advertising. Left: book cover designed by John Heartfield, 1929. This pioneer of photomontage sometimes incorporated typography in his pieces in the manner of the work with photography – cutting up and ironically juxtaposing elements, or squeezing meaning out of forms that was never to be seen in the familiar context. Here the black-letter calligraphy is fairly straight, but is deliberately chosen for its association with German nationalism. Some characters are given extra emphasis, drawing them into the image, as with the final "s".

1930

TIMES

The decade that endured the Great Depression and ended with the start of the Second World War also saw an increase in international communication and travel. The representation of time and human action – whether through print, cinema or broadcast – moved ever faster and farther. The evolution of a world market, of huge forces at work in controlling demand and supply, gave the collapse in the financial markets the potential for an earth-shattering impact. The international communications and culture could help destabilize nations – and could also be manipulated to help control nations through mass propaganda.

These major themes had their bearing on typographic development. Nowhere more so than in the path taken by the apostle, then apostate, of the new typography, Jan Tschichold. From 1926 until 1933 Tschichold taught and worked in Munich, where he also wrote and published *Die Neue Typographie*. In 1933 he was arrested and removed from his job by the new Nazi government; his ideas were considered *Kulturbolschewismus* ("cultural bolshevism"). The attack was part of the clampdown on all manifestations of Modernism that led to the closure of the Bauhaus in 1933 and the mounting of the Degenerate Art exhibitions, and later to the destruction of modern works of art. Tschichold moved to Switzerland where he taught, and wrote *Typographische Gestaltung*, published in 1935. While still advocating many of the ideas of the earlier work, Tschichold now showed an appreciation for the finesse of classical typography. The title page, with its combination of a swash italic for the author's name, block serif for the title and Bodoni bold for the printer's name, laid out in a balanced composition of symmetrical and asymmetric elements, displays Tschichold's change of heart. The text is also in Bodoni, with block serif headings.

Speaking at a Type Directors' Club seminar in 1959, Tschichold described *Typographische Gestaltung* as "more prudent" than the earlier book:

"... to my astonishment I detected most shocking parallels between the teachings of *Die Neue Typographie* and National Socialism and fascism. Obvious similarities consist in the ruthless restriction of typefaces, a parallel to Goebbels' infamous *gleichshaltung* ('political alignment'), and the more or less militaristic arrangement of lines. Because I did not want to be guilty of spreading the very ideas which had compelled me to leave Germany, I thought over again what a typographer should do. Which typefaces are good and what typefaces are the most practicable? By guiding the compositors of a large Basel printing office, I learned a lot about practicability. Good typography has to be perfectly legible and, as such, the result of intelligent planning. The classical typefaces such as Garamond, Janson, Baskerville and Bell are undoubtedly the most legible. Sans serif is good for certain cases of emphasis, but is used to the point of abuse."[1]

Tschichold's experience of the changed climate of 1930s Germany was, of course, one shared by all who held beliefs not countenanced by the Nazis. The wave of repressive activities that grew in Germany, and later Austria, Holland and France, under the Nazis forced the spread of the ideas pioneered in and around the Bauhaus group of artists and designers. Many went into exile, chiefly to Britain and the United States.

The same was true of Tschichold's adopted homeland of Switzerland, where the first signs of a typographic approach that would influence a whole generation of postwar designers became apparent in the 1930s in the emergence of Swiss Style, later to be called International Style. From the teaching of Ernst Keller (1891–1968) and Alfred Williman at the School of Applied Art in Zurich after the First World War came a practical development of the new modular order expressed in the work of the De Stijl artists and the Constructivists. The establishment of a system for a flexible but firm underlying structure for typographic layouts complements the push to simplify and purify the form of type, as seen in the promotion of new sans serif faces. One student at the Zurich school was Theo Ballmer (1902–65), who went on to study at the Bauhaus. From the late 1920s, he used a visible grid to underpin the typographic order. This anticipates one of the most distinctive ideas associated with the Swiss school of the 1950s and 1960s. The process of deriving the grid and then applying it to order information was a major contribution to the structuring of a typographic designer's work. Ballmer's ideas were mapping out the way ahead. The grid idea, itself, was of course in no way new – a grid underlies the layout of the first book printed with movable type, Gutenberg's 42-line bible of 1452 – but in this era the grid was restated as the bedrock on which typography could be constructed.

Another Swiss student out of the Bauhaus was Max Bill (1908–94). He combined a severity in type choice – Akzidenz Grotesk to the fore – with an approach that created posters that are almost purely typographic and, even then, consist of few words. This was in the tradition of the German Plakatstil artists, given a new twist through Bill's minimalist take on Bauhaus theories. The posters of another leading Swiss designer, Herbert Matter (1907–84), for the clothing company NKZ and then for Swiss tourism, combined an appreciation of the art movements of the time with the development of the typographic craft. All the elements of the image were integrated in one powerful piece, sometimes with no distinct line of type but with the typographic elements worked into the picture.

Matter was one of many designers to go to the United States when it became difficult to work in Europe. Few were under more pressure to leave Germany than those associated with the Bauhaus, and Gropius, Moholy-Nagy, Bayer and van der Rohe all ended up in the United States. Two significant American appointments of Europeans not from the Bauhaus were that of Mehemed Fehmy Agha (1896–1978) to art director for *Vogue* (from 1929 until 1942), and Alexey Brodovitch (1898–1971) to art director for *Harper's Bazaar* (from 1934 until 1958). Although the Great Depression provided the economic backdrop to their first years on these glamour titles, their early work dramatically enlivened and accentuated the fashionable qualities of the magazines, and from this vantage point propagated new ideas in the

Fette Fraktur *28pt*

Left: cover of *Deutschland Ausstellung* prospectus designed by Herbert Bayer, 1936. The Nazi-forced closure of the Bauhaus in 1933 led to the diaspora of Modern designers from Germany, spreading the new ideas. Before Bayer left for the United States in the late 1930s (in 1938 he helped organize the famous Museum of Modern Art Bauhaus exhibition in New York) he can be seen to have compromised his work with this promotion for a Nazi-organized German culture show. It uses his condensed modern (sub-Bodoni) face Bayer-type. Above: Fette Fraktur, a popular nineteenth-century black-letter and the type of face seen as essentially Germanic in the 1930s. In 1941 it was cast out by the Führer as betraying Jewish origins and also being unsuitable for imposing a global message.

Left: the second issue of a short-lived Barcelona periodical espousing the Modern movement in architecture, and also flying the flag for a new typography. It explored an unusual square format and held firm to the grid, with Futura as the sole typeface. Below: promotion for the highly stylized face Independent from the Amsterdam Type Foundry, designed by G. Collette and J. Dufour, 1930 – a playful extreme of Deco hinting at the abstraction of character forms.

relationship of type and image. Each had worked in Paris and brought with them an awareness of Bauhaus thinking, along with the experience of the lively French commercial poster scene. Neither designed type or kept to strict rules on which types were acceptable, but both helped forge the new idea of the art director as one who directed layout, photography and illustration, rather than crafting every element. Both challenged magazine design conventions by using large photographs and white space, and sought to represent content through typographic expression.

At the Italian office equipment manufacturer Olivetti the strong design culture extended to graphics. The corporate typography was allied with ideas of industrial design and exhibition display in the work of Giovanni Pintori, Xanti Schawinsky and Nivola, among those graphic designers who worked for Olivetti under its Development and Publicity Office, established in 1931. The relationship between the potential of type and the nature of the typewriter-written word and how those words are produced (at some point, from the imagination) is demonstrated in a 1934 folder designed by Schawinsky (a former Bauhaus student) and targeted at selling typewriters to doctors. It layers text over headline, sets type flush against a curve, dramatically contrasting typographic and photographic elements, and uses lines of type as pointers for the reader. In another Olivetti project, Schawinsky's fundamental questioning of typographic principles is flourished by the distinction of having no words other than the logotype in an image – a woman rests her hands on the petite form of a typewriter, the product's own

Campo Grafico
RIVISTA DI ESTETICA E DI TECNICA GRAFICA
ANNO 5 N. 1 . GENNAIO 1937-XV . SPEDIZIONE IN ABBON. POSTALE
DRADI-ROSSI
FOTOCOPPOLA
BUENOS AIRES

Left: cover for *Campo Grafico* from 1937 by Attilio Rossi. This Modernist Italian designer helped found the pioneering Modern architecture journal and spread Modernist graphics to Buenos Aires when he moved there in 1935 in despair at Italian politics.

branding (the Olivetti name being boldly displayed in two places) sufficing to make the advertising statement, the image bound together by the use of the same colour for the machine and the woman's lipstick. Schawinsky was one of a number of prominent designers who worked with Antonio Boggeri (1900–90). Studio Boggeri opened in 1933 and became a focal point for new graphic design in Italy, drawing on contact with the Bauhaus set.

The foundries responded to the demand for creating "the Bauhaus look" by creating numerous sans serif and block serif faces, usually drawing on Futura, but not exclusively. Erbar was a popular geometric sans serif released during the 1920s, and Rudolf Koch's distinctive Kabel face also had followers. Key designers who added their contribution to the foundry catalogues at this time included Herbert Bayer (Bayer Type); Lucian Bernhard (Bernhard Gothic); William A. Dwiggins (Metro); Frederic Goudy (Goudy Sans); and R. Hunter Middleton (Stellar). The block serif revival followed on as, in effect, serifs were added to the Futura model to produce a new form of the traditional "Egyptian" face: Memphis, City, Beton, Cairo, Karnak, Rockwell (a revival), Pharaon and Scarab are some of those from the largest suppliers (these suppliers had the best distribution and this in turn influenced tastes). Cutting these faces was part of the response of type foundries to meet the burgeoning needs of advertising typographers as clients became more sophisticated and the demand for graphic communications increased.

Bayer-type *38pt*

a b c d e f
g h i j k l m
n o p q r s t
u v w x y z

City *21pt*

ABCDEFGHIJKLMNOPQRSTUVWXYZ
abcdefghijklmnopqrstuvwxyz

Opposite: Peignot, a highly original twist on the search for the universal alphabet, was designed by A.M. Cassandre for Deberny & Peignot, Paris, 1937. Originally distributed in three different weights, this sans serif dispensed with lower-case letters for all but "b", "d" and "f", and created a new lower case with ascenders and descenders added to capitals. Cassandre believed he had drawn a purer form of the alphabet which bore the "essential character" of roman letters. He intended Peignot for text and was disappointed at its low adoption. Left: Bayer-type, 1931, by Herbert Bayer, an experimental universal type design digitized by The Foundry, 1990s. The mono-alphabet Modern appears to have influenced the more conventional Bayer-type issued by Berthold in 1935 (used on the Bayer-designed prospectus shown on page 69). Below left: City, a 1930 design by George Trump, was a stylized take on the Modernist love of geometry. Essentially it was a fresh twist on the old slab serif. Memphis and Rockwell were other popular 1930s revivals of this type form.

ALPHABET
MEDIUM 72 POINT
Aa Bb Cc Dd Ee Ff Gg
Hh Ii Jj Kk Ll Mm Nn
Oo Pp Qq Rr Ss Tt Uu
Vv Ww Xx Yy Zz
1234567890
1234567890

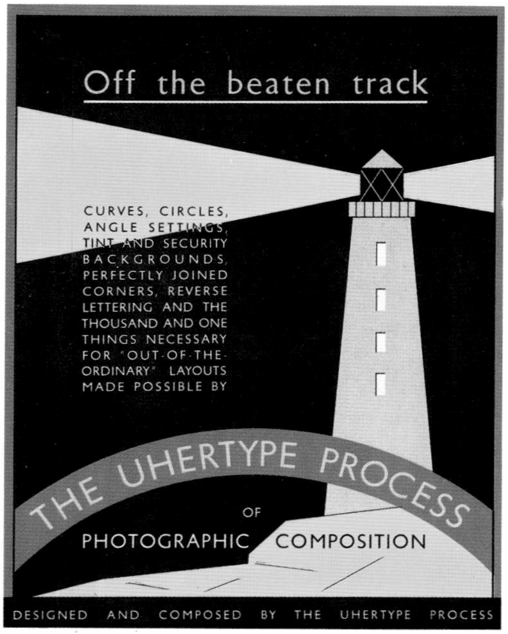

One of the most distinctive sans faces was Cassandre's Peignot for the foundry Deberny & Peignot. This questioned the existence of different forms for upper and lower case, seeking to do away with most of the different, supposedly corrupt, lower-case forms. However, as an acknowledgement of reader expectations, the face maintains the concept of ascenders and descenders and also has contrasted thick and thin strokes as a nod to ideas about legibility. Cassandre was insistent that this was not a decorative face, but a more pure form of the alphabet than tradition had led to thus far. The single alphabet concept was not carried through to its ultimate implication, however, as both upper- and lower-case forms were cut.

Not all development was so fashionable or dramatic. In the

Libra *21pt*

abcdefghij
klmnopqrs
tuvwxyz

libra-medium

abcdefghij
klmnopqrs
tuvwxyz&
æ œ ch ij ß $ £
1 2 3 4 5 6 7 8 9 0

Copyright by the Amsterdam Typefoundry, Amsterdam-Holland

libra a new typeface
presented by the amsterdam typefoundry

in recent years it has become evident that the fundamental differences in form between capitals and lower case letters does not give general satisfaction · typographers, in an endeavour to achieve freshness and better balance in general work have made many interesting experiments · for example the attempt to suggest harmony in type by using lower case exclusively has aroused much controversy · the device of using capitals alone is familiar but it is usually considered to fail from the standpoint of legibility, as well as harmony. it will be agreed that the lower case used exclusively, lacks distinction · in creating libra the guiding principle has been to secure the balance previously unattainable.
this new type is based on the same forms those of as the so-called 'uncials' which were used in the early middle-ages. 'libra', which means balance, is an epoch-making typeface which gives users extensive scope for the development of modern typographic styles · the handwritten form is one of its further characteristics which lends to 'libra' a vivacity and charm of its own.
in presenting our 'libra' we feel confident that it will meet with the approval of printers and general public alike.

amsterdam typefoundry
amsterdam-holland

Opposite top: advertising for Uhertype photocomposition, 1939. Edmund Uher was one of the early experimenters with phototypesetting, trying manual and keyboard processes. He commissioned Jan Tschichold, among others, to design new faces for his technology in 1935, but these do not survive. Opposite centre and below: Libra, an intriguing sport from 1938 designed by S.H. de Roos for the Amsterdam Type Foundry. It draws on uncial script – the rounded letterform of early Latin manuscripts. This occasional inspiration to type designers has yet to win any popular revival. Above left: front and back cover of S. I. Kirsanov's *The Word Belongs To Kirsanov*, designed by Solomon Telingater, 1930, in Moscow. The Constructivist meets Dadaist as Telingater explores the diagonal, montage, and deliberately crude juxtapositions of different fonts, weights and sizes. Left: everyday Dada from Max Ernst in 1934 with a poster for an exhibition in Zurich. The exotic, decorative, shadowed headline type and silk-screened colours over the standard repeated printer's hands insert elaborate jokes about the vernacular within a simple composition.

design of type for text there was a search for higher standards in traditional faces, as well as faces that combined the best of the old with the ideas of the new. Stanley Morison was brought in as typographic consultant to *The Times* newspaper in London after complaining about the newspaper's setting – this despite *The Times* having a high standard among newspapers. Morison saw a text face that was inadequate for the tasks placed upon it, and a sloppy sense of typographic discipline. His advice led to a decision to go for a different but extant revival face; tests were carried out with some of Monotype's recent revivals and new faces: Plantin, Baskerville and Perpetua (Gill's latest). The drawbacks of these when used on newsprint helped Morison argue the case for a new face. It was decided that this should be based on Plantin, the main merit being that Plantin was more condensed and took up less space than Baskerville and Perpetua.

The resulting Times New Roman is a loose revival, with reference to the sixteenth-century face of the Amsterdam printer Christophe Plantin and with key qualities of twentieth-century typeface design. Morison aimed to improve newspaper type to a quality comparable to that in average book production; in that way he would bring the finer craft standards into the realm of mass production. That few lay people would spot his changes was for him a mark of achievement, not criticism: *The Times* is said to have received only one letter of complaint after the new face was introduced in the issue of 3 October 1932. In his "First Principles of Typography" essay Morison asserted: "for a new

f

Caledonia *48pt*

A B C D E F G H I
J K L M N O P Q
R S T U V W X Y Z
a b c d e f g h i j k l m n
o p q r s t u v w x y z

Above: Caledonia, 1939/41, by William Addison Dwiggins for Linotype. This re-drawing of nineteenth-century Scotch roman provided a robust, readable face that quickly gained wide use in book production, rivalled only by Times New Roman, opposite, which thanks to the extent of the British Empire became perhaps the most widely read typeface mid-century. It first appeared in 1932 in *The Times*, London, designed by Stanley Morison and Victor Lardent from the inspiration of sixteenth-century Plantin. Morison, like Dwiggins, sought to create a readable, "transparent" type.

A B C D E F G H I
J K L M N O P Q
R S T U V W X Y Z
a b c d e f g h i j k l m n
o p q r s t u v w x y z

fount to be successful, it has to be so good that only very few recognise its novelty".

In fact the font was not so successful with other newspapers as they used poorer paper than *The Times* and required type with less contrast of stroke and fineness of serif. However, it was widely adopted for books – indeed the renowned American type historian and small-press printer D. B. Updike used it for the final book from his Merrymount Press, *Some Aspects of Printing, Old and New*, in 1941. This was quite an honour for a face that Morison himself would later sum up as being "by the vice of Mammon and the misery of the machine...bigoted and narrow, mean and puritan".

Awareness of unsatisfactory standards in type in the 1920s had led newspaper proprietors in the US to call for the likes of Linotype and Intertype to improve what was workable on their high-speed letterpress machines. Ionic, cut in 1925, was a key development, being a throwback face that drew on the Victorian Clarendons for a rugged look distinguished by an almost even stroke line and a high x-height. It was swiftly adopted by newspapers internationally. In 1931 Linotype's Excelsior came out as a design developed to overcome the ink-trap effect on counters of tighter characters. Then came Paragon and Opticon, the latter opening out its characters even more to work with heavily inked newspapers. This series was part of Linotype's Legibility Group of new faces tackling the need for a type culture specifically suited to the needs of newspapers and other large-run, low-cost text printing. The culmination of this

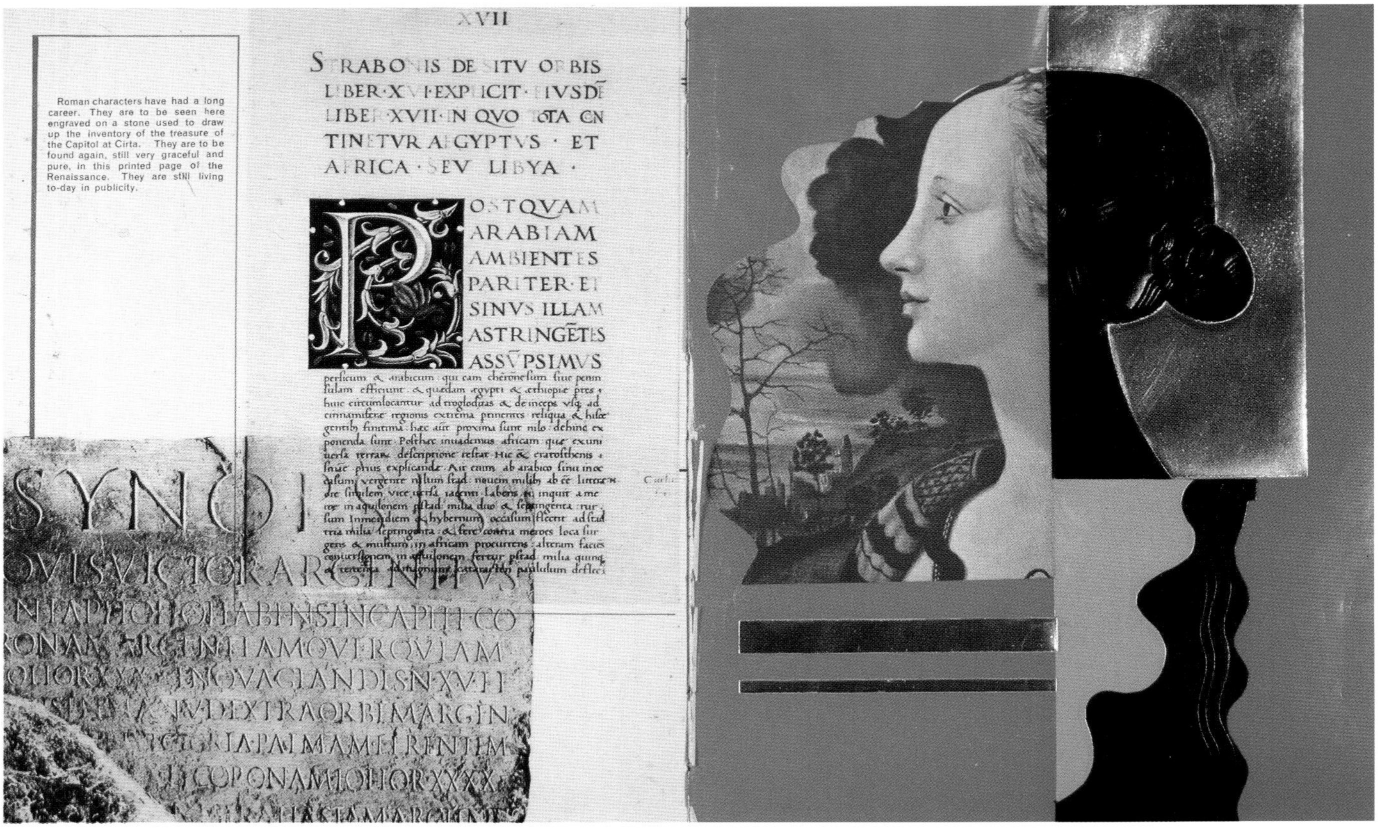

period of development was the issue of Corona in 1941, a face that became immensely popular with American newspapers.

In the background there was the emergence of the early phototypesetting systems. Edmund Uher took out international patents for a system with both a keyboard and manually set method of instructing the exposure of type design (carried on a glass cylinder) on to photosensitive paper. Tschichold designed the promotional material and around ten faces for Uher in 1933, but none of the drawings appear to have survived after a later change of policy at the company. In 1935 a specimen book of Uhertype hand-settings was released, designed by Imre Reiner to show how flexible the process would be for innovative typography.

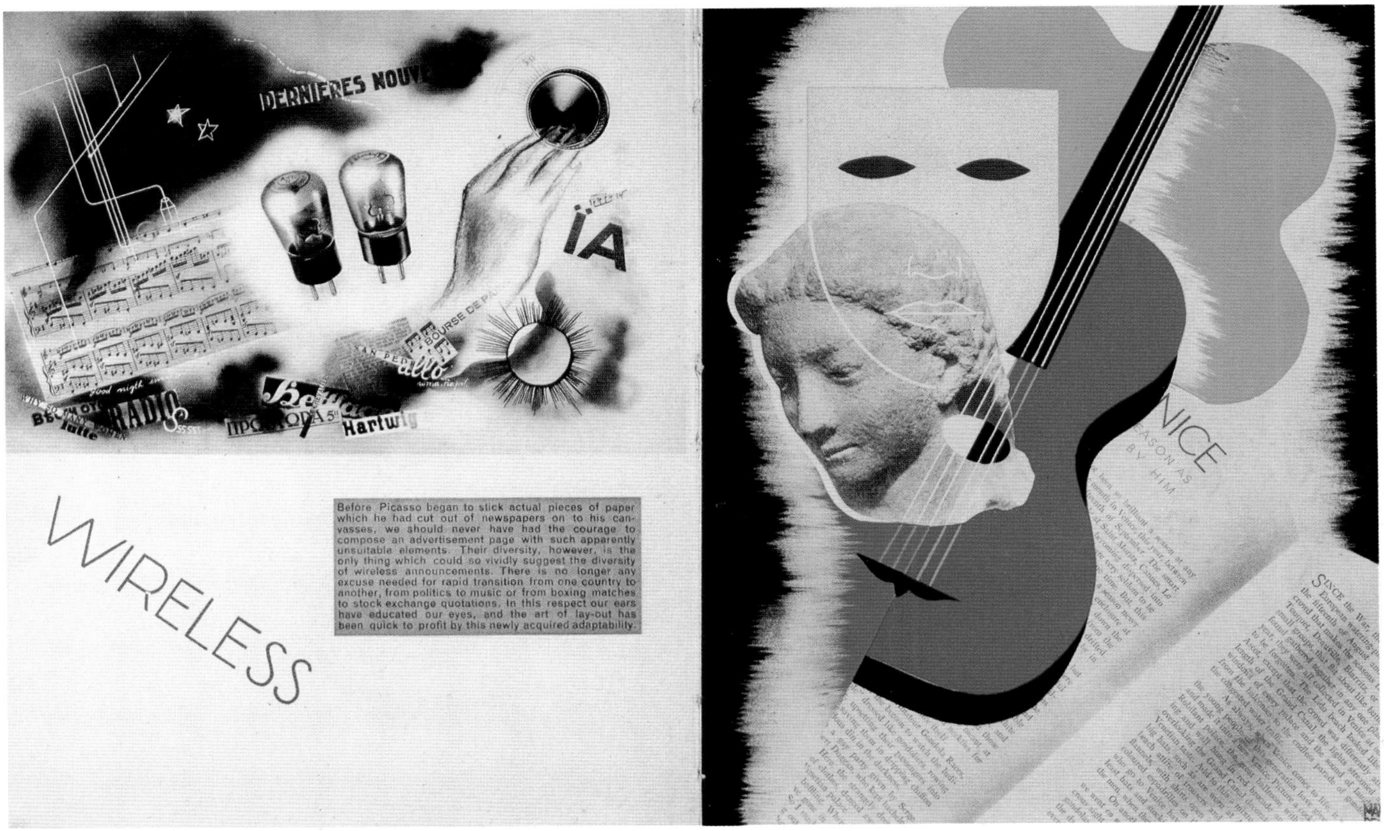

Spreads from *Mise en Page*, 1931, a guide to new layout ideas for the printer and the designer. Written, designed and produced by Parisian printer Albert Tolmer, it sought to blend the Bauhaus and commercial printing.

Uher's was not the only phototypesetting development. In New York, Photo-Lettering Inc. offered a service of photocomposed display lettering using the Rutherford Photo-Letter Composing Machine, launched in 1933. This machine had similarities with the Uher invention in that it used a glass slide to carry the character images, which was moved in front of the light source to expose characters, the images passing through a focusing lens on to photosensitive paper. The method and control was crude, there was still plenty of development to be done, but the basis for a new understanding of type was being born, through the embrace of photography.

This was the decade when men and women in the Western world began to see that world more through the camera, as represented in the cinema, and hear about it through their ears (radio) rather than relying on print and word of mouth. Indeed, the unsung designers of Hollywood movie titles were really getting to grips with expressive lettering as much as the celebrated heroes of modern design mentioned above. Print was still growing, but was no longer so dominant: for every daily newspaper bought in Britain (the country with the highest readership of newspapers) in the 1930s, two cinema tickets were sold.

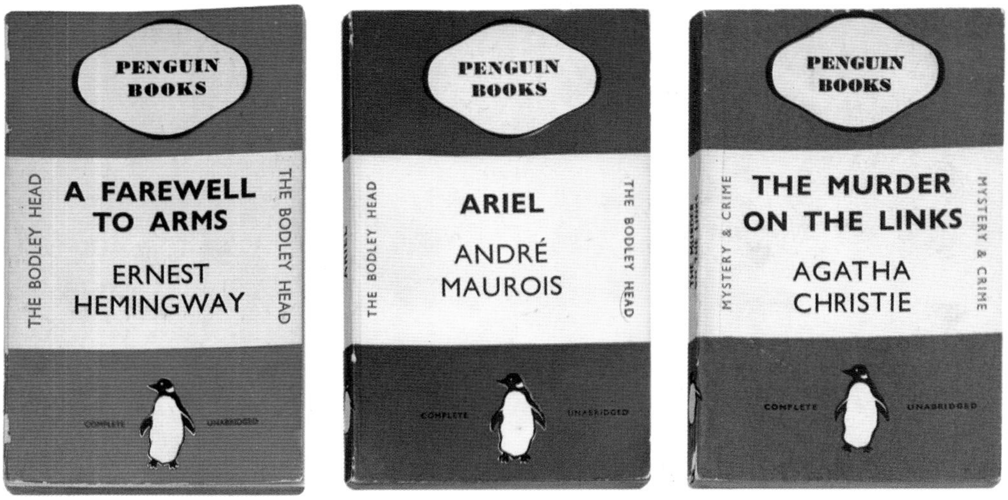

Above: early Penguin book covers from 1935 onwards. This London publisher took the paperback format upmarket and sought a new graphic language in the process. Gill Sans was used for the covers and Times New Roman for text, these new faces helping brand the offer. The publisher Allen Lane and designer Edward Young drew on the pioneering Tauchnitz editions, right, and the crisp typography and colour-coding of the Hamburg-based Albatross editions, far right, whose designer was the German/Italian fine printer and type designer Hans "Giovanni" Mardersteig.

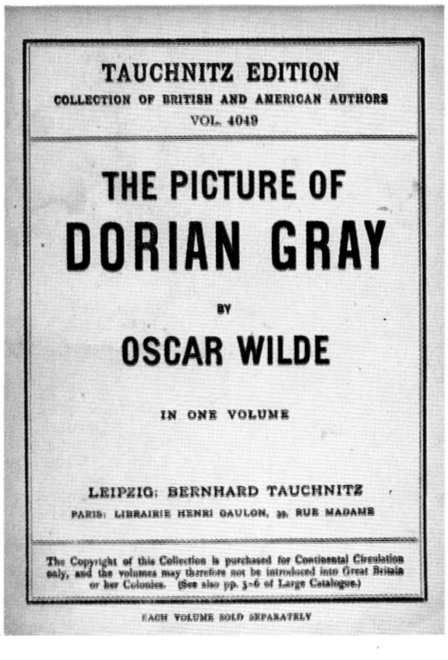

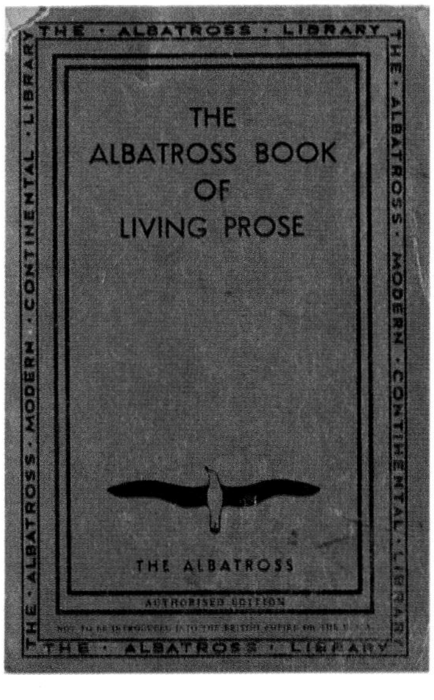

Above: two forms of a poster designed by Herbert Matter, 1935, for the Swiss tourist office. A single colour change of the red plate enables this poster to work in different languages, while the type remains integrated in the composition. The considerations of international business life are not to be under-rated as a spur to the development of form – the later success of the International Style is partly because it helped deliver efficient graphic design. Left: Motor by K. Sommer for Ludwig & Mayer, 1930 (called Dynamo in its unshaded version), is a "techno" font. It celebrates the car; now it is the computer.

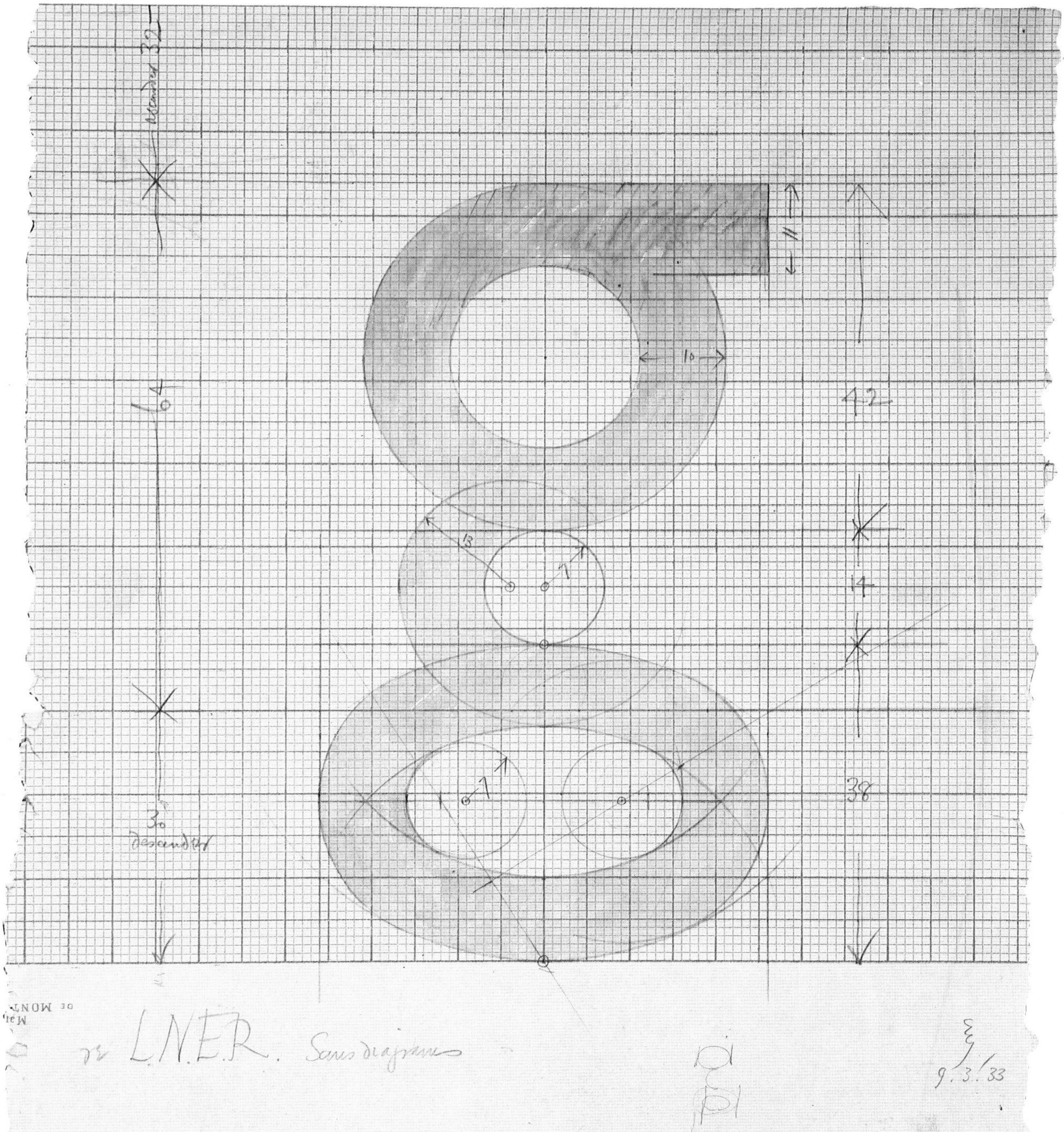

ascender 32
40
30
descender
11
10
42
13
7
14
38
L.N.E.R. Sans diagrams
9. 3. 33

Gill Sans *24pt*

a b c d e f g h i j k l m n

o p q r s t u v w x y z

A B C D E F G H I

J K L M N O P Q

R S T U V W X Y Z

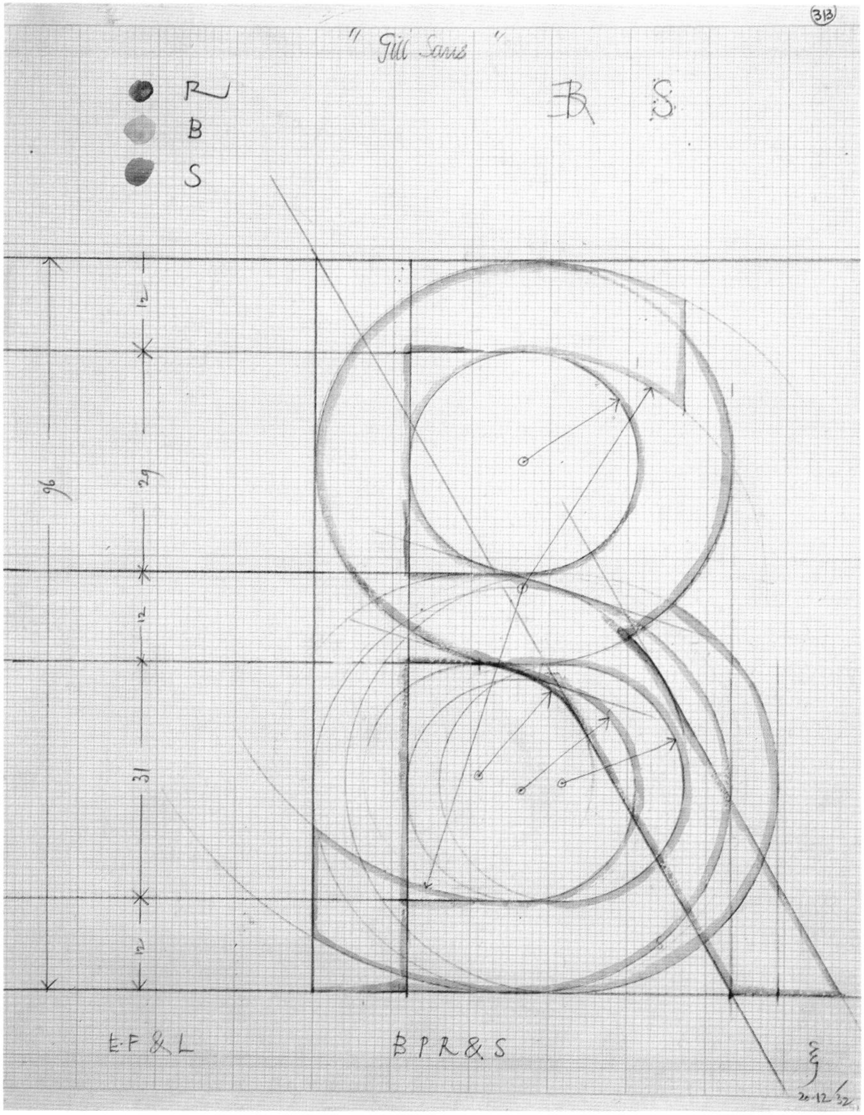

Left and opposite: drawings made by Eric Gill for the first version of his famous eponymous sans serif type, produced for the London & North Eastern Railway. One shows the "g" and was drawn in 1933; while the combined "B", "P", "R" and "S" dates from 1932. The LNER adopted Gill Sans for all signage, advertising and timetables.

OF 'Enola Gay'
29
Atomic Bomb
On HIROSHIMA
20144185
1
9
247

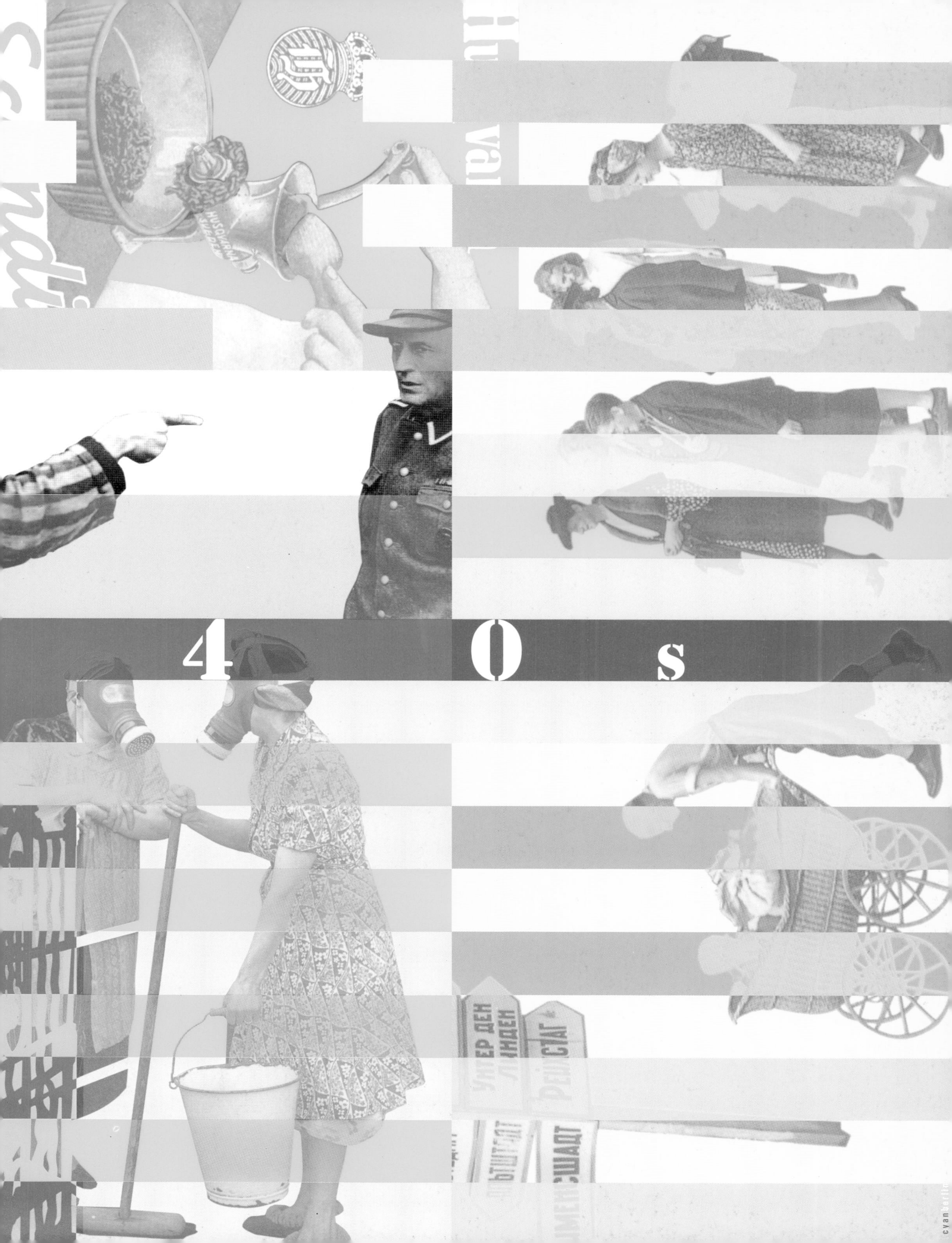
4 0 s

The Second World War delayed the advance of many ideas vaunted in the years before 1939. As resources and markets for new typefaces disappeared in the all-consuming war efforts, so too did the climate for experimentation: the early efforts at photosetting would have to wait twenty years for fulfilment, while aesthetic discussion also settled into entrenched positions for want of pioneers in education or the fuel of consumer demand for the new.

War produced its own distinct contribution to the demand for graphic design in the form of government information, particularly the propaganda poster. This was the last hurrah for the poster medium, which was increasingly undermined by the growth in magazine and newspapers and cinema, and soon to be knocked into a minority medium by the arrival of television as the means of mass communication.

The movement towards integrated image and type had taken root in much commercial work in the 1930s, but information posters were a different challenge: with scant resources, designers were often required to present complex messages that would be quickly understood. Some of the most noted posters of the period were produced by leading European designers of the prewar era – many of whom were working in exile in the US or Britain. In the US young American Modernists joined European exiles: the Office of War Information commissioned prominent designers such as the Austrian Joseph Binder, the Italian Leo Lionni and the Frenchman Jean Carlu to create posters. Exiles like Bayer and Matter, among others, produced designs for the Container Corporation of America's innovative series of promotions, in which the commercial purpose was largely subsumed within messages in support of the war effort.

The immigrant designers arrived with a vision that had an immediate impact on the American scene. A new typography acceded to power in the world's most powerful economy. The radical was becoming the mainstream. But these designers did not simply impose their beliefs; they were also changed by the experience of being accommodated within the framework of largely unfettered capitalism. This evolution would take the idealism of the 1920s into a creed of Modernist communication for the world. The brutal simplicity of high Bauhaus work developed into a more subtle, studied display of Modernist key principles. Sans type, the stripping-out of ornament and concentration on a core message gave fresh impetus to the punching out of war propaganda or commercial messages.

New York was the centre of graphic design activity and was the proving ground for the interplay of the new ideas and the vernacular. The results are apparent in the work of the "New York School" of American designers – Lester Beall (1903–69), Paul Rand (1914–97) and Bradbury Thompson (1911–95) being the most renowned. Rand's working life stretched over sixty years, from art directing *Apparel Arts*, *Direction* and then *Esquire* magazines in the late 1930s to doing corporate consultancy work for the likes of IBM and writing in the 1980s, to producing some final fiery polemics right up to the time of his death. In his work as an advertising art director at the Weintraub agency in the 1940s he pushed the standard of advertising layouts. His partnership with Bill Bernbach (1911–72, the founder of the advertising agency Doyle Dane Bernbach) helped lay the basis of the current concept of the art director and copywriter team: where the copywriter was once king in advertising, it increasingly became apparent that a full integration of the copywriter and art director's ideas enabled a more expressive approach to be taken towards type and image, allowing them to contain the idea, not simply carry it.

In 1946 Rand published *Thoughts On Design*. This book was an influential statement of his principles and also a sign that American graphics was maturing – it no longer needed to take all its direction from the European imports. Rand's career is marked by a bringing together of ideas from fine art while advancing the argument for an almost scientific approach to the issue of legibility with type. In *Thoughts On Design* he mixed commonsense practical notes with a mystical demand for typographic and visual communications to display "the integration of the beautiful and the useful".

The high point in Bradbury Thompson's contribution to typographic thought came through his editing of the promotional publication *Westvaco Inspirations*, between 1939 and 1961. His adventurous experiments with layouts explored the processes of print and punned on the potential of type and image. But they were more than just fun: they sought out a deep appropriateness of form for the subject. Thompson also designed *Mademoiselle* magazine from 1945 to 1959, was art director of *Art News* for twenty-seven years, and later in his career became a prolific designer of fine books. But his most provocative contribution was his development of the single alphabet idea promoted by Bayer and others with the 1946 publication of his "mono alphabet". Like Bayer, Thompson proposed that only the lower-case alphabet should be used. Experimenting with Futura, his proposal included beginning sentences with a full stop and using bold instead of capitals. In 1950 he presented a further refinement on the simplified alphabet idea called Alphabet 26. Instead of the forty-five different characters that exist in the upper- and lower-case alphabets, Thompson took the twenty-six that he saw as the most distinctive symbols for each letter. He used Baskerville for the exercise to show that the project was not about radical innovation but about concentration on what is at the heart of familiar type forms.

Rationed paper, conscripted troops and the removal of other resources for print and design work restricted the designers remaining in Europe. But as in the US, there was some poster art of note: in Britain, Modernist design was encouraged when the Ministry of Information asked the young designers Tom Eckersley, Abram Games and F.H.K. Henrion to produce posters. Their work displays an illustrative style that draws on art movements from Cubism to Surrealism, but there is a fresh voice in the type: as with the American designers of the same period, there is a deliberate, playful reference to a vernacular in the lettering. Stencil cuts and Victorian-style playbill lettering found new uses, as did older sans faces and a few others.

Stencil *36pt*

ABCDEFG
HIJKLMN
OPQRSTU
VWXYZ

Above: R. Hunter Middleton's Stencil, designed in the late 1930s, was an ironic nod to a vernacular that was to become only too relevant in the next six years. Stencilled characters are emblematic of the1940s – the characters detailing military equipment, a mix of the industrial (the stencil) and the hand-crafted nature of its operation. World War made typeface production a luxury in work and in materials. Right: cover of a publication from 1942 recording the Autocar Company's production of vehicles for the war effort – an authentic stencil being used by designer Paul Rand for the effect here. Inside spreads are in a typewriter face, without margins. Brutal crops and stark contrasts in shape are given the ultimate functional flourish with a spiral binding, implying the book was more a useful manual than a self-congratulatory brochure.

There was little incorporation of the new with the old for Jan Tschichold, though. His development was an abrupt move from one to the other. During the war years his work included a series of book covers for the publisher Birkhäuser as well as research into type and calligraphic areas, the results of which appeared in his own books and articles. The Birkhäuser books are the blueprint for the work Tschichold would do when he was invited in 1946 to develop the design of the fast-growing paperback publisher, Penguin.

His impact can be seen easily by contrasting the previous Penguins with the new: new type, new spacing, even a new penguin. But the neatly centred, generously spaced, almost understated covers are unassuming from the perspective of the designer's ego – the effect is the assertion of many classic values of book design. Besides the link with the Birkhäuser work, there is a debt to the work of Giovanni Mardersteig (1892–1977) on the 1930s Albatross books. As with the typographer and fine printer Mardersteig, Tschichold believed the key to the efficient typography of mass-production books was to devise an approach to communication, design and implementation that was rigorously applied. The Penguin Composition Rules were the result of Tschichold's concern to ensure that the various printers and typesetters who took on Penguin work would understand his requirements and work to them. Grids were produced for the different series, an innovation for the publisher. No hard and fast rules were set for typefaces – each book was tackled on its own merits, albeit jacket design elements fitted in with the identities for the various series. But every cover, title page

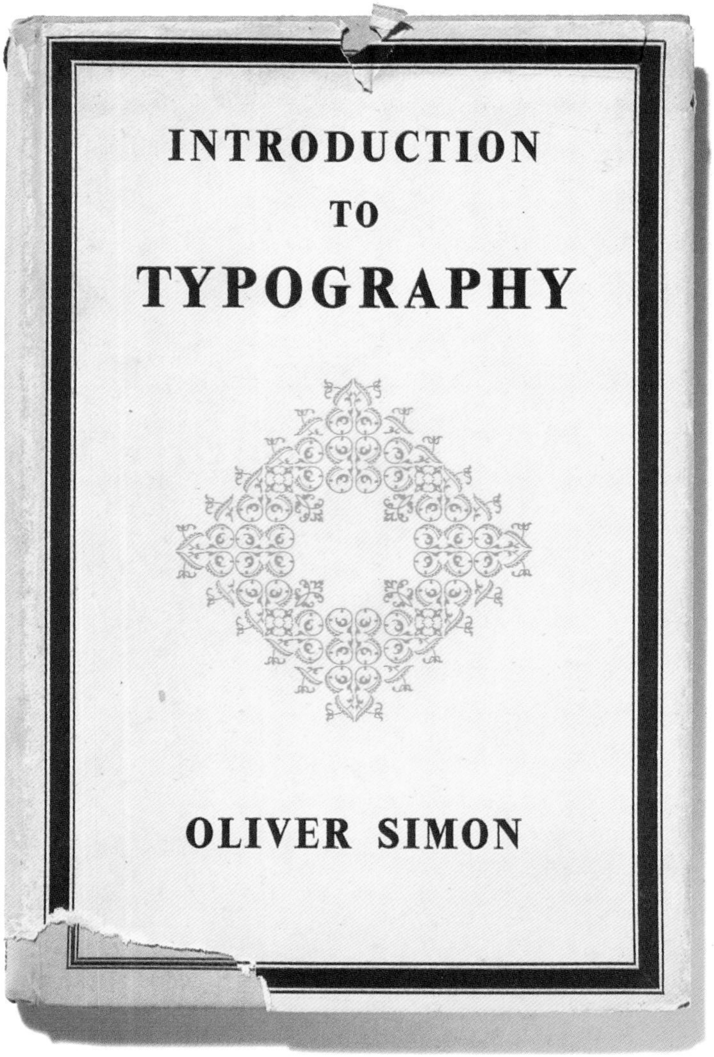

Left: Oliver Simon's *Introduction to Typography*, published 1946, was a slim bible of 138 A5 pages for the jobbing British printer. It set out the rules of quality typographic practice at the mid-century point. Below is a sample spread encouraging the proper use of printers' "flowers" – wholly at odds with Modernist thought.

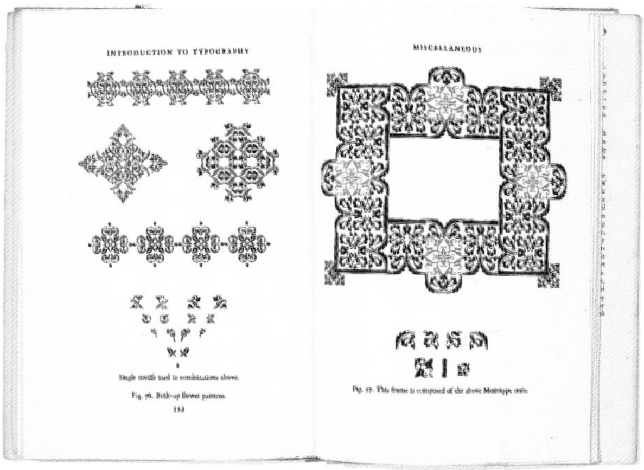

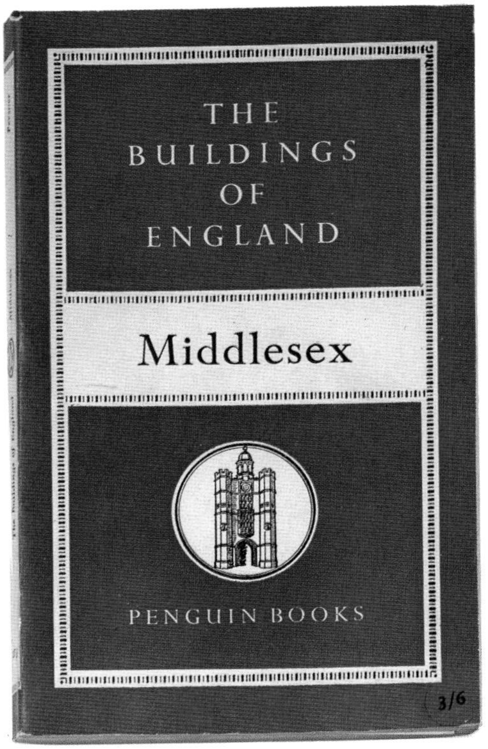

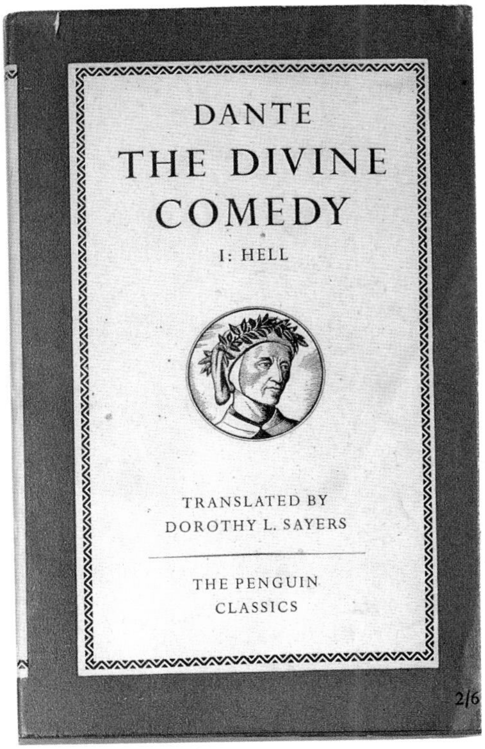

Above: Etruria Vetulonia, one of the first of the many type designs by Aldo Novarese (1920-97) for Nebiolo in Turin. Etruria was the name for the land occupied by the Etruscans, the most ancient Italian culture and a touchstone for Mussolini's rabid nationalism. Right: Jan Tschichold's work for Penguin from 1946 demonstrated his apostasy from 1920s new typography and embrace of the fine detail of classicism. He built this into the cornerstone of a corporate identity, closely controlling the image of the various sub-brands (as here with The Buildings Of England series, and Penguin Classics) and imparting a sense of the cohesive values.

Van der Leck *24pt*

ABCDE
FGHIJK
LMNOP
QRSTU
VWXYZ

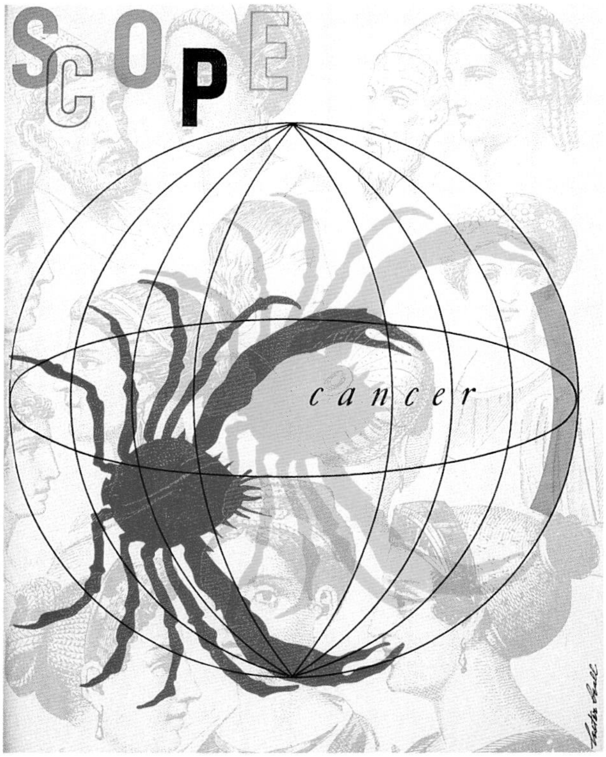

and run of body text was deemed to be part of an individual work that had to have its own coherence. Legibility, clarity and elegance were watch words. Tschichold worked on more than five hundred books before returning to Switzerland in 1949, and his rules continued to be applied after he left by his successor Hans Schmoller.

Tschichold's rejection of his earlier principles and embracing of traditional forms brought him into open conflict with the Swiss designer Max Bill. In 1946, following the report of a lecture Tschichold had given, Bill wrote an open letter attacking the "threadbare" and "reactionary" quality of Tschichold's arguments. This prompted the victim to hit back with a long reply outlining his position on Modernism versus classicism and implying that the threadbare and reactionary was apparent in his critic's arguments.[1] Tschichold positions traditional typefaces and layouts as representative of a rich, organic process understood and appreciated by many and in contrast to the arcane and absolute new rules of the Modernist typography. The celebration of mechanization is attacked as a dehumanizing and essentially pointless concern. Tschichold criticizes the obsession with sans faces, saying it is fine for some display work, but is unsuitable for text. He praises the removal of superfluous elements (such as numerous faces and sizes) advocated by the new typography and recognizes its awareness of compositional quality. But, with a sense of irony, Tschichold points out that he himself set down many of the new typography rules obeyed by the likes of Bill, and asserts that he had kept to the key rules in his apparently "reactionary" move.

Bill *24pt*

abcdefghijklmnop
qrstuvwwxyz

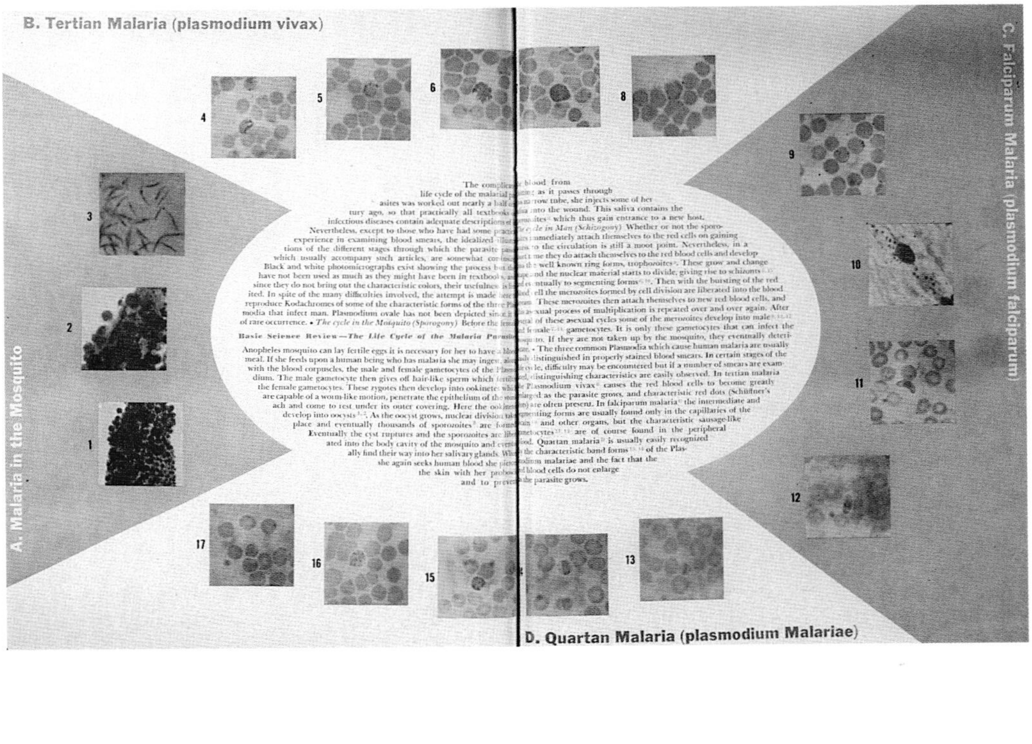

For all that there was a hiatus in new type, and a backlash against the Modernist innovations of the pre-war years, experimental lettering in the 1940s survived in pockets. Opposite left: De Stijl influenced lettering by the painter Bart van der Leck for a 1941 edition of a Hans Andersen story. Above: Max Bill's lettering for a 1949 exhibition stand, with geometry meeting calligraphy. Both these have been made into digital type Architypes in the 1990s by The Foundry in London. Opposite and left: cover (March 1948) and a spread (June 1944) from the magazine *Scope* designed by Lester Beall for the Upjohn Corporation in the United States. Beall's use of a minimal palette of typeface, in size and form, was enlivened by a masterly use of tints and of half-tones, showing the emerging opportunity for and awareness of the extra power of colour in editorial. The spread here shows the life-cycle of the malaria parasite.

Bringing together the two strands of typographic development, Tschichold acknowledged a debt to Stanley Morison and his colleagues at Monotype for the rebirth and development of classic types which had "brought with it a typographic revival the world over that is as important as the cleaning-up process of the new typography was for Germany". In 1946 the principles of the "rebirth" were crystallized in a slim volume written by the man who was instrumental in advising the choice of Tschichold for the Penguin job, Oliver Simon. In the 1920s he had edited the first four issues of *The Fleuron*, preceding those edited by Morison, and in the 1930s he had run another typographic magazine, *Signature*, as well as carrying out his work as director and typographer of the fine book printer The Curwen Press. Now, in his *Introduction To Typography*, Simon set down the principles of good practice in book typography of the kind Tschichold and Morison admired and good printers knew by heart. It was written for the young printers, publishers and other interested parties who would be involved in the rapid growth of postwar printing. It went into several editions, and was a further propagator of the orthodox standing firm against the Modernists. It did not even mention the New Typography or those designers associated with it. World conflict had ended, but design was still at war.

Trade Gothic *24pt*

ABCDEFGHIJKLMNOPQRSTUVWXYZ
abcdefghijklmnopqrstuvwxyz

G

Opposite: in this poster for motor racing at Monza in Italy the foreshortened projection of the words helps create both the sense of depth and speed. Meanwhile the red, green and white suggest the colours of the Italian flag; but it is the red, blue and green speeding arrows that suggest the cars; while the green and blue are the type (suggestive of sky and countryside?). The enigmatic yet highly reduced mix of figurative and abstract makes this poster by Max Huber a masterpiece of mid-century graphics, realizing the new ways of seeing within a real commercial setting. Left: Trade Gothic, first released in 1948 by Linotype and added to in succeeding years to produce an extensive family of variations. Designed by Jackson Burke, this is a utilitarian face (condensed even in its standard form) that mixed Modernist tweaks into a basic nineteenth-century sans.

Gran premio
dell' Autodromo
17 ottobre 1948
Monza

"As there are many splendid types of earlier centuries that we still gladly use in printing, it may perhaps be asked why new types are designed. Our time, however, sets the designer other tasks than did the past. A new type must, along with beauty and legibility, be adapted to the technical requirements of today, when high-speed presses and rotary presses have replaced the hand press, and machine-made paper supplanted the handmade sheet. Just as musicians and artists seek to create some new expression of our time and link it to a rich past, so too must the work of type designers and type founders remain bound to the great tradition of the alphabet."

In his 1954 book of typographic quotes and exercises, *Manuale Typographicum*, Hermann Zapf (1918–) noted the inevitable requirements for change wrought by new audiences, new media and new technology. The 1950s were the last years of hot metal's unchallenged leadership in typographic communication. By the end of the decade photosetting had gone beyond the experimental and was delivering radical change in the process of generating type.

Growing audiences for, briefly, cinema, and then the explosion of television as the mass medium of choice, threw up new challenges for the application of type and lettering that broke free of the restrictions and labours of metal setting. Movie titles of the 1950s began to integrate type and images in ways dreamt of by Moholy-Nagy in the 1920s. The work of the designer and director Saul Bass (1920–96) on films such as *The Man With The Golden Arm*, *Walk On The Wild Side*, *Psycho* and *Vertigo* fully integrated lettering and image into time-based experiences capable of setting the mood and suggesting a story. But while the creative vision was in tune with the times, the process of creating type was still stuck with materials and processes that were in keeping with nineteenth-century knowledge. Lettering for titles and other screen imagery was more easily drawn by hand than done by hot metal or handsetting, which created a proof that had to be transferred to film.

While there were many individual contributions made by designers, such as the noted typefaces of Hermann Zapf and Roger Excoffon (1910–83) (see illustration), who both explored and mixed tradition, calligraphy and modern demand in their work, this period stands out for the emergence of the school that came to dominate typographic layout worldwide – the Swiss/International Style. The designers in this group had a massive impact, projecting theories that still underpin much that is taught and practised despite years of reaction against the approach. The International Style is based on the creation of a grid for all designs, and the concentration on sans serif faces and asymmetric layouts. Its roots can be seen to relate clearly to the work of Theo Ballmer (see page 68), but it is also a derivation and pursuit of the ideals espoused by the Bauhaus and the young Tschichold, and it has links with the De Stijl artists' reduction of form to rectangular blocks and lines. One teacher in particular would later have a major influence: from 1918 until 1956 Ernst Keller taught at the Kunstgewerbeschule in Zurich (Applied Art School). Among his early pupils were Ballmer, and later Adrian Frutiger and Edouard Hoffman (designers of the ground-breaking 1950s faces Univers and Helvetica). Keller preached clarity and simplicity, restricted styles and close letter fit. These principles aimed for communication divorced from the baggage of tradition and the clutter of unnecessary associations.

Layouts designed by Ballmer and Max Bill in the 1930s were early intimations of this approach. By splitting the page or poster into a grid, modules were arrived at that could be used to articulate clearly proportion, balance and perspective. In 1950 Bill began teaching at the Hochschule für Gestaltung in Ulm, Germany, developing a curriculum that united his background of Bauhaus training and Swiss-style schooling with an attempt at a universal statement about typography. His search for a rigorous, mathematical logic to graphic design was similar to the teaching of Emil Ruder (1914–70) in Basel around the same time, who sought to pare down the thinking of students to an appreciation of the value of white space and formal rhythms in relation to the type. He stressed that the empty space was as crucial a part of the design as the printed areas and encouraged a limited selection of faces, weights and styles. But he also appreciated novelty and dynamic qualities in layouts. This did not permit unaccountable idiosyncrasy, though. Unlike some other Swiss theorists, Ruder was not opposed to justified setting, seeing it as sometimes preferable to ragged right as it balanced blocks of text and prevented setting from being a dense mass.

Joseph Müller-Brockmann (1914–96) was a Swiss designer whose visual ability, manifested in poster work and books, gave dramatic beauty to the reductive principles behind International Style. He went further than Ruder and Bill in laying down laws, proposing "objective design" that was freed from designers' subjective expressions and taste and instead represented a purely functional communication. He opposed the combining of different type families, or even different forms of the same family. Different sizes were also to be avoided, and the type area should be as compact as possible. Line spacing should not permit any line to be isolated and inter-word spacing was to be uniform. He preferred sans serif faces for their avoidance of "decorative" contrasting stroke weight and the "ornament" of the serif, believing they functioned as well as romans for most tasks.

These views went from being essentially Swiss-based to being discussed and followed worldwide. This was partly due to the movement of influential designers around Europe and to the United States but also to the promotion of these principles in the magazine *Neue Grafik*, launched in 1959. Edited by Müller-Brockmann, Richard Lohse, Hans Neuberg and Carlo Vivarelli, it was written in German, English and French and illustrated these design principles by using the best new Swiss typography.

The argument for sans serif faces promoted by the Swiss typographers built on the earlier influence of the Bauhaus which had led all the major foundries to turn out copies of

Left: promotional image by Roger Excoffon (1910-83) of his brush-stroke type Choc of 1953. Released by the Fonderie Olive, this was one of a series of joyful and ingenious types by Excoffon that managed to retain the sense of the calligrapher's freehand within the constraints of metal type. These brush scripts were designed primarily for advertising and quickly gained popularity, giving the opportunity for fresh expression in an era wishing to break from the drab and imposed utilitarianism of the near past.

Optima *18pt*

ABCDEFGHIJKLMNOPQRSTUVWXYZ
abcdefghijklmnopqrstuvwxyz

Melior *18pt*

ABCDEFGHIJKLMNOPQRSTUVWXYZ
abcdefghijklmnopqrstuvwxyz

Top left: two faces by Hermann Zapf, the innovative Optima (1958) and Melior (1952). Melior was designed as a tough text face, such as on newsprint, with designs based on the rectangle. Optima explores the area between serif and sans serif, creating the stressed sans serif. Zapf's great calligraphic skills enabled him to combine modern geometric forms with the Venetian type examples he also admired, achieving a highly readable yet radical new form. Left: cover of *Rassegna Grafica*, 1955, by Franco Grignani (born 1908). The cover also demonstrates the impact that photographic manipulation was beginning to have on typography, even before photosetting arrived. Far left: the new discipline of corporate identity drew heavily on new typography in devising memorable marks that spoke of modernity. At the core of identity programmes were typographic rulebooks. Paul Rand's work for IBM, 1956, developed the existing slab serif initials, but the breakthrough point in giving character was to make the form from lines, memorably striping the whole logo block, giving it greater harmony and originality.

Above: Saul Bass (1920–96) pioneered film titles and posters as a field of evocative graphic design, producing creative ideas that worked as campaigns across film and into print. His work in the 1950s and early 1960s continues to be influential to the present day, with the above work having been taken as inspiration for at least two advertising campaigns in recent years. He combined type, calligraphy, illustration and photography – appreciating the flexibility of film and feeding that back into his print imagery.
Left: Roger Excoffon's Banco of 1951 is manifestly hand-drawn and yet suggests cut forms, strips of material laid down. Almost all his fonts were for display use, through Fonderie Olive. As a graphic designer, Excoffon saw the opportunity for more exuberant display faces in advertising (he worked for Air France among others).

Futura quickly in the late 1920s and 1930s. By the 1950s Futura and its copies had become a leading choice for advertising. Contemporary reviews of typeface usage and change of fashion in advertising noted that whereas in the UK in 1929 Cheltenham, Goudy and an unspecified sans serif grouping were first, second and third in popularity, by 1953 the figures had swapped around so that contemporary sans cuts were the first choice, followed by revived gothics, followed by Monotype's Plantin. In the US, Garamond, Caslon and Bodoni were the top three in 1929, but Bodoni, Century and Futura were leading in 1952.[1]

This demand fed the creation of Helvetica and Univers, two faces most emblematic of type design in the twentieth century. Neither could be mistaken for the product of an earlier century, but neither was so radical as to prevent quick adoption. Both were to be enormously successful. Their origin lay in the enthusiasm of designers for sans faces and the growing dissatisfaction with geometric sans serifs. It was not Futura or one of the post-Bauhaus faces that the Swiss typographers favoured above all – instead the 1896 Berthold face Akzidenz Grotesk (or Standard, in a copied version) was the constant choice of designers like Max Bill. Being a "modern gothic", Akzidenz Grotesk does not have the squared, contrasting stroke style associated with gothics such as Benton's ever-popular Franklin Gothic, and it was favoured over the geometrics for its ability to provide a more comfortable close fit of letters, with a rhythm and character the geometric faces lacked (there is a slight contrast of stroke, and tails to letters such as "a", "j", "t" and "u").

aLPHaBeT 26

Throughout this issue, only one symbol for each of the 26 characters of the alphabet is used. Ordinarily, 19 of these characters are represented by two symbols quite unlike in appearance. The other seven characters are essentially identical in both upper- and lower-case design. This experiment is based on the logic, represented by these seven letters and by the illustration at right, that a symbol or trade-mark of any kind, to be efficient, should be constant.

In observing the earliest reading efforts of children today who are taught to recognize words even before memorizing individual letters of the alphabet, one may see a fallacy in single characters having two designs. [See below.]

a previous experiment in Issue 152 entitled the "Monalphabet" suggested the exclusive use of the lower-case design for all characters. To provide large letters performing the function of capitals, that plan requires the redesign of traditional letters with ascenders or descenders to enable them to fit on the customary type body. With "alphabet 26," as this present experiment is called, the problem is avoided by eliminating designs having ascenders or descenders. The alphabet at lower right employs some upper-case and some lower-case versions.

Of important consideration are the letters "a, e, m and n." The lower-case designs are selected because they do not

Continued on following page

Design and Typography of This Issue: Bradbury Thompson

Run Pal.
See him run.
Go Pal.
See him go.

From the above page of a First Reader, a child learns to recognize the words "Run" and "Go" only to be confused in the lines below because the same words are different in appearance, as upper- and lower-case "Rs" and "Gs" are unlike.

aBCDe
FGHIJK
LmnOP
QRSTU
VWXYZ

Upper-case design is used for these characters
Lower-case design is used for these four characters
Only one design exists for these seven characters

Above: the CBS "eye" logo of 1951 by Robert Golden worked across media – being a powerful device in television and in print, with a typographic pun (the C of CBS is also the pupil of the eye). Left: Alphabet 26 by Bradbury Thompson, as he presented it in Westvaco Inspirations 180, 1950. Thompson proposed merging the "best" of the upper and lower cases of Baskerville, selecting one form of a letter from each case. Capitals were set larger. Opposite: combined catalogue and exhibition poster by Marcel Duchamp, 1953. In contrast to Dadaist art, the poster is highly rational, working as advertising, but also giving a list of exhibits and four features on the event.

DADA
1916-1923
sidney janis
15 east 57
new york
april 15
to may 9
1953

Eduard Hoffman at the Haas foundry noted the popularity of Akzidenz Grotesk and commissioned Max Miedinger to refine it and give Haas a version of it to sell: this resulted in Neue Haas Grotesk (1951–53), later renamed Helvetica when sold to Stempel (1957) and then Linotype and produced in a full family of variants. This was a face that was developed neither as an experiment nor as a punt into the marketplace, nor as a sport, nor simply as a copy of somebody else's success (although there is an element of that), but rather as a clear response to overwhelming demand. It became the most popular face for many advertising typographers, while also finding usage in text settings.

Left: "You too are liberal" poster by Karl Gerstner, 1956. Swiss style at its most reductive, with just the single bleed image taken to a hard graphic, and the brief copyline placed confidently between the focal points of the image (the finger tip and the eyes) and set in lower case except for the attention drawn to the "you" by the upper-case "D". The suggestion is clear: the subject of the piece is the viewer rather than the man pointing.

Systematische Grafikerausbildung
A Training System for the Graphic Designer
Formation méthodique des graphistes

33

la pratique et prennent conscience de leur futur métier. Les exemples représentés sont des travaux caractéristiques exécutés durant les quatre ans d'apprentissage. Leur présentation n'emprunte rien à la chronologie, mais elle est divisée selon les différentes disciplines. Le premier essai important confié à l'élève qui entre dans la classe de graphisme ne constitue nullement un travail très attrayant et qui exige néanmoins une attention soutenue: il consiste en la définition des propositions de formes et de volume afin d'en trouver une application pratique. Telle qu'elle se présente, à l'aide de dessins et de photos de modèles, la tâche comprend les problèmes essentiels suivants:

1. Huit surfaces en forme de cercle doivent être trouvées dans des grandeurs différentes, mais ayant une proportion réciproque entre elles. Ces proportions doivent répondre à un principe logique et satisfaire l'esthétique.
2. Ces huit cercles sont posés chacun sur une surface carrée. Les huit surfaces carrées ainsi obtenues sont disposées sur la feuille de dessin de telle façon que les espaces, les carrés et les marges constituent également une proportion bien définie.
3. Avec les huit cercles, il convient de créer une composition. Cette composition ne doit pas choquer la logique, c'est-à-dire qu'elle devra se conformer à la forme et à l'esthétique. Les distances qui séparent les cercles seront conformes à des proportions définies.
4. La composition avec les huit cercles est assujettie à une projection de plan. Parmi les huit corps à trois dimensions, il convient de définir la forme et la grandeur. Chaque dimension doit donner une mesure logique de proportion.
5. La composition des trois dimensions est exécutée dans une matière que l'élève choisira lui-même si possible (bois ou métal, matière plastique, etc.).

M.
Rein zeichnerische Versuchsarbeiten
167
Eduard Müller
Diese als Werkzeichnung ausgeführte Arbeit symbolisiert die Präzision des SKF-Kugellagers. Die Typografie ist organisch dazu in Beziehung gebracht
168
Alois Märchy
Zeichnerische Formulierung einer Hallenkonstruktion
169
Gianfranco Verna
Konstruktionszeichnung, grafisch überarbeitet

M.
Work consisting of pure drawing
167
Eduard Müller
This drawing symbolises the precision of SKF ball bearings. The typography is organically related to the drawing.
168
Alois Märchy
Drawing for the construction of a hall
169
Gianfranco Verna
Drawing for a construction retouched

M.
Travaux résolus par le dessin
167
Eduard Müller
Ce dessin d'usine symbolise la précision des roulements à billes SKF. La typographie est en rapport direct avec le dessin
168
Alois Märchy
Construction d'une halle figurée par le dessin
169
Gianfranco Verna
Dessin de construction travaillé par le graphisme

Left and above: from *Neue Grafik*. Published 1958-66, the magazine set out the philosophy of Swiss Style typography, while its ambitions to internationalism were expressed through the use of three languages throughout. The journal was edited by Zürich-based designers Josef Müller-Brockmann, Richard Lohse, Hans Neuberg and Carlo Vivarelli. There is a severe organization around the grid, with Akzidenz Grotesk the only face used, and just two sizes (headline and body text). The layout above features concert posters by Müller-Brockmann and the poster in the layout left is by Eduard Müller.

Univers was less a market-led product and more a fulfilment of functionalist ideals – it offered an integrated family that took the basic desire for a modern, lightly stressed gothic and produced it in a comprehensive range of twenty-one variants presented in a nomenclature that attempted a revolution in type description. It was designed by Adrian Frutiger (1928–), originally as an experimental project before he was invited by the foundry Deberny & Peignot to advise on typefaces that could be transferred to photocomposition. Univers was launched in 1954 by Deberny & Peignot with a distinctive specimen sheet that presented weight and width in a logical palette, with reference numbers rather than imprecise names such as "extra bold". This idea did not catch on because printers were not interested in changing their language, however modern and logical it might be for a modern and logical face such as Univers.

Univers was distinctive in being produced in both a photosetting and a metal version. The booming demand and the new phase of type design and typographic debate of the 1950s was accompanied by radical change in the means of production. Although there had been experimentation since the turn of the century, photocomposition was not really practical until the 1950s. The process involved exposing a master negative of the characters on to photographic film in the required size. Focus, alignment, consistency of exposure and spacing had been problems before, but these were tackled until a range of competitive machines came on to the market. Different methods of storing type information were used, some using disks, some using grids. From experiments at the beginning of the decade, the systems had advanced to real commercial application by the end – in 1959, National Geographic installed the first full production model of a

Univers, designed by Adrian Frutiger for Deberny & Peignot, 1954-7. As the name suggests, it was intended to be universal, and the diagram and numbering system Frutiger devised, right, set out the principle of the 21 variations and how they related. This was a revolutionary concept for how families related, doing away with terms such as "bold", "italic", "extended" and "condensed". At the centre is Univers 55, the equivalent of standard book setting. The vertical axis shows weight, while the horizontal notes perspective. All even numbers are italic.

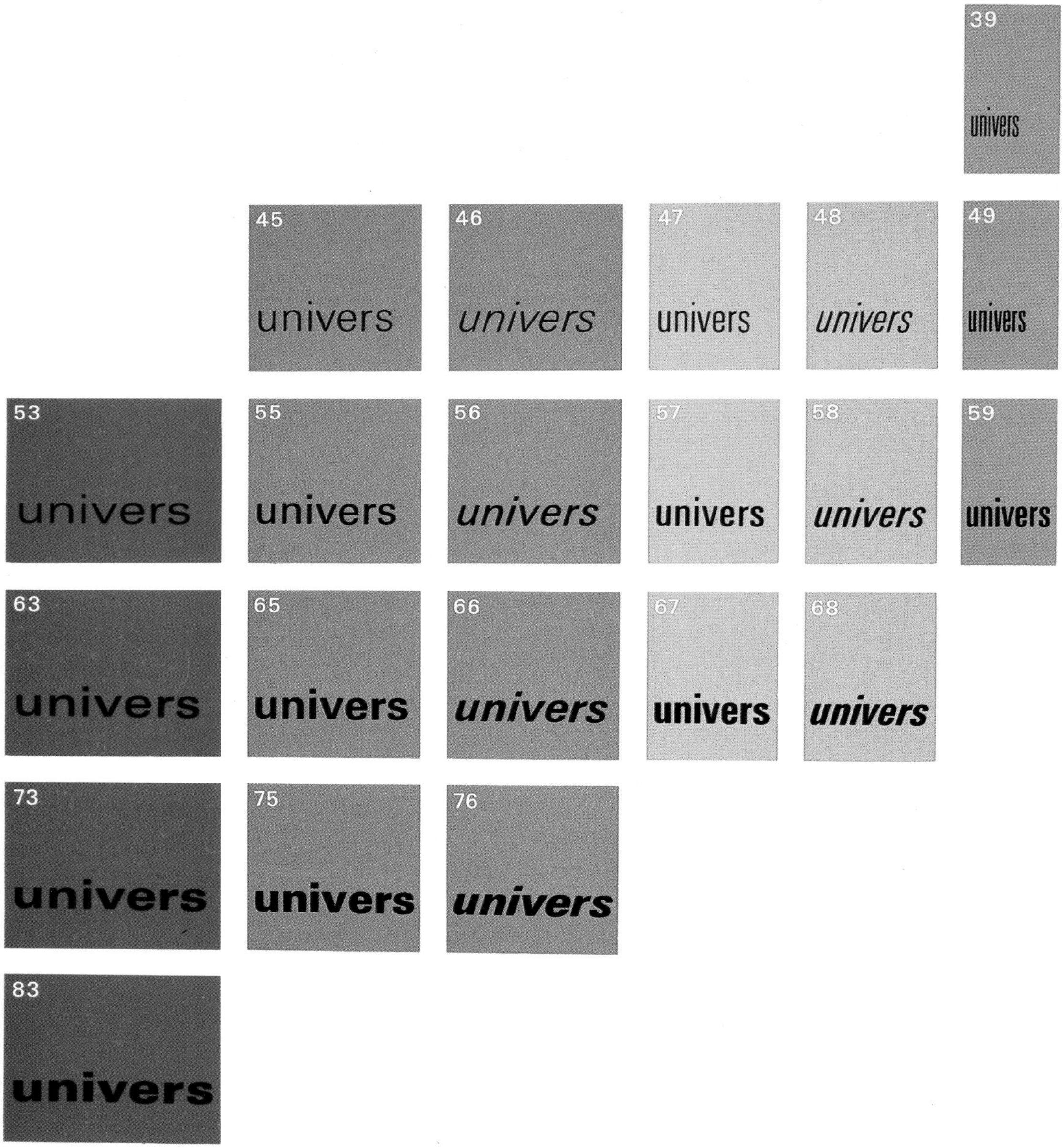

Linofilm. Photocomposition promised a cheaper, cleaner and faster way of typesetting in a form that was easily applicable to advances in film science as applied to offset lithography. But in typography the benefits would prove less certain: while the flexibility of type positioning had been improved (kerning was easier), the tendency of enlarging type to different sizes from a master, rather than holding different cuts in different sizes, would lead to the degradation of letterform quality.

Computer setting was also pioneered in this decade. It held out the prospect of saving the labours of justifying type, but it was apparent that the human eye and intelligence were not easily replaced with the achievement of consistent line setting: gaping spaces between words, and inadequate and insensitive hyphenation became associated with computer setting into the 1990s (particularly in newspapers).

Much less sophisticated, but nevertheless highly significant, Letraset instant lettering was made into a viable commercial proposition in the 1950s, the company being properly set up to exploit the process in 1959 when it offered a wet transfer method of obtaining camera-ready type. Dry transfer followed in the early 1960s. This was a vital contributor to the spirit of eclectic adventure that would in the following years shake out the staid, craftsman-like associations of graphic design, bringing typographic experimentation into the hands of anyone who could afford a sheet of rub-down letters.

Univers 55 *24pt*

A B C D E F G H I J K L
MNOPQRSTUVWXYZ
abcdefghijklmnopqrs
tuvwxyz

u

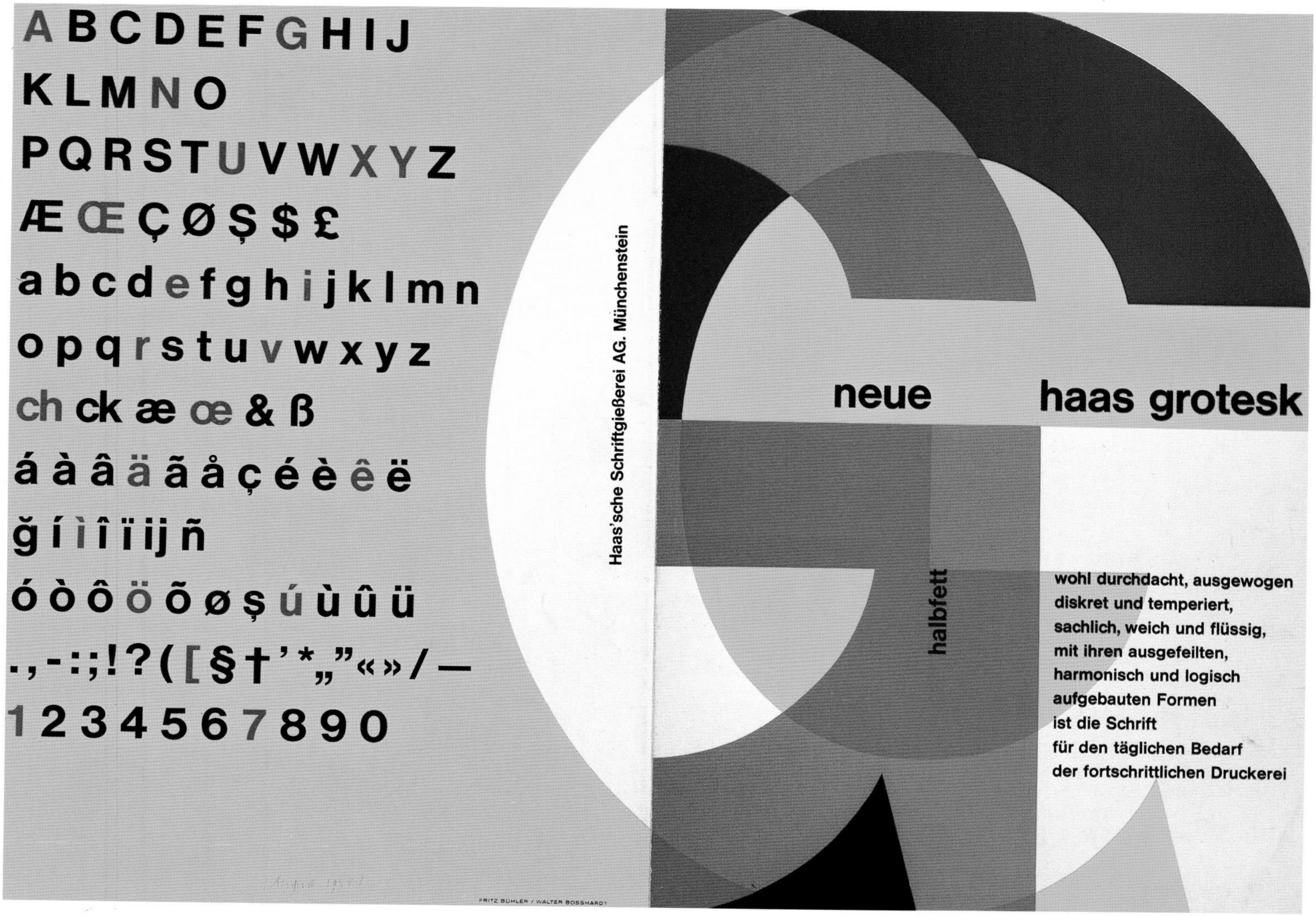
ABCDEFGHIJ
KLMNO
PQRSTUVWXYZ
ÆŒÇØŞ$£
abcdefghijklmn
opqrstuvwxyz
ch ck æ œ & ß
á à â ä ã å ç é è ê ë
ğ í ì î ï ij ñ
ó ò ô ö õ ø ş ú ù û ü
.,-:;!?([§†'*„"«»/—
1234567890
Haas'sche Schriftgießerei AG. Münchenstein
neue haas grotesk
halbfett
wohl durchdacht, ausgewogen
diskret und temperiert,
sachlich, weich und flüssig,
mit ihren ausgefeilten,
harmonisch und logisch
aufgebauten Formen
ist die Schrift
für den täglichen Bedarf
der fortschrittlichen Druckerei
FRITZ BÜHLER / WALTER BOSSHARDT

Helvetica roman *24pt*

ABCDEFGHIJKLMNOPQRSTUVWXYZ
abcdefghijklmnopqrstuvwxyz

Opposite: promotional material for Neue Haas Grotesk (1958), the typeface designed to replace Akzidenz Grotesk in the favour of Swiss designers. Eduard Hoffman of the Haas foundry asked in-house designer Max Miedinger to develop the face, which has a higher x-height than AG and takes slight influence from the more geometric sans serifs that had come after the then 50-year-old AG. Designed by Miedinger and Hoffman in 1951-53, it was licensed to Stempel and to Linotype, who renamed it Helvetica (Latin for Switzerland). Left: an early 1960s promotional piece for Helvetica. In the 1960s Helvetica rose to become the most popular of all sans serifs, with its modern cut aided by a name that tied in with a belief in Swiss graphics.

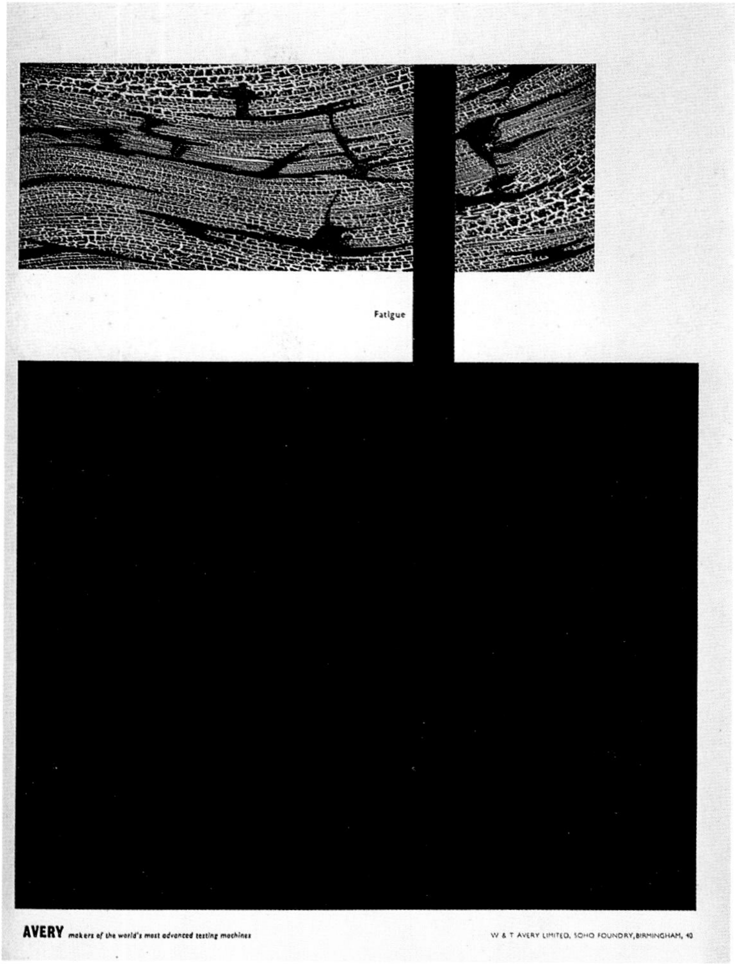
Fatigue
AVERY makers of the world's most advanced testing machines
W & T AVERY LIMITED, SOHO FOUNDRY, BIRMINGHAM, 40

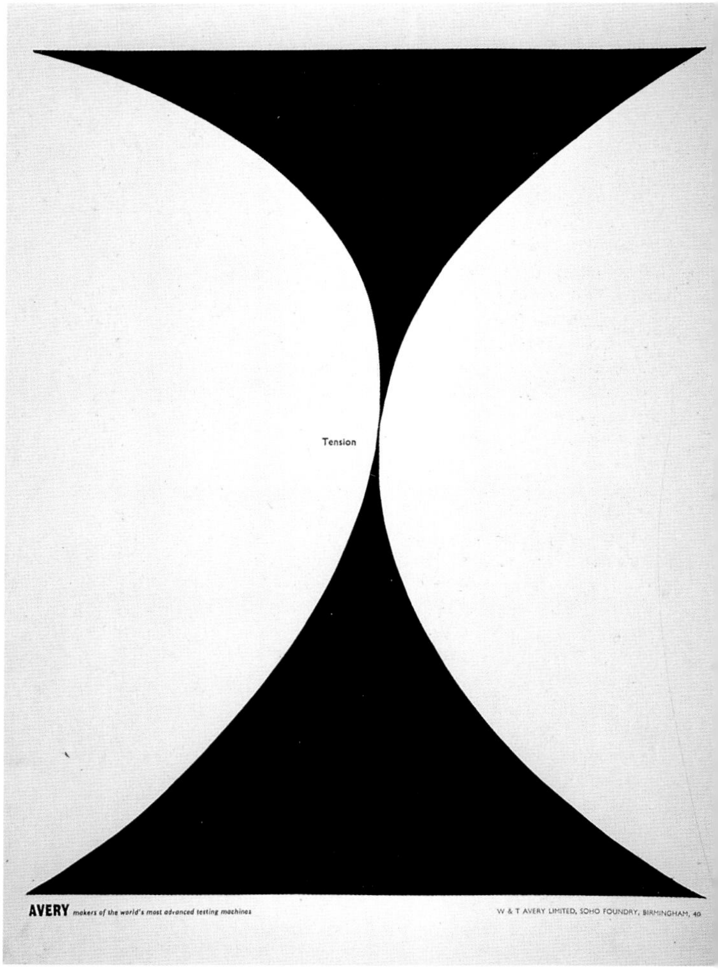
Tension
AVERY makers of the world's most advanced testing machines
W & T AVERY LIMITED, SOHO FOUNDRY, BIRMINGHAM, 40

Opposite: during the 1950s advertising design began to move forward, as the growth in printed material and competitive advertising demanded more brand difference to be demarcated graphically. Gradually, more radical ads started to emerge, few more extreme than these press advertisements from the W. S. Crawford agency in London, designed by Paul Peter Piech. A remarkable absence of type or of product shots opens the way for powerful abstract forms to be used to illustrate the concepts behind the value of Avery scales. A single word – "tension" or "fatigue" – is expressed in black and white composition. Piech, an American soldier who stayed in Britain after the war, later worked on personal posters without type, shaping his own linocut letters. Right: an advertisement for the Italian printers Alfieri & Lacroix, 1960, by Franco Grignani, explores the flexibility of film to express the motion of the press by rotating and reversing the name of the advertiser.

Simbolo delle rotative
dell'inchiostrazione fluida
delle carte calandrate
dei quartini ottavi
sedicesimi
dei controlli elettronici
della velocità
della perfezione
questa è
la *vostra* Alfieri & Lacroix
grignani

FOR A TYPOGRAPHICAL CELEBRATION OF THE 1960S, M/M (PARIS, FRANCE) OFFERS YOU A TYPOGRAF
AND MATHIAS (BORN THE 04/04/1967) EXECUTED FOR 28OFF (£32) IN FRONT OF THE POMPIDOU CEN

ITAL REMASTERISED VERSION OF A PORTRAIT OF MICHAEL (BORN THE 02/06/1968)
RIS, FRANCE) BY AN ANONYMOUS ARTIST (ON THE 18/03/1995). THANK YOU!

The emerging force of "youth culture", the rapid growth of television and change in type technology made this a decade that would re-invent the nature of typography. Unlike the radical experiments of the 1920s, in this period the scientific, social and political shifts prompted typographic novelty.

From the late 1950s onward there was a rush to market photocomposition machines: some found success and helped the development of new companies that supported type design programmes (such as Compugraphic and Hell); some met with failure – notably American Type Founders, which emerged at the end of the nineteenth century from the implications of hot metal, but disappeared under a takeover from Lanston Monotype after an unsuccessful investment in its own photocomposition machine.

The uncertainty of business was due to more than changing production methods. The type consumers, the publishers and their designers, were taking in new influences and were pushing for effects that were difficult to achieve with metal, while also being prepared to see a loss of some traditional qualities of metal setting because of cost or other practical and non-aesthetic reasons. That photosetting led to a drop in typographic skill was often lamented, but it was a chosen consequence. Suddenly type was becoming a flexible right-reading image that could easily be photographically manipulated, instead of being a rigid, wrong-reading relief letterform. Characters could be enlarged or shrunk, kerned or spaced almost at will, overlapped and positioned in a few moments rather than through hours of setting and construction on the printer's stone.

All this was encouraging for those seeking novelty and was dispiriting for those concerned with the traditional details. Poor fit of letters and ugly letterforms began to be seen, fed by the practice of generating a whole range of point sizes out of a single matrix, which inevitably distorted the face. It was also perpetuated by the ignorance of the user: with hot metal, much skill resided with the compositor, skill that a typographic designer could rely on, even take for granted to some extent. Niceties such as ligatures disappeared, partly because the ease of kerning should have overcome some of their need, partly because character sets did not extend that far, but it was a point that fine typographers missed.

The new systems began to chip away at the knowledge base of the compositor, bringing them closer to a glorified typist. Initially cold composition worked in a similar way to a Monotype machine, in that it produced a tape that drove the setting machine (but the subsequent setting was not as easily corrected: a new piece of film bromide being required to change one letter, rather than the insertion of the single letter). During the 1960s, though, computers began to impact upon this operation, offering systems programmed to assist with the justification of setting and memories that could deliver an image on a CRT (cathode ray tube) screen as reference. But this reliance on early computer programs brought problems, too, with the programmers and their systems often being unable to offer the spacing and word-break control that a good compositor would have supplied previously. Nevertheless, hot metal was increasingly frozen out by the costs and convenience of cold type, matched by the growing drift from letterpress printing to offset lithography, which was better suited to meet the growth in quality and demand for colour printing.

There were other signs of how increasing demand for print and business communication and new methods of satisfying it threatened the print establishment. In 1961 the IBM Selectric golfball typewriter was launched, offering an office machine with the capability of changing its characters to a different face: an early sign of the move of improved output into the hands of the office worker and a step towards today's desktop publishing systems.

Another development, launched in 1961, had more creative impact – Letraset's instant dry transfer lettering. The company had marketed wet transfer lettering from 1959, but failed to crack the American market. The dry method was cleaner and simpler to use and succeeded in the US: designers realized it empowered them to produce the artwork for headlines and other display elements, bringing down time and costs; indeed, it brought fancy display setting into the reach of many areas that would never have had access to it. Early Letraset advertising presented it as something for everyone, suggesting that typography was open to anybody. One over-enthusiastic piece of copywriting even stated that there was "no talent needed" to achieve fine results.

Letraset's library grew quickly, not just with copies of existing faces (often good cuts, taken under license from the original foundry drawings), but also under its own design programme. The first, and one of the most distinctive period faces, was Countdown. Designed by Colin Brignall, who went on to be appointed design director at the company, the face suggests 1960s science fiction and was the inspiration for many shop signs, particularly boutiques that wanted to shout their futuristic modernity. Other wacky faces were produced that may now seem ephemeral gimmicks but were notable in their quick response to the spirit of the age. Letraset had an impact on everything from magazines to posters, mass advertising to local newsletters. The company also worked to commission for companies that required their logo and other artwork in rubdown form. The lettering was much used in television, being ideal for producing titles and information graphics.

Technological change supported a questioning climate for design that was fuelled by the ending of postwar austerity in Europe and came as a reaction to the brasher consumerism of the 1950s in the US. Pop Art, the major art movement of the time, was built out of or against the dominance of abstraction, and many of the artists who came to be grouped under the label used elements of vernacular typographic and popular graphics within their work (processed into paint on canvas by Andy Warhol, Roy Lichtenstein and Robert Indiana in the US, and earlier, in montage by Eduardo Paolozzi and Richard Hamilton in Britain). The ironies, mixture of visual and verbal wit, and

Antique Olive *Nord* *18pt*

ABCDEFGHIJKLMNOPQRSTUVWXZ
abcdefghijklmnopqrstuvwxyz

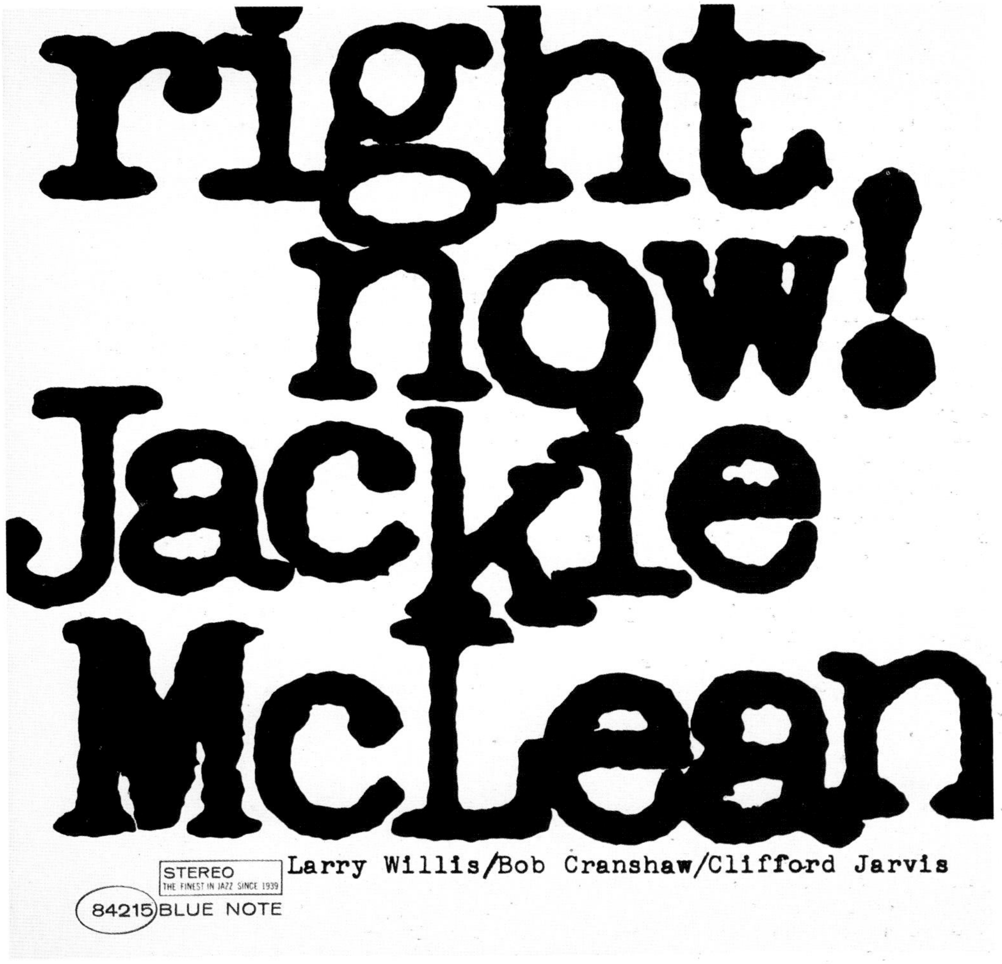
right now!
Jackie McLean
STEREO
THE FINEST IN JAZZ SINCE 1939
84215 BLUE NOTE
Larry Willis/Bob Cranshaw/Clifford Jarvis

Top: Roger Excoffon's Antique Olive was an attempt to offer a more refined sans serif than that presented by Helvetica and Univers – but it was too characterful and too late to be adopted widely outside France. It has a more calligraphic line than its rivals. Left: record sleeve by Reid Miles for Blue Note records, from 1964-5. Miles used type in highly inventive ways to illustrate the sleeves he created for the jazz label from 1954-69. He explored many forms of type or lettering technology, here grossly enlarging and reworking an image originated on a typewriter.

CHARLES TOLLIVER HERBIE HANCOCK CECIL MC BEE ROY HAYNES
STEREO
84179 BLUE NOTE
JACKIE McLEAN
"it's time!"...!!!!!!!!!

JOE HENDERSON
Kenny Dorham Richard Davis Elvin Jones etc.
STEREO
84166 BLUE NOTE
in'n
OUT

Eurostile *24pt*

ABCDEFGHIJKLMNOPQRSTUVWXYZ
abcdefghijklmnopqrstuvwxyz

ABCDEF
GHIJKLM
NOPQRS
TUVXYZ
W abcdef
ghijklmno
pqrstuvx
yzw 1234
567890

EUROSTILE (NEBIOLO) DISEGNATO DA A. NOVARESE · 1962

316

Gli esempi che abbiamo raggruppati sotto il titolo: « forme quadrate », sono tipiche espressioni della tendenza del nostro secolo, e sono sorte per ambientare il carattere all'estetica architetturale contemporanea.

La forma quadrata e compatta, infatti, ci è ormai familiare: essa è presente, direi, predominante, in ogni cosa che ci circonda. Ed il carattere, oggi — come fu per il passato — si fonde e si mimetizza nelle espressioni dell'epoca attuale. Gli esempi, anche pregevoli, delle pagine d'un tempo dimostrano che ogni stile — sia esso bodoniano, veneziano, egiziano, o lineare — può modificare, cambiare forma, specialmente per quanto riguarda le curve, passando da quelle tondeggianti a quelle più angolose e quadrate, senza alterare di molto l'originaria forma.

HO
ho
ho

La forma quadrata è tipica espressione architettonica del nostro secolo, come lo fu l'arco a tutto sesto dal quale derivò il carattere lapidario romano; ed anche l'arco a sesto acuto che originò, a sua volta, il carattere gotico.

317

exploration of throw-away consumer culture found in much of this work is echoed in the puns and ironies introduced into graphic communication at the time. Advertising was at the fore in expressing this change, the "golden age" of "big idea" advertising in America being led by the work of the agency Doyle Dane Bernbach. The Volkswagen Beetle campaign, which began in the late 1950s and ran through the 1960s, not only shook up car advertising by puncturing the hype of others in a self-effacing pitch, but projected this attitude in clean, restrained typography. The use of a specially cut geometric sans (based on Futura) suggested the modern, German origins of the car and the sense of good engineering. Type was being used for its cultural associations, not its inherent graphic qualities or legibility. Similarly, in DDB's ads for Levy's rye bread, the thick, soft but strong contours of Cooper Black suggest the wholesome product.

A new adventurous expressiveness was apparent in the work of many of the leading graphic designers of the era. Reid Miles' work as art director of record covers for the Blue Note label from the mid-1950s through the 1960s developed an increasingly strong relationship between type, layout and photography, with sympathetic play between the elements, often chopping up type or photography, often merging the two. These techniques were startlingly advanced compared with many of the other sleeves in the rack. The strength of the work reinforced the whole label's identity, and heralded the realization in the music industry that graphics could sell the music, rather than just showcase the recording artist.

Opposite top: two more Reid Miles covers for Blue Note (see previous caption also). Despite not being much of a jazz fan, Miles improvised around the words of a title or an artist's name in a way not dissimilar to the method of themes being explored in a jazz composition. Opposite: Eurostile, designed by Aldo Novarese in 1962 for Nebiolo, with the explanatory display he created for it in his book *Alfa Beta*. He shows how it is in keeping with the design of the age – with modern buildings, trains and television screens – rather than the classical or gothic characters of earlier type. Left: New York advertising swung into its heyday in the 1960s, with the apotheosis of the "Big Idea", and none bigger than in the Volkswagen campaign, from which "Lemon" is one of the most famous ads. The typographic identity of this work still survives in contemporary VW ads, the special cut of Futura semi-bold suggesting some Germanic know-how. The consistency of keeping the type "cool" when advertising is usually "hot" has given VW a very distinct identity.

Herb Lubalin (1918–81), who moved across from an advertising background in the 1950s to a type design career in the 1970s, produced some of his most memorable work in the 1960s, often through the reliance on typographic puns to reinforce a strong concept. His famous proposed magazine logo "Mother & Child", in which the child is an ampersand sitting in the bowl – or womb – of the "o" in mother, is trite, but saved by the perfect matching of the visual forms. Indeed, much of the visual punning of the period can seem rather laboured, but the best work goes beyond this to explore the double meanings, the ironies possible when presenting imagery to an audience that was becoming increasingly sophisticated – and jaded – in its consumption of mass communication.

The typography used in conceptual American advertising by its numerous art directors crossed the Atlantic and found its strongest response in Britain, notably with the partnership of Alan Fletcher, Colin Forbes and Bob Gill (the origins of the design group Pentagram). Their work displayed a similar ability to reduce the statement of a piece of commercial art to a key point that was boldly presented, often through typographic wit. This reductive, conceptualizing approach was a new influence overlaid on the still advancing Swiss school and the International Style. For ordering a mass of information and sorting out a typographic hierarchy, the commandments of Müller-Brockmann and his colleagues on *Neue Grafik* promised a revelation of the underlying order within a brief, a way of containing the given material clearly and with a logic. It was a creed that increasingly sat at odds

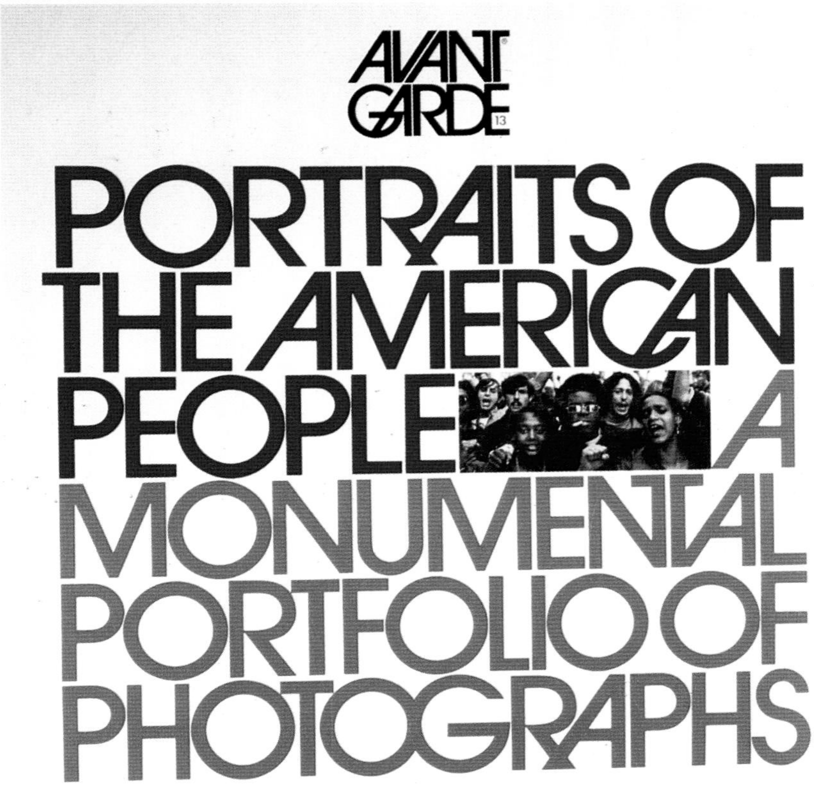

with the *laissez faire* graphics of popular culture. The rules of International Style did not provide a method for popular entertainment, which commercial communication demanded increasingly, as it was realized that to stand out amidst the growing mass of mass communication, advertising needed to appeal, not hector.

A key development of the 1960s was the flowering of the phenomenon since labelled "youth culture" – the culture created by and for teenagers and twenty-somethings, products of the postwar baby boom and a generation crucially free from the experience of war and the values of the earlier era. The spending power of this group differed markedly from antecedent youth as they benefitted from near full employment and a general rise in living standards, and

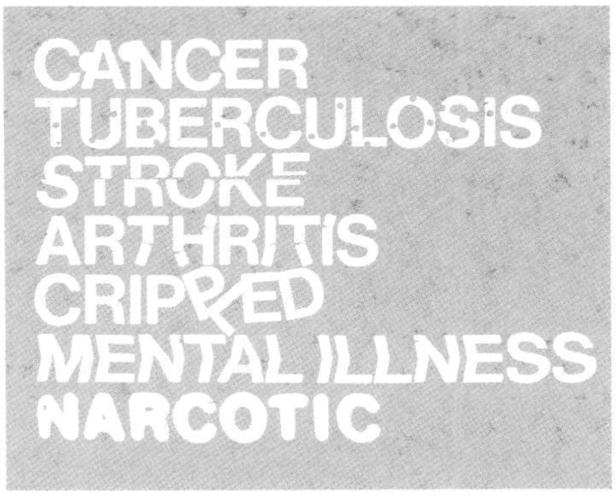

Families

A READER'S DIGEST PUBLICATION

Avant Garde *24pt*

ABCDEFGHIJKLMNOPQRSTUVWXYZ
abcdefghijklmnopqrstuvwxyz

Opposite left: logo for the 1968 Olympics in Mexico, designed by Lance Wyman. International Style, psychedelia and an attempt to draw from the bold stripes in traditional Mexican patterns all converge. The mark was at the heart of a programme praised for its comprehensive approach to the huge event. Opposite right: cover of *Avant Garde* magazine, designed by Herb Lubalin. His art direction of the magazine led him to create the face Avant Garde (left), which is remarkable for its ligatures and tight fit. The incredibly close characters are typical of Lubalin's work – seen also in the masthead he created for *Families* magazine (above left). Top: advertisement for the Photo Typositor system, 1961, plays with effects and tricks popular also in early digital typography.

they displayed a growing desire to stake their own place in society. This found graphic expression most notably through music and fashion, the hot industries in free-market capitalism which now emerged as standard-bearers for the avant-garde in communication, a position they have retained.

In the mid and late 1960s, record sleeves branched out into a whole range of eclectic type designs, often borrowing ideas and imagery and redrawing letters (Letraset was invaluable). Calligraphy (of a kind) was revived with strange new psychedelic twists courtesy of airbrush artists. "Underground" magazines and other expressions of protest broke the rules wilfully: articles in the magazine *Oz*, for example, could and did appear with almost unreadably long lines, ranged right with a ragged left stepping out, and all this

This page: 1960s counter culture, particularly around rock music, developed its own graphic expression, utilizing silk-screen printing for psychedelic posters. The leading work came out of San Francisco. Clockwise from right: Procol Harum at the Fillmore by Lee Conklin; The Doors at the Avalon Ballroom by Victor Moscoso; The Yardbirds, The Doors and others, by B. McLean. The power of the incredible silk-screen colours is only hinted at by photography and four-colour process print.

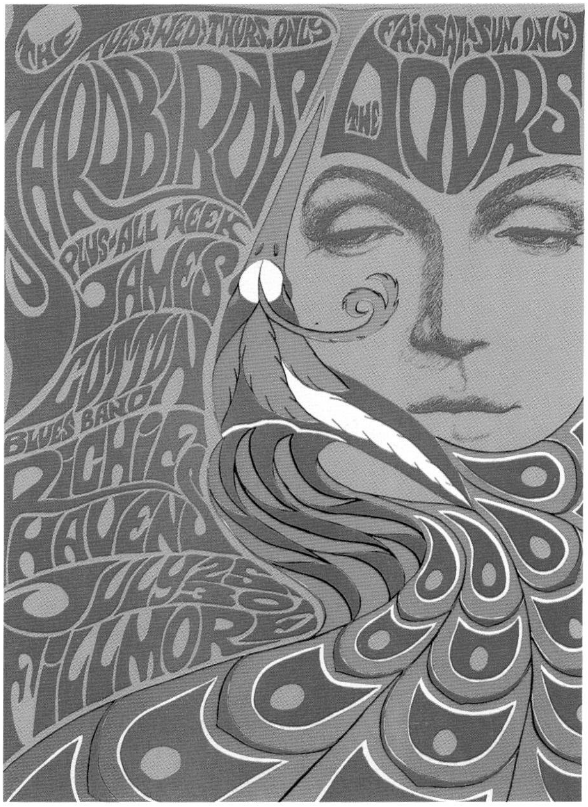

reversed from a sludgy photograph. The point was not to read it in a hurry, or perhaps at all: the protest was in the way it looked. Typewriter text was popular, partly because it avoided typesetting and was thus accessible and cheap for offset lithography, but it also contained the right associations in rejecting a smart business image.

Poster art for rock concerts and festivals produced some of the most remarkable, unreadable but communicative, calligraphy, with elaborate hand-drawn or photographically stretched words suggestive of the tricks of distortion that computers and photocopiers would make much easier to explore a few years later. Victor Moscoso and Wes Wilson's psychedelic posters in the US were the most polished examples, although it was a style widely copied, with different variations – in Britain, a revival of Art Nouveau led to an expansion of the florid lettering of that period into more psychedelic forms.

In magazine work one of the most influential practitioners was Willy Fleckhaus (1925–83). His design of *Twen* through the 1960s showed the art director in the ascendant (Fleckhaus trained as a journalist and his input in the magazine extended into the origination of ideas and treatments). He ferociously cropped photography for dramatic effect, cleared body copy from visual spreads and on to dump pages of solid text, and used blocks of type as building blocks to construct the page, suggest the grid, or challenge order. Dramatic contrasts in the scale of type often added tension to the page, with Fleckhaus elaborately

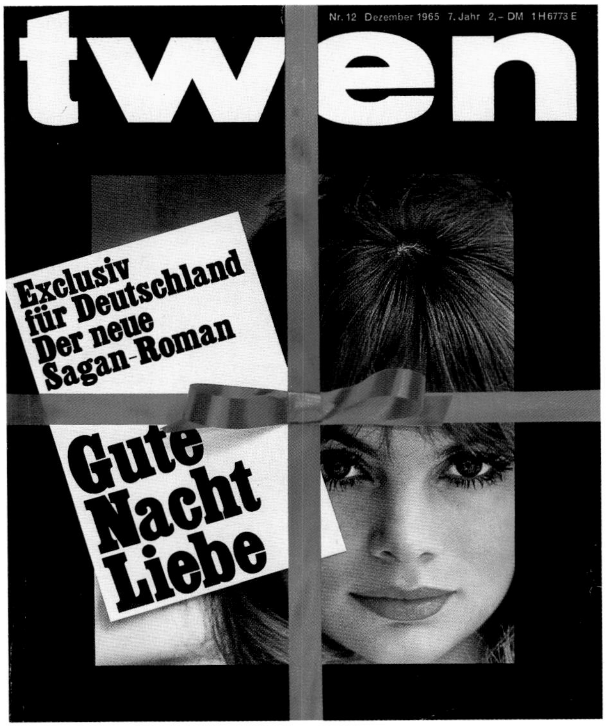

Far left: cover of promotional brochure for *Ad Lib*, designed by Freeman Craw for American Type Founders in 1961. This display face drew on nineteenth-century wood letter and the idea of the crude paper cut shapes. Craw offered alternate letters, with variations that even allowed letters to be turned upside-down without losing alignment. His was a reaction against the neutrality of modern sans serifs and a questioning of conventions, that finds an echo in the organic, "random" fonts of the 1990s. Above left: *Twen*, December 1965, art directed by Willy Fleckhaus, an art director's art director who emphasized photography and tended to consign typography to a means of text delivery.

cutting and adjusting type to fit his intentions and the space allotted. In Britain, echoes of this work could be seen in the fresh look of *Nova* magazine, which also targeted the younger set with provocative features that devoted opening spreads to strong photography, paring the text back and playing with different typefaces to convey a more emotive kick to the beginning of an article and merge more fluidly with the illustrative content.

Fleckhaus designed book covers for the publisher Suhrkamp which were exclusively typographic, the type on or out of a deliberately restricted palette of background colours. Despite the simplicity of the elements to which he confined himself, he produced highly expressive and varied covers, all reinforcing a distinct identity for the publisher.

OCR-A *18pt*

ABCDEFGHIJKLM
NOPQRSTUVWXYZ
abcdefghijklm
nopqrstuvwxyz

OCR-B *18pt*

ABCDEFGHIJKLM
NOPQRSTUVWXYZ
abcdefghijklm
nopqrstuvwxyz

CMC7 *24pt*

1234567890

E13B *36pt*

1234567890

But it was not all about a quest for personal or corporate individualism. The decade also saw international alignments of experts collaborating on communications technology. Committees considered research on computer-type (optical character reading). OCR–A was issued in 1966: it is an extremely coarse design, with characters produced on a 4 by 7 grid. OCR-B, issued in 1968 (with Adrian Frutiger as a consultant) works to a finer grid (18 by 25), enabling more sophisticated curves. OCR-A and its forerunner, E13B (used by banks on cheques), were a genuine machine-driven aesthetic that found a stylistic echo in the aforementioned Countdown or the more elegantly squared-off designs of Aldo Novarese's Eurostile, extended from his earlier Microgramma.

There were advances in faces that could work for screen display as well as input. Here, simplicity was used not only to create distinctions that the machine could read but to make clear forms that the human eye could swiftly assimilate. The Dutch designer Wim Crouwel (1928–) was committed to the idea that in the not too distant future the screen would be the pre-eminent source of typographic communication and was concerned that more effort should go into developing appropriate designs. His Neue Alphabet of 1967 simplified the alphabet to horizontal and vertical elements, removing diagonals and curves. All characters are the same width, and to make "m" and "w" he had to underline the "n" and "v", respectively. There was only one alphabet, not an upper and lower case.

New Alphabet *40pt*

The development of computers that could read led to, first, computer-readable code, then typefaces that could be read by intermediate technologies, before gradually spawning an aesthetic. Opposite: CMC7 was a face developed for use with magnetic inks in the early 1960s (designer unknown). It was only briefly promoted, being quickly superseded. E13B was a machine-recognized set of numerals developed by the American Bankers' Association in the mid-1960s and is still seen on cheque books. The minimal grid idea links with that behind the poster of 1968, left (which inspired the cover of the last edition of this book, see page 173) designed by Wim Crouwel (born 1928). In 1967 Crouwel designed the minimalist New Alphabet, which reduces characters to essential distinguishing elements. Opposite top: OCR-A and OCR-B came as a result of standards laid down in 1965 by the European Computer Manufacturers Association for computer-readable type. ECMA engineers developed OCR-A in 1966, while OCR-B emerged with Adrian Frutiger's assistance in 1968 – a finer face that demands greater processing power.

But with all this talk of technological change and of "Swingin' Sixties" libertarianism, what did the traditionalists think? One could always rely on Stanley Morison, responsible for reviving classic faces at Monotype, to present a sober argument for classical values. In a 1967 new edition of his 1930 essay "First Principles of Typography", he added a response to International Style and to the new wave of sans serif faces:

"Claims are made that the style appropriate for the time consists not only in the choice of sans serif type but that it be composed in asymmetrical form, without recourse to italics. Paragraphs are to be closely set without indentation, and the whole appearance of the page must depart wherever possible from age-old custom. The twentieth century would thus mark itself off by its distinctive typography as the great period of revaluation....Tradition itself is not well understood at the present day in some quarters. If it were a reflection of the stagnation or prejudice of past ages of printers, little attention need be given to it by historians and none by practitioners of the arts and crafts. But tradition is more than the embalming of forms customary in states that have been long since cast aside. The sum of experience accumulated in more than one man's lifetime, and unified by succeeding generations, is not to be safely discarded. Tradition, therefore, is another name for unanimity about fundamentals which has been brought into being by the trials, errors and corrections of many centuries. *Experientia docet*."

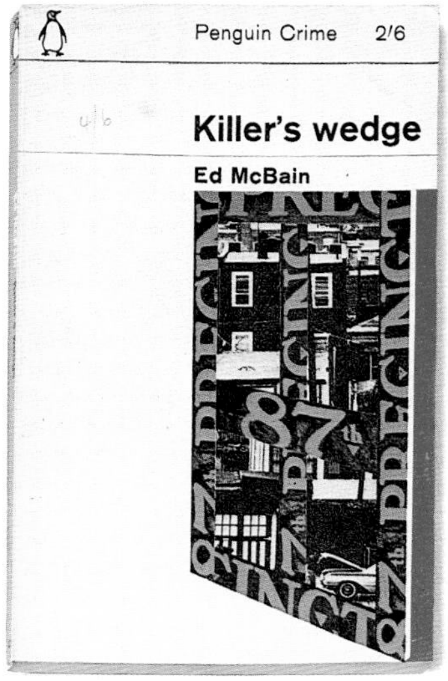

Sabon *24pt*

ABCDEFGHIJKLMNOPQRSTUVWXYZ
abcdefghijklmnopqrstuvwxyz

Appropriately perhaps, Morison ended on a note that, with the decline in a classical education, would be savoured by few of the new generation of typographers. For them, the reality of the typographic context was increasingly of non-print media, of communication that mixed the alphabet with sound and motion in the full fluidity of film and video and, soon, computer-based communication.

Right: Letraset's transfer lettering was quick, cheap and could even be fun – truly type for the Pop era. Faces included Milton Glaser's Baby Teeth and creative director Colin Brignall's Countdown, ready-to-rub for sci-fi covers and fashion boutiques. Opposite: commercial graphics exploded into brighter colours as print technology improved in the 1960s and Western markets became more consumer-driven. Here cutting through the noise was a Shredded Wheat pack by British design trio Fletcher Forbes Gill, a reaction that said "value" against over-packaging. Even Penguin books caught the marketing bug, allowing new art director Alan Aldridge to try more varied directions (the cover near left is his design, while Romek Marber and Alan Spain designed *Killer's Wedge*, both 1964). In 1967 he resigned when a rigorous typographic scheme was reasserted. Opposite below: Sabon, 1966, by Jan Tschichold. Just as hot metal was about to be replaced by photosetting, a group of German printers asked Tschichold to create a "unified" face that worked across both Monotype and Linotype hot metal systems and also in foundry type for handsetting. Monotype Garamond was the basis for this difficult marriage.

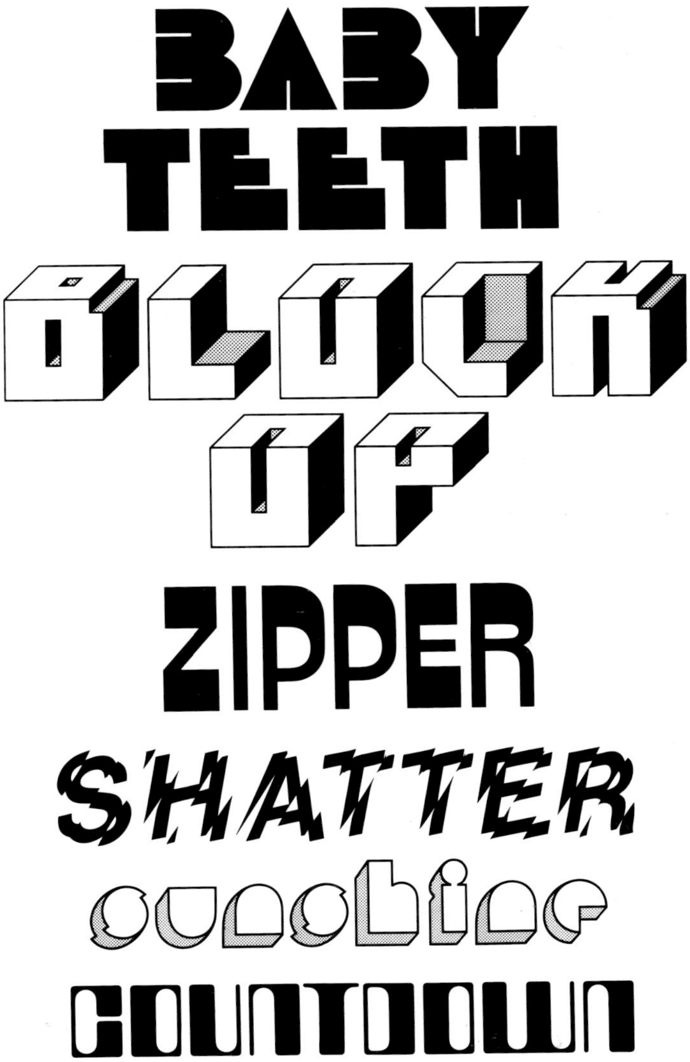

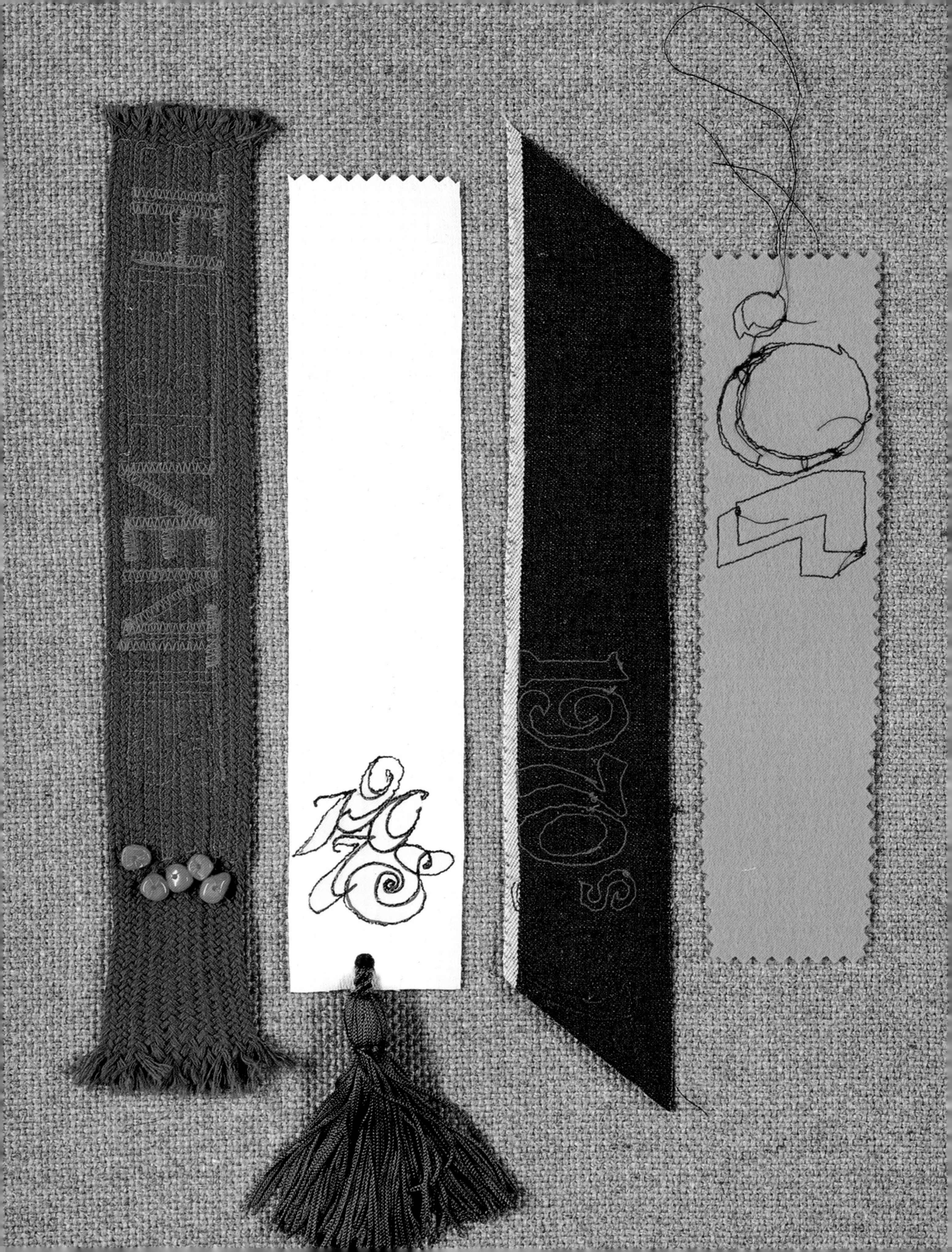
1970s

1970s
the
nine
teen
sev
en
ties

The 1970s have been dubbed "the decade that fashion forgot" and this label might also be extended to graphics. But with due warning: anything that seems irredeemable is usually soon to be recycled, and in music and fashion some aspects of this decade already have been. It might be a while before ITC Souvenir becomes widely used again, but don't count it out.

While rock music and clothing stretched the late 1960s visions, so in typography the promise of the preceding years turned to baroque extravagance. Experimentation with the new systems led to type being spaced so tightly that letters overlapped and words became squeezed and only semi-legible. Whatever its merits and faults, it created a distinctly contemporary form.

There was perhaps more to tight letterspacing than fashion jumping on to a new technique. Underlying some experimentation is the continuing quest for archetypal letterforms. The idea that sans serif faces produced the most functional letterforms was reinforced by a technology that increased their legibility. An argument for serifs is that they help guide the eye along the line and join letters into words, but as photocomposition provided potential for closing up sans serif faces into tight "word images", it gave new material to arguments on the relative readability of forms.

For all Modernism's love of geometric forms, such geometry bears no inherent relationship to the nature of the alphabet, which was drawn from calligraphic and (much earlier) pictogram roots. In the 1970s Adrian Frutiger demonstrated that when characters from some widely read typefaces were overlaid (Garamond, Baskerville, Bodoni, Times, Palatino, Optima and Helvetica), the skeletal forms that emerged from the superimpositions corresponded closely to faces then used in mass-market newspapers (Excelsior, Caledonia). The sans serifs Helvetica and Univers matched the basic outline exactly, but deviated, of course, in lacking serifs and having a more constant stroke thickness. For Frutiger, this illustrated that "the foundations of legibility are like a crystallization, formed by hundreds of years of use of selected, distinctive typefaces. The usable forms that have stood the test of time are perhaps permanently accepted by humankind as standards conforming to aesthetic laws." He pointed out that "where there are excessive innovations of form or designs of poor quality, the typeface encounters a certain resistance in the reader and the reading process is hindered."[1]

Note the concern about "designs of poor quality". Manufacturers had rushed to offer an impressive range of familiar faces on their phototypesetting systems, plus whatever was new and different. This led to the supply of many poorly drawn faces. There were the inevitable distortions resulting from not supplying masters in different sizes but instead requiring one size to be enlarged to all sizes. This meant that the need for a change of balance in a cut at different sizes to preserve characteristics was ignored. The decline in typographic quality was not only the result of the methods of generating type, but also of printing: the transfer of most printing from letterpress to offset lithography, as well as the advent of inkjet and laser printing technology, unleashed type in areas where traditional typographic controls and skills were absent.

But there was a growing awareness of the graphic design *profession*. In type this was signified by the arrival of a type producer that expressed both the changing needs of the type specifier and the potential of the technology – the International Typeface Corporation. ITC was formed in 1970 by designers Herb Lubalin and Aaron Burns who joined forces with Ed Rondthaler, of Photo-Lettering Inc., to set up a company that would market new typeface designs as artwork supplied to other type and typesetting equipment manufacturers. In effect, ITC was a type design agency, building on the expertise and archive that the Lubalin and Burns partnership had already created, but also bringing in new designers and designs to license across manufacturers. Royalties would be paid on the usage of the face, and the success of the design would directly benefit its creator. This model, with adaptation, has inspired the subsequent growth of designer-led type distribution companies.

This organization responded to the prevailing trend of piracy in new typeface design. If one supplier had a design that another did not have, photo-technology made it easy to duplicate the master matrix of characters and re-name the design and then avoid paying any royalties to the originators of that face. It was not in the interests of good typeface designers or manufacturers for such a situation to continue, but neither was it desirable or practical to expect good designs to be tied to only one system.

ITC's type library began in 1971 with Lubalin's Avant Garde Gothic, drawn from his work for *Avant Garde* magazine in the 1960s. Next was a recut extended family designed by Ed Benguiat of a turn-of-the-century design, the notorious Souvenir, originally carried by American Type Founders (which had effectively disappeared in 1970 with the merger with Lanston Monotype). New faces, recut faces and extended families poured forth thereafter. ITC was a publisher, not a seller of systems – this was a radical new model for type distribution, Letraset excepted. Each new face was effectively a new title and needed to perform through different retailers (or type manufacturers) for ITC to be profitable.

In the 1973 launch edition of its own publication, *U&lc* magazine, ITC began a campaign against type piracy. An article by Rondthaler admitted that copying faces was as old as typefounding itself (and was certainly very much a part of the hot-metal era) but insisted that it was only the arrival of "phototypography" that had brought the time and costs down to the point where the pirating of type became a real threat to the origination of new work. He commented that "photography has been the technological salvation of the typesetting business, but when used unethically it can rob the type designer of his livelihood. It can do worse than that. It is now threatening to throw the creative arm of the industry into chaos." He called for designers to boycott suppliers who did not use properly licensed designs and compared the use of anything else as being akin to passing off counterfeit money. Without

A Fox is quick (0 to 50 in 10 seconds).
It's surefooted (front-wheel drive).
This sly, cunning sedan can take the sharpest turns nimbly (sports car type steering and suspension). It can stop practically in its tracks (power front disc brakes). And it doesn't eat much (23 miles per gallon).
Best of all, for under $3,200* you can catch the Fox.
YOUR HUNT IS OVER. THE QUICK, SLY, CRAFTY,
CUNNING FOX BY AUDI IS HERE.
*Suggested Retail Price $3199 East Coast P.O.E. (West Coast slightly higher.) Price subject to change without notice. Local taxes and other dealer delivery charges, if any, additional.

Herb Lubalin acclaimed this early 1970s use of his Avant Garde. He praised the DDB art director Helmut Krone for setting the headline so tight that the letters join up and overlap.

strong action, warned Rondthaler, there was no reason why designers, foundries or manufacturers should consider investing in the design of new typefaces. The 1970s could either mark the demise of type design or the beginning of a renaissance, he concluded.

As it turned out, the latter was the case. There were moves in international copyright law to clamp down on such piracy, and there were followers of ITC's initiative – other type licensing enterprises and new manufacturers such as Hell and Compugraphic – investing in design. ITC's practices were not uncritically received, however; the ubiquity of its faces meant that if it marketed a bad design, then that could end up being widely adopted at the cost of a better, earlier precedent. The American graphic designer Paula Scher later commented that "ITC had an enormous impact in this country because it was a national type business. It sold to all the small suppliers, but it destroyed the face of Garamond and it destroyed the face of Bookman."[2] ITC designs tended to have a large x-height (which aided readability in smaller sizes) and a close character fit, restrictions that eroded many distinguishing qualities of classic designs.

The high ground of detailed care in transferring and evolving type design was held by Berthold, and the torch was carried by Gerhard Lange, whose career began in 1950 and lasted into the 1990s. He oversaw the creation of a library of classic faces transferred first to photosetting, and later to digital form. Berthold's "diatronic" system of photosetting, with a

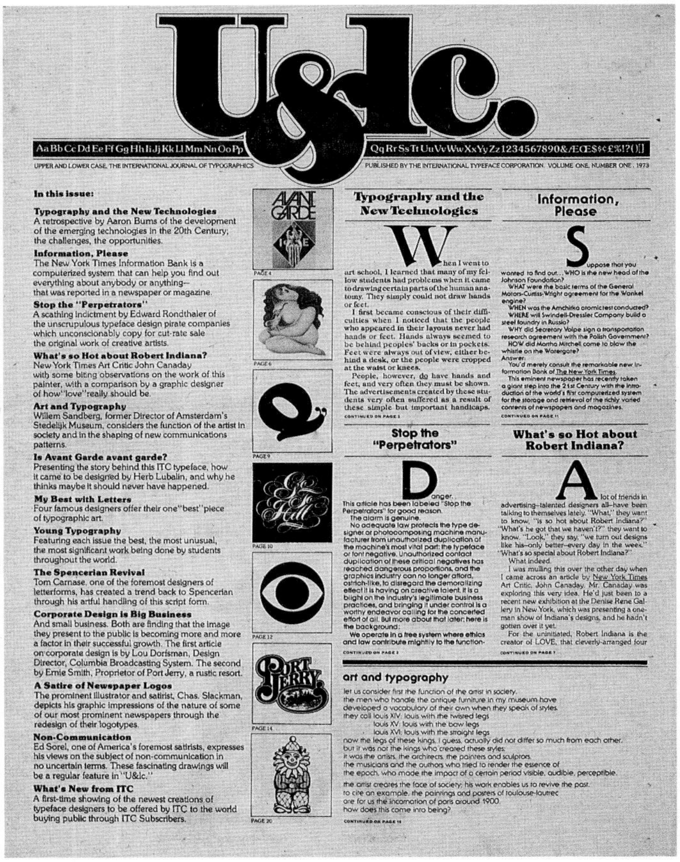

U&lc.

Aa Bb Cc Dd Ee Ff Gg Hh Ii Jj Kk Ll Mm Nn Oo Pp Qq Rr Ss Tt Uu Vv Ww Xx Yy Zz 1234567890&ÆŒ$$¢£%!?()[]

UPPER AND LOWER CASE, THE INTERNATIONAL JOURNAL OF TYPOGRAPHICS

PUBLISHED BY THE INTERNATIONAL TYPEFACE CORPORATION. VOLUME ONE, NUMBER ONE, 1973

In this issue:

Typography and the New Technologies
A retrospective by Aaron Burns of the development of the emerging technologies in the 20th Century; the challenges, the opportunities.

Information, Please
The New York Times Information Bank is a computerized system that can help you find out everything about anybody or anything– that was reported in a newspaper or magazine.

Stop the "Perpetrators"
A scathing indictment by Edward Rondthaler of the unscrupulous typeface design pirate companies which unconscionably copy for cut-rate sale the original work of creative artists.

What's so Hot about Robert Indiana?
New York Times Art Critic John Canaday with some biting observations on the work of this painter, with a comparison by a graphic designer of how "love" really should be.

Art and Typography
Willem Sandberg, former Director of Amsterdam's Stedelijk Museum, considers the function of the artist in society and in the shaping of new communications patterns.

Is Avant Garde avant garde?
Presenting the story behind this ITC typeface, how it came to be designed by Herb Lubalin, and why he thinks maybe it should never have happened.

My Best with Letters
Four famous designers offer their one "best" piece of typographic art.

Young Typography
Featuring each issue the best, the most unusual, the most significant work being done by students throughout the world.

The Spencerian Revival
Tom Carnase, one of the foremost designers of letterforms, has created a trend back to Spencerian through his artful handling of this script form.

Corporate Design is Big Business
And small business. Both are finding that the image they present to the public is becoming more and more a factor in their successful growth. The first article on corporate design is by Lou Dorfsman, Design Director, Columbia Broadcasting System. The second by Ernie Smith, Proprietor of Port Jerry, a rustic resort.

A Satire of Newspaper Logos
The prominent illustrator and satirist, Chas. Slackman, depicts his graphic impressions of the nature of some of our most prominent newspapers through the redesign of their logotypes.

Non-Communication
Ed Sorel, one of America's foremost satirists, expresses his views on the subject of non-communication in no uncertain terms. These fascinating drawings will be a regular feature in "U&lc."

What's New from ITC
A first-time showing of the newest creations of typeface designers to be offered by ITC to the world buying public through ITC Subscribers.

PAGE 4

PAGE 6

PAGE 9

PAGE 10

PAGE 12

PAGE 14

PAGE 20

Typography and the New Technologies

When I went to art school, I learned that many of my fellow students had problems when it came to drawing certain parts of the human anatomy. They simply could not draw hands or feet.

I first became conscious of their difficulties when I noticed that the people who appeared in their layouts never had hands or feet. Hands always seemed to be behind peoples' backs or in pockets. Feet were always out of view, either behind a desk, or the people were cropped at the waist or knees.

People, however, do have hands and feet, and very often they must be shown. The advertisements created by these students very often suffered as a result of these simple but important handicaps.

CONTINUED ON PAGE 3

Information, Please

Suppose that you wanted to find out... WHO is the new head of the Johnson Foundation?

WHAT were the basic terms of the General Motors-Curtiss-Wright agreement for the Wankel engine?

WHEN was the Amchitka atomic test conducted?

WHERE will Swindell-Dressler Company build a steel foundry in Russia?

WHY did Secretary Volpe sign a transportation research agreement with the Polish Government?

HOW did Martha Mitchell come to blow the whistle on the Watergate?

Answer:

You'd merely consult the remarkable new Information Bank of The New York Times.

This eminent newspaper has recently taken a giant step into the 21st Century with the introduction of the world's first computerized system for the storage and retrieval of the richly varied contents of newspapers and magazines.

CONTINUED ON PAGE 11

Stop the "Perpetrators"

Danger.

This article has been labeled "Stop the Perpetrators" for good reason.

The alarm is genuine.

No adequate law protects the type designer or photocomposing machine manufacturer from unauthorized duplication of the machine's most vital part: the typeface or font negative. Unauthorized contact duplication of these critical negatives has reached dangerous proportions, and the graphics industry can no longer afford, ostrich-like, to disregard the demoralizing effect it is having on creative talent. It is a blight on the industry's legitimate business practices, and bringing it under control is a worthy endeavor calling for the concerted effort of all. But more about that later; here is the background:

We operate in a free system where ethics and law contribute mightily to the function-

CONTINUED ON PAGE 2

What's so Hot about Robert Indiana?

A lot of friends in advertising–talented designers all–have been talking to themselves lately. "What," they want to know, "is so hot about Robert Indiana?" "What's he got that we haven't?" they want to know. "Look," they say, "we turn out designs like his–only better–every day in the week." "What's so special about Robert Indiana?"

What indeed.

I was mulling this over the other day when I came across an article by New York Times Art Critic, John Canaday. Mr. Canaday was exploring this very idea. He'd just been to a recent new exhibition at the Denise Rene Gallery in New York, which was presenting a one-man show of Indiana's designs, and he hadn't gotten over it yet.

For the uninitiated, Robert Indiana is the creator of LOVE, that cleverly-arranged four

CONTINUED ON PAGE 7

art and typography

let us consider first the function of the artist in society.
the men who handle the antique furniture in my museum have
developed a vocabulary of their own when they speak of styles.
they call louis XIV: louis with the twisted legs
louis XV: louis with the bow legs
louis XVI: louis with the straight legs
now the legs of these kings, i guess, actually did not differ so much from each other,
but it was not the kings who created these styles:
it was the artists, the architects, the painters and sculptors,
the musicians and the authors who tried to render the essence of
the epoch, who made the impact of a certain period visible, audible, perceptible.

the artist creates the face of society; his work enables us to revive the past.
to cite an example, the paintings and posters of toulouse-lautrec
are for us the incarnation of paris around 1900.
how does this come into being?

CONTINUED ON PAGE 15

Souvenir *18pt*

ABCDEFGHIJKLM
NOPQRSTUVWXYZ
abcdefghijklm
nopqrstuvwxyz

Serif Gothic *18pt*

ABCDEFGHIJKLM
NOPQRSTUVWXYZ
abcdefghijklmn
opqrstuvwxyz

American Typewriter *24pt*

ABCDEFGHIJKLM
NOPQRSTUVWXYZ
abcdefghijklm
nopqrstuvwxyz

Opposite: The first issue of the ITC magazine *U&lc*, 1973. Designed by Herb Lubalin, it contained a blistering attack on type piracy – an issue that was to become increasingly important as type broke away from being the proprietary design with a particular system. Copying was an irritating, parasitic problem in the photocomposition era, but this would become pandemic with the ease of duplication made possible by digital information technology of the late 1980s onwards. Early ITC faces – shown here Souvenir (Ed Benguiat, 1970), American Typewriter (design by Joel Kaden and Tony Stan, 1974), Serif Gothic (Herb Lubalin and Tony DiSpagna, 1972-4) – tended to an exaggerated x-height and a narrow body, the compacted, close-set appearance being a look that became associated with the decade almost as much as tight flared trousers and large collars. Right: Strong designs carried on the promotional brochures used to launch ITC faces.

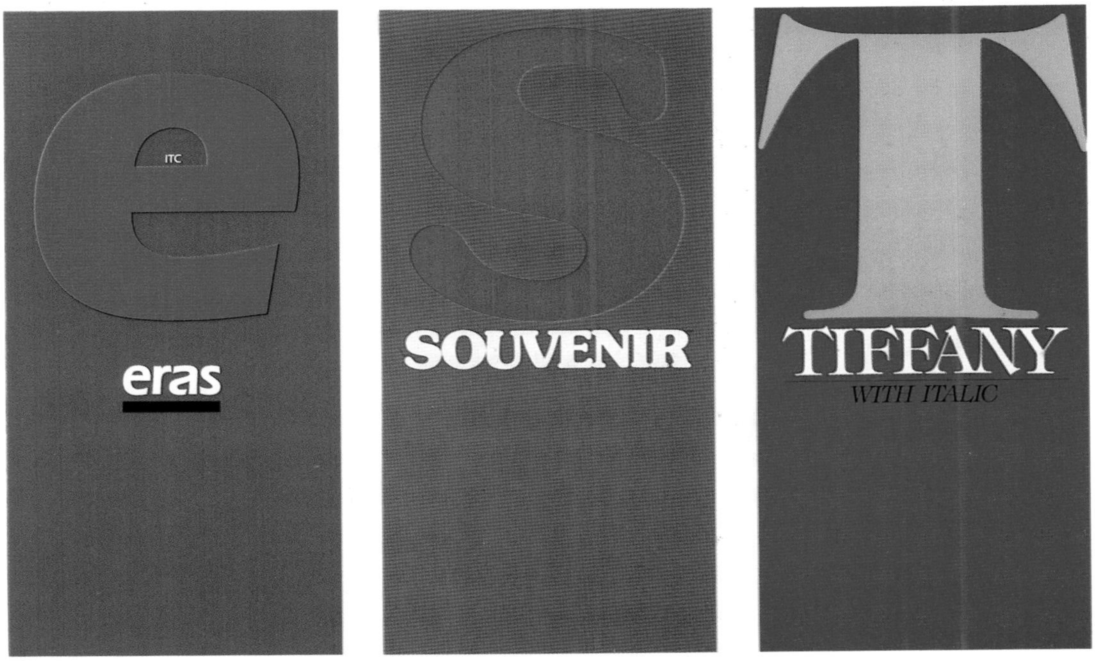

glass negative image of the font, was remarkable for its sharpness and accuracy of output.

The process of drawing type began to undergo significant change with the arrival of on-screen computer-aided design. To the fore was the Ikarus system developed by Peter Karow in Hamburg. Launched in 1974, it was adopted by Berthold and Linotype and soon found users across Europe, the US and in Japan. It offered a way of converting screen-designed images to line drawings; converting drawings to digitized information for screen working, and a way of automatically developing variants around the key design, so assisting production of a comprehensive type family. Other systems were launched with comparable facilities, but updated forms of Ikarus remained the most widely employed at the top end of type-design programs into the 1990s, although in the late 1980s Fontographer emerged as the most commonly used program on the personal computer.

Besides the changing methods, the meaning of design was also shifting. After almost two decades of the International Style gaining strength, its beliefs were now seriously questioned. The key reaction started in its homeland, with ideas that were later seen as the New Wave. The key instigator was Swiss designer Wolfgang Weingart (1941–).

In 1968 Weingart began working at the Basel School of Design, whose teaching he had rejected as a student in opposition to the dogmatic approach identified with the Swiss typography of Emil Ruder and Armin Hofmann, both

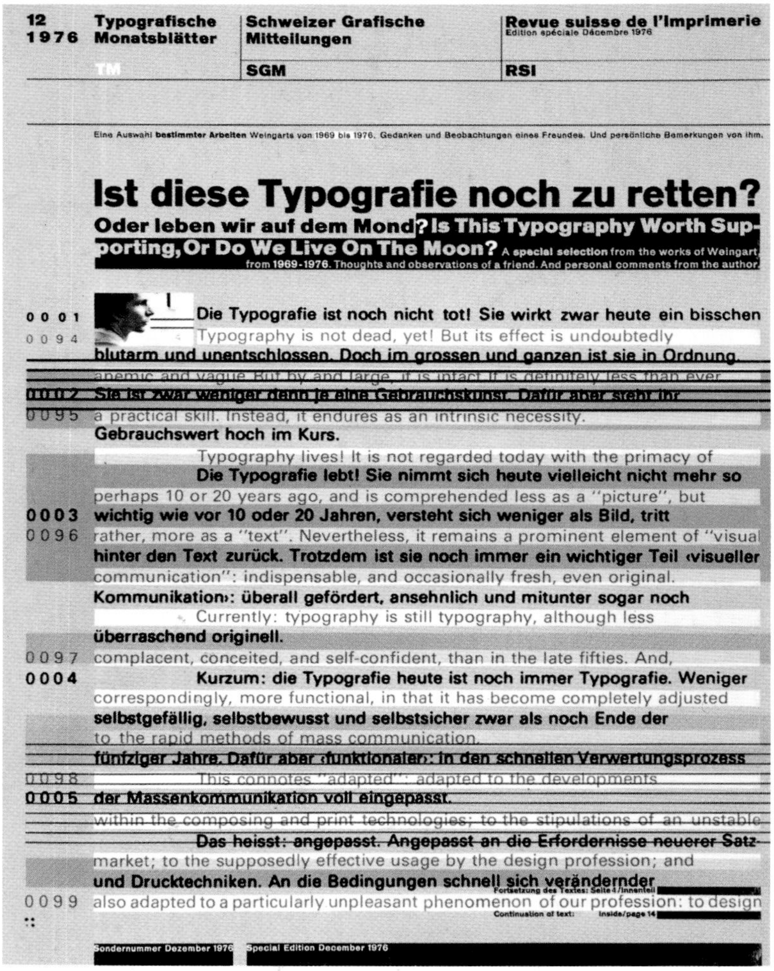

Left: from a special edition of *Typografische Monatsblätter*, December 1976, designed by and featuring the work and writings of Wolfgang Weingart. Broken and cut grids, reversed and stepped blocks, different ranging points for text – such devices and more became part of Weingart's mannered response to the dominance of Swiss Style reduction. Weingart's search to revive expression gave birth to the New Wave typography and became an important influence in the US. Under the provocative pyrotechnics with type that his imitators made into mere style, Weingart was investigating the potential of changing media. Opposite: in *Typografische Monatsblätter* 12, 1972, a special section on education co-edited by Weingart featured studies by his colleague at Basle, Peter von Arx, who argued "the prospective designer should become familiar with the factors of movement, time and speed" as seen in film.

on the staff. But their recognition of his talents led to an invitation to come back and present an alternative voice. In so doing he placed himself at the centre of a new orthodoxy and circle of influence that stretched across Europe to the West Coast of the US (Dan Friedman and April Greiman being his most noted followers).

Weingart rejected the reductive approach that had taken Swiss typography to its position of pre-eminent intellectual credibility. Where Josef Müller-Brockmann reduced type to one face in two sizes (text and headline) positioned in a clear relationship and organized around the right angle and placed on a grid, Weingart asked his class to find principles of typographic composition that did not rely on any systematic approach, but drew from the structures suggested by the production processes of the piece itself. He wanted typographic design mixed in as part of a range of tools within the graphic designer's control. His students studied other areas such as photography, drawing, colour theory and packaging.

From this dedication to the potential of the tools and their expressive qualities emerged an introspective form of design in keeping with the mood of an era. Self-conscious forms were apparent in metafictional literature and films, and music that questioned music structure. This trend was followed by three-dimensional design (with works by the Memphis group in the early 1980s) and postmodern architecture.

Such radicalism soon became formulaic. Weingart has admitted that the experimentation he sought to foster, and which

is apparent in his own work, was inspired by the potential of pushing hot-metal processes to the limit and standing them on their head. This led to stylized features – stepped blocks, bold reversal out of type, varying letter spacing and underlining, to name but a few tropes – becoming associated with the "New Wave" typographers. A common visual emphasis would be heavily screened photography with the halftone dot size visible so that the picture self-consciously displays its method of illusion.

The Swiss origins are still there. Weingart favoured certain families and tended to stick with them, his preferred faces being Akzidenz Grotesk, Helvetica and Univers of the sans serifs (mostly used for the poster and other display work emanating from his class and studio) and Times and

Left: 1971 poster by A. G. Fronzoni (born 1923). This Italian Minimalist probed the boundaries of type size, of print colour, of the edge of the medium, and to what reduction characters could be taken while still being readable. Below: Frutiger, designed by Adrian Frutiger, 1973-6. Created for signage at Charles de Gaulle Airport, Paris, it was issued by Linotype in 1976. A descendant of Univers, it is more open (note the "c" and the "e") with small capitals and longer ascenders and descenders. Frutiger looked back to Roman capitals and away from geometric sans. Opposite top: Bell Centennial, 1975-8, and Galliard, 1978, by Matthew Carter for Linotype. The first was commissioned by AT&T as a directory face to fit more into less space. Carter designed forms that retain distinctions even when degraded. The exaggerated cut-aways in small sizes allow for inkspread. Galliard was a revival of a sixteenth-century design by Robert Granjon, more true to Garamond than the many other revivals. Opposite: pictograms by Otl Aicher for the Munich Olympics, 1972, based on a 20x20 grid, a key contribution to the international language of non-text marks. Far right: Mobil identity newsletter, from 1975, design by Chermayeff & Geismar Associates, spreading the culture of global typography.

b

Frutiger *18pt*

ABCDEFGHIJKLMNOPQRSTUVWXYZ
abcdefghijklmnopqrstuvwxyz

Bell Centennial *24pt*

ABCDEFGHIJKLM
NOPQRSTUVWXYZ
abcdefghijklm
nopqrstuvwxyz

Galliard *18pt*

ABCDEFGHIJKLM
NOPQRSTUVWXYZ
abcdefghijklm
nopqrstuvwxyz

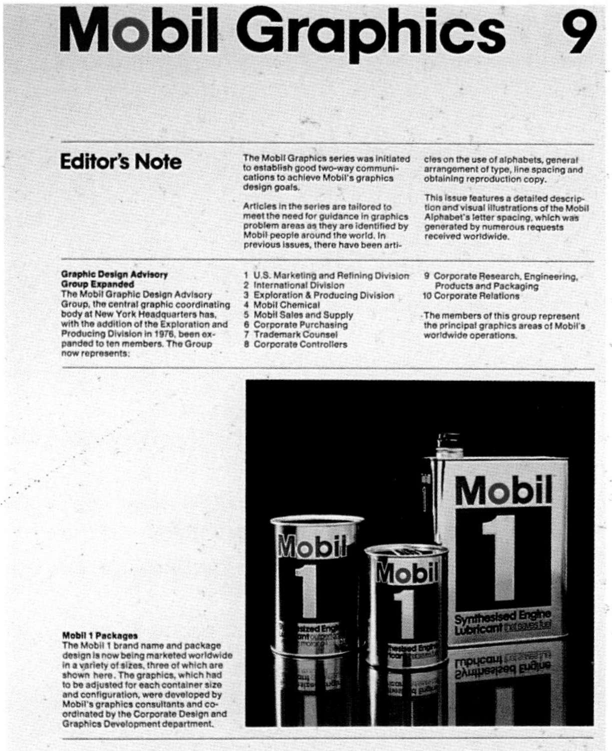

Mobil Graphics 9

Editor's Note

The Mobil Graphics series was initiated to establish good two-way communications to achieve Mobil's graphics design goals.

Articles in the series are tailored to meet the need for guidance in graphics problem areas as they are identified by Mobil people around the world. In previous issues, there have been articles on the use of alphabets, general arrangement of type, line spacing and obtaining reproduction copy.

This issue features a detailed description and visual illustrations of the Mobil Alphabet's letter spacing, which was generated by numerous requests received worldwide.

Graphic Design Advisory Group Expanded
The Mobil Graphic Design Advisory Group, the central graphic coordinating body at New York Headquarters has, with the addition of the Exploration and Producing Division in 1976, been expanded to ten members. The Group now represents:

1 U.S. Marketing and Refining Division
2 International Division
3 Exploration & Producing Division
4 Mobil Chemical
5 Mobil Sales and Supply
6 Corporate Purchasing
7 Trademark Counsel
8 Corporate Controllers
9 Corporate Research, Engineering, Products and Packaging
10 Corporate Relations

The members of this group represent the principal graphics areas of Mobil's worldwide operations.

Mobil 1 Packages
The Mobil 1 brand name and package design is now being marketed worldwide in a variety of sizes, three of which are shown here. The graphics, which had to be adjusted for each container size and configuration, were developed by Mobil's graphics consultants and coordinated by the Corporate Design and Graphics Development department.

Garamond (for text). Weingart's aim was to break free of the "stiff and boring" orthodoxy that he felt slavish adherence to Swiss Style had led typography into: although his direct influence has been to create a new style, New Wave, the thrust of his teaching was actually anti-style.

Reaction and rejection of a different order was apparent in the style of graphics associated with the punk and new music scene of the late 1970s. Here, again, the music industry showed it had the ephemeral, inquisitive, novelty-seeking nature to throw up challenges. The work of young designers in the UK, the main ground for the short-lived movement, stands out. Designers like Barney Bubbles (Colin Fulcher), Jamie Reid, Malcolm Garrett and Peter Saville launched their reputations, not by creating a prevailing aesthetic, but by a wave of invention, of pillaging history and vernacular without excessive respect. Like the music they were packaging, they celebrated the idea that their medium was more about emotion in communication than reason.

Right: the extremes of the 1970s: the International Style rules of control even extended to this self-conscious range of "Basics" packaging from Sainsbury supermarkets in Britain in the early 1970s. The own-brand products were colour-coded with mostly sans serif typefaces and minimal graphic elements to suggest good value. In contrast, establishment values of all kinds were under attack by punk graphics, opposite right, which were like the music in determinedly kicking at conventions. Leading the charge were Jamie Reid's covers for the Sex Pistols, here the back of the 1977 album *Never Mind The Bollocks*. Its "ransom note" style typography was part of a general strategy of appropriation and subversion, ideas taken in part from the 1960s Situationist movement. Opposite left: somewhere in between, the experimental could also be seen in the convergence of graphics and film with computer effects. The movie titles of R/Greenberg Associates in the late 1970s were among the first to use super-computers to to drive out graphic effects on sequences for *Alien* (as here) and *Superman*, both big budget spectaculars. This was part of the groundwork for tools that would become commonplace in computer manipulation.

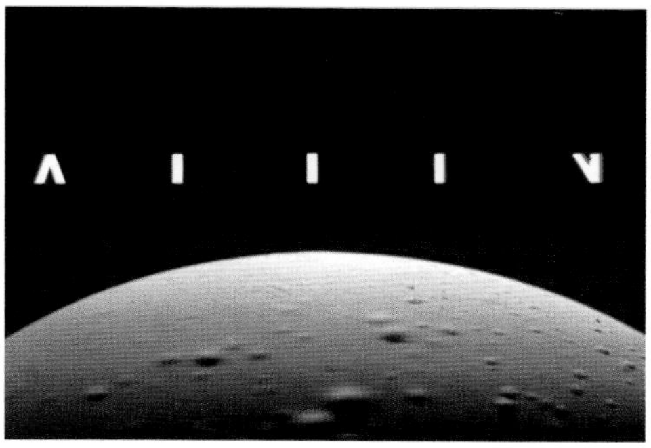

A L I E N

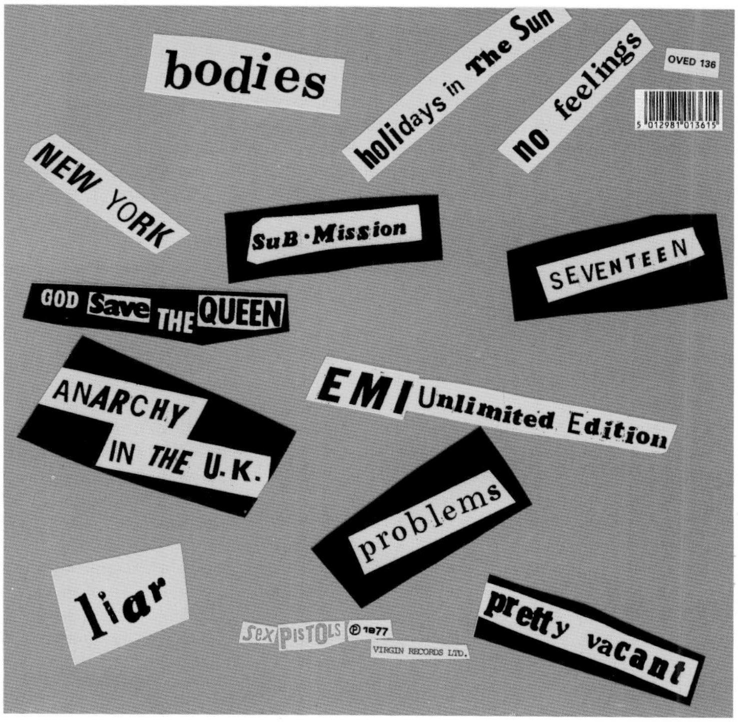
bodies
holidays in The Sun
no feelings
OVED 138
NEW YORK
SuB·Mission
SEVENTEEN
GOD Save THE QUEEN
ANARCHY IN THE U.K.
EMI Unlimited Edition
problems
liar
SEX PISTOLS ℗ 1977
VIRGIN RECORDS LTD.
pretty vacant

1980
1981
1982
1983
1984
1985
1986
1987
1988
1989

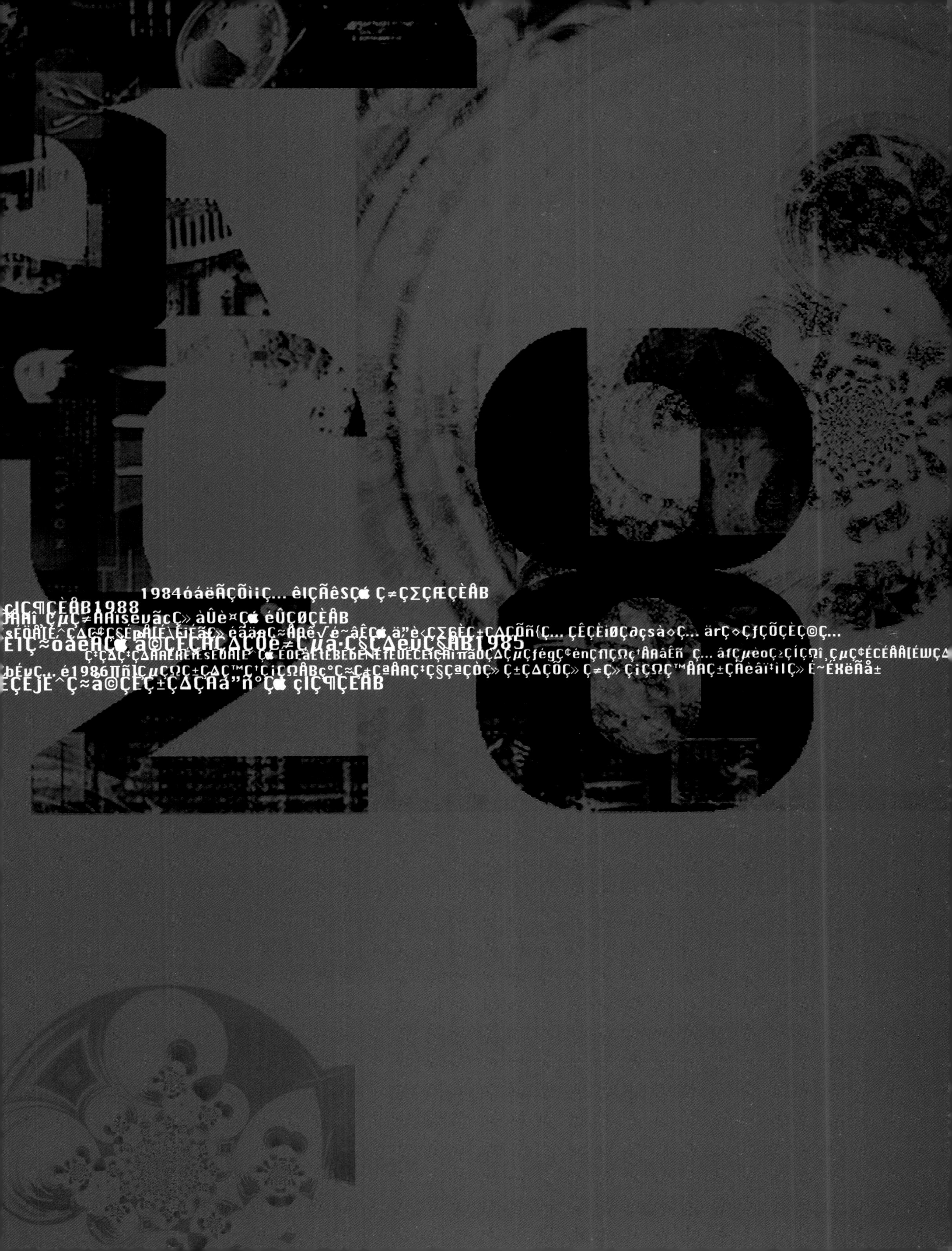
1984óáëÃÇÕì¡Ç… êIÇÃêSÇ Ç≠ÇΣÇÆÇÈÅB
çIÇ¶ÇÈÅB1988

"Most of my life," recalled Matthew Carter in the late 1980s, "I dreaded situations like dinner parties where people ask you what you do for a living. People had no idea what a type designer actually did. Nowadays I'll be in a restaurant and a waiter will come up to me and ask, 'Did I hear you talking about fonts?'"[1]

An exceptional waiter, perhaps, but such was the radical shift in the access to typographic decision-making in the 1980s. From being an arcane area that many graphic designers had only elementary knowledge of, typography was, by the end of the decade, being practised in millions of homes and offices.

This was due to the arrival of the personal computer. The PC was launched by IBM in the early 1980s and became widely "cloned", in other words, copied by much cheaper rival products being sold that were capable of running the same software. No longer did users need a degree in computer science to operate such a machine, and users could afford to buy the tools to add functions to their computer. This separation of the functionality of software from hardware was a development that underpinned the new form of type design and layout. Typographic control was no longer related to the use of large systems, as with hot metal or photosetting.

The launch of the Apple Macintosh personal computer in 1984 set the pace for developing user-friendly systems: it featured wysiwyg presentation ("what you see is what you get"), not only for showing text but for simulating the wider creative working environment. This made possible the practice of "desktop publishing", a much-used phrase applied to the potential given by the new systems for creating and outputting publishable material, either in finished form (via a desktop printer) or ready to give to an external printer. Typesetting and other print-room skills were merged into the same process as that required for designing on-screen. Designers began to do their own typesetting. Software layout packages, such as PageMaker and QuarkXPress, simulated the graphic designer's work tools and desk on-screen. Initially crude in their typographic sensitivity, these packages were rapidly upgraded in response to both user demand and to take up the benefits of the fast-advancing technology.

Besides the transfer of fonts to the digital environment, and the growth of font vendors in this environment (see Bitstream and Emigre below), the fact that type choice, however crude, was commonly available on-screen, created a new perception of this subject. The "Mac" came bundled with a clutch of fonts as part of its system software: these included versions of Courier (a backwards reference to the typewriter), Helvetica and Times, and also new screen fonts that worked at the low-resolution (72 dots per inch) of on-screen display – Chicago (used on the system display itself), Geneva, Monaco and New York. They were not for printing, but existed only for the on-screen world.

The "Mac" and related software were by the end of the decade developed to such an extent that the graphics industry was switching over rapidly to the control, speed and economy it made possible. Diverse software for handling the input of words and pictures into the on-screen layout was produced, increasingly releasing functions only half-dreamed of pre-digitally. To some degree the new processes were driving the graphics (a simple example of this would be that the default settings and screen display suggestions within a program would encourage designers to take up certain options). In other words, decisions were constructed around the parameters laid down by the program writers. Lower-cost scanners and easier links with other programs provided the means for integrating the computer with the mass of other print, photographic and film information that a designer may need to draw on. At the same time developments in software for related areas of activity, notably word processing, supported the transfer of the material handled by typographers into the new technology. For the first time there existed a seamless production process in which all the material could be generated in the same format – digitally – and pulled together in one creative production centre, the desktop computer environment.

This did not happen overnight, but nearly. Into the early 1990s the majority of print production took place with traditional methods heavily involved. But the rapid adoption and development of the technology happened at a pace much faster than the move to previous technologies in print and communications. Where hot metal took decades to become established and gain the support of a wide variety of typefaces, and photosetting took twenty years to turn around from initial take-up to dominance, the digital revolution prevailed within a decade. From virtually zero computing in design at the start of the 1980s, by 1990 a survey in the US reported that 68 per cent of graphic designers used computers and a further 26 per cent were in the process of buying a system.[2]

"Within my experience, the time taken to conceptualize and produce a real letter character has gone from a year to a day," Matthew Carter commented, contrasting the beginnings of his type design career (learning punchcutting at the venerable Dutch printing firm Enschedé in the 1950s) with the power that off-the-shelf font design programs gave designers by the mid-to-late 1980s.[3] Carter's career neatly encapsulated the changes. After working for Crosfield and then Linotype as a designer who adapted and developed types for photocomposition, he formed Bitstream in 1981, with colleagues from Linotype. To a degree it followed the route mapped out by the International Typeface Corporation, that of a system-independent type supplier. Bitstream sold digitized typefaces to the new companies that were launching electronic imaging equipment and needed type libraries to make their systems viable. Rather than each individual manufacturer having to develop libraries, Bitstream launched a rapid programme of digital face development and licensed the faces. Many of the classic faces had to be incorporated to offer a useful library, and so the great majority of Bitstream faces are those whose basic forms are in the public domain or are licensed from others. Over the decade the library grew to more than a thousand faces, which were

Left: poster by April Greiman for the Pacific Design Center, 1983. From the basis of studies under Wolfgang Weingart in the 1970s, Greiman (born 1948) developed her own West Coast spin on these ideas, forming an approach she dubbed "hybrid imagery", which drew on the language of video and computer as well as print graphics. The self-consciousness of the work is to the fore, with suggestions of colour registration, of the dot of half-tone screen, and cutting away at the printed plane. At the same time there is a degree of rigour to the ordering of the various blocks of information that harks back to the Swiss Style.

licensed to around three hundred manufacturers – an indication of the explosion in options available for outputting type, when compared to the small group of manufacturers seriously able to invest in hot metal and then photocomposition technology.

The library includes important new designs, beginning with Carter's own Charter (1987). This was one of a number of faces designed to tackle the challenge of variable printer quality and how it could degrade a face. With a high-resolution typesetter, 1200 dpi (dots per inch) or more, the finer points of a design will be reproduced. But with the 300 dpi printers (and some even lower resolution) that were common, many faces broke up. This was an acute problem in smaller sizes where the number of dots drawing the design of, say, an eight-point character, would be insufficient to render fine serifs. Charter responded to these conditions by offering a limited family (regular, bold, black and italic) that had sturdy, open letterforms, that do not lose definition or fill in when produced on standard low-resolution printers.

Early ground rules for coping with low-resolution output were presented in Gerard Unger's family of faces (Demos, Praxis and Flora), released between 1976 and 1980 while he was working with the pioneering German digital typesetting manufacturer Dr. Ing. Rudolf Hell GmbH. The three, respectively, serif, sans serif and italic forms, demonstrated the large x-height, openness and sturdiness seen in the later Amerigo, Charter and other digital faces intended for wide-ranging application. Unger noted that the requirements of

Opposite: Lucida, designed by Charles Bigelow and Kris Holmes for Adobe in 1985, was the first original face designed for laser printers, being tolerant of different resolutions of output. Stone Sans was part of an 18-font family designed in 1984–7 by Sumner Stone for Adobe which was intended to work on digital technology for anything from low-resolution display advertising through to fine text in books.
Left: in the mid to late 1980s Studio Dumbar in The Hague was at the forefront of a wave of influential design coming out of The Netherlands. Led by Gert Dumbar (born 1941), who built on the Dutch Modernists such as Piet Zwart, the studio often used constructions that mixed flat art with staged photography, playing with the viewer's perspective.

these faces was not so dissimilar to the basic parameters of effective, straightforward typeface design of the last four hundred years.

Kris Holmes and Charles Bigelow's Lucida family (1985) for Adobe Systems (which had a type-design programme in support of its graphic design-related software products) took this idea further, drawing on legibility and readability research to develop a simplified sans serif and serif that would reproduce the preferred characteristics of classic typefaces but through the terms of the new low-resolution technology, rather than against it. Holmes explained that:

"The basic Lucida letterforms are purposely free of complexity and fussiness so that the underlying letter shapes can emerge legibly from the 'noise' of the printer-marking techniques. Certain traditionally complex details, such as swelling stems, brackets, and serifs are rendered diagrammatically as polygonal shapes rather than as subtle curves. In small sizes and low resolutions, these produce clear forms; in larger sizes and higher resolutions, they reveal interesting modulations."

Holmes and Bigelow created a comparable range of bitmapped screen fonts called Pellucida, conceived to best express the different qualities of the family on the poor resolution of the monitor (72 dpi equivalent on a typical display). All faces for digital setting need to have a screen font version, but the inaccuracy of many made them difficult to work with as what you saw was not what you got.

Lucida *30pt*

A B C D E F G H I J K L M
N O P Q R S T U V W X Y Z
a b c d e f g h i j k l m n o p
q r s t u v w x y z

Stone Sans *30pt*

A B C D E F G H I J K L M
N O P Q R S T U V W X Y Z
a b c d e f g h i j k l m n o p
q r s t u v w x y z

A problem with screen fonts, besides their low resolution, was that they were often partly drawn by the computer from knowledge of the nearest sizes: this can lead to highly unattractive renditions of the face on screen as the computer may "refine" the wrong elements of the design. Adobe, the company behind Lucida, pioneered a method called "hinting" to overcome this drawback. This process builds information into the type that automatically adjusts the face in small sizes to combat low-resolution problems, putting in elements to retain characteristics, but it does so at the cost of some of the original character of the design. However, with the launch of its program Adobe Type Manager the company delivered an industry-standard technology that removed the troublesome "bitmapping" effect of enlarging fonts beyond the size at which they were originally constructed. The proliferation of digital software and hardware also created a demand for a common language for type information in computer files. Different languages were developed, but the victory went to Adobe's PostScript, launched in 1983. Rather than working with a bitmapped image, PostScript draws and fills in Bezier curves to achieve a better print image.

While many designers could – and did – go on producing work that looked pretty much as it would have using photosetting or even hot metal, a new generation of designers picked up on the freedom with which typographical form could now be exploited, aided and abetted by other media technology advances in photographic and film form.

The West Coast magazine *Emigre* was important as both a demonstration of new ideas and a rallying point for debate on digital type and design-related issues. Initially an attempt at a lifestyle magazine when launched in 1984, it moved increasingly to being a design, then a typographic, magazine. This was related to the growth of the digital font business of *Emigre* founders Rudy VanderLans and Zuzana Licko. With Licko as chief designer and other designers' faces included in their distribution, their fonts began with raw explorations of the bitmap structure and moved on to address aesthetic issues that responded closely to the potential of the systems and the concerns of the design community.

A highy influential figure in this period was Neville Brody, whose work on the British style magazines *The Face* and *Arena* became internationally known – an effect propagated by the growth of general media interest in fashionable graphics, along with the publication in 1988 of a book, *The Graphic Language of Neville Brody*, and a world-touring exhibition. Such a phenomenon was, arguably, a result of the new generation of graphic producers enfranchized by digital technology: now typography was not remote, graphic style was more accessible – almost like fashion or food, just one more aspect of taste to understand and explore.

Crudely measured, the results of the "Brody school" could be seen in the exploitation of letterforms as graphic devices, the do-it-yourself design of new display forms (Brody drew the Constructivist-influenced typefaces he used on *The Face* by hand, but they have an aesthetic that relates to the bitmap

Industria Solid *21pt*

ABCDEFGHIJKLMNOPQRSTUVWXYZ
abcdefghijklmnopqrstuvwxyz

Insignia *21pt*

ABCDEFGHIJKLM
NOPQRSTUVWXYZ
abcdefghijklmnop
qrstuvwxyz

Opposite: after Neville Brody built his reputation, Brody-like typography was commonplace – this advertisement is one of the few he designed, rather than being a pastiche of his work. Above: two of his early pre-digital typefaces. Right: record sleeve by Vaughan Oliver, 1988 – florid type and dark imagery were trademarks in his influential output for 4AD records.

fonts) and in the reliance on typographic elements as expressive features of the page. In its picking up of the language of digital typography as something to exploit and express, there were connections, albeit unspoken, with the New Wave approach of expressionist typography taught by Wolfgang Weingart.

Another designer involved in the influential batch of "style magazines" of the 1980s was Terry Jones, who launched *i-D* magazine. Here legibility was questioned in a manner akin to the psychedelia of the late 1960s, with text subverted by garish overprinting and crude typewriter text, copy reversed out from four colour, photocopier distortions added and many more graphic experiments thrown into the pot besides. All this "noise" was part of the message, of course. For the audience of *i-D*, typographic quality involved view-ability as much as legibility in creating readability. Style magazines such as *i-D*, *The Face* and *Blitz* in England, or related magazines such as *Actuel* in France or *Wiener* in Germany, were badges of affiliation to be worn as well as to read.

Teaching practice was falling a generation behind what was happening around new technology and the style magazine typography. With colleges and their staff largely wedded to older technology and teaching programmes related thereto, they had difficulty, both conceptually and economically, in embracing the latest equipment as freely as had ambitious studios or publishing operations. But one school that did make its mark was the Cranbrook Academy of Art in the US, where the postgraduate teaching and work of Katherine

Matrix *21pt*

ABCDEFGHIJKLMN
OPQRSTUVWXYZ
abcdefghijklmnop
qrstuvwxyz

Above and opposite: examples of the early output of Emigre Graphics, the company set up by Rudy VanderLans and Zuzana Licko in 1984. Beginning with the early Macintosh as the design tool, Licko produced a range of bitmapped fonts, such as Emigre Eight, in the mid-1980s. Her designs developed with the technology; Matrix, above, shows an attempt to create a face with serifs that would be extremely robust for low-resolution output. Left: questioning Modernism, American designers were exploring their vernacular as a rich source of typography – and Tibor Kalman (born 1949) was among the most witty, as with this menu for an up-scale diner which takes the letter board of a down-scale diner, but introduces Apollinaire-like typographic puns. Opposite right: New Order Confusion cover, 1983, by Peter Saville, a pioneer of typographic cool.

McCoy in graphics during the 1980s, supported by key students such as Jeffery Keedy, Edward Fella, Scott Makela, David Frej and Allen Hori, was to have an influence beyond its small academic environment. In the following years its students would feed out to head up many of the leading graphics courses in the States. McCoy's direction can be seen in an early pre-digital project with the design of an issue of the academic communication theory magazine *Visible Language* in 1978, where the text was deconstructed by a variety of typographic devices (such as reversals, hugely exaggerated word spacing and ragged margins, all showing the influence of Weingart). McCoy explored the "linguistics" of typography, seeking to isolate the "hardware" – the basic structure of the communication – from the "software" – the meaning in the work. The dislocation sought to prise loose

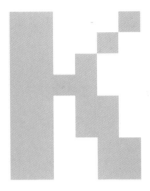

Emigre Eight *42pt*

ABCDEFGHIJKLMNOPQRSTUVWXYZ
abcdefghijklmnopqrstuvwxyz

an awareness of the signified from the signifier, to use the terminology found in the writings of a Cranbrook influence, pioneering language theoretician Ferdinand de Saussure (the notoriously long reading list of the school drew heavily on structuralist and deconstructionist thinkers). While most of the work did not depend on new technology for its execution, in its diversity and intellectual drive, the Cranbrook Academy sought to present a new agenda for typography. Not entirely coincidentally, there was an emerging technology ready to help this happen.

In televisual graphics, new systems fostered new techniques during the 1980s – notably the image-manipulation and retouching machines pioneered by Quantel (Paintbox and, later, Harry) that offered a powerful method of manipulating frame-by-frame movement, integrating graphic effects and live action. But there was still little effort applied to generating new faces specially created for the unique conditions of television, despite this being the prime medium of communication. Type would tend to be a bold face with crudely spaced and leaded lines ("TV spacing", as it was commonly known), or there would be an attempt at something more adventurous that would fall foul of the unsuitable nature of print faces on screen. Fine weights and serif forms do not survive the 625-line-or-less boiling mass of information supplied by the rolling scan of television image-construction.

Besides the innovation in technology and the work of those designers attuned to it, there were eclectic revivals and

The 1980s threw up questions that bypassed type design history, with the "transparency" of type and its fine history in metal becoming increasingly redundant in electronic media. Opposite top: The time-based dot matrix of indicator boards (as with the London Underground signage introduced in the late 1980s) demands viewer participation and awareness of the moment of the message. This has prompted art works such as Jenny Holzer's piece from 1988, a slogan in Spectacolor above Piccadilly Circus, right. Such conceptual pieces of typographic-based art have probed the relationship between text, image and viewer, bringing an awareness of dimensions beyond the print tradition of type. Opposite: The dislike of Chicago in the typographic establishment has no effect on its prevalence or strong functionality as the default font on several generations of Macintosh computers, and representing the operating system. Chicago is one of the original "city" fonts supplied with the Macintosh in 1984, designs intended for high legibility on a 72dpi screen and not for print.

Chicago *48pt*

File Edit View Label Special

ABCDEFGHIJKLM

NOPQRSTUVWXYZ

abcdefghijklmn

opqrstuvwxyz

cross-fertilizations of graphics. This was aided by the ease with which scanners made it possible to suck material into a computer layout. Typographers could take old faces that may exist only in a specimen book or a piece of print and scan and rework them to create either one image or a new font. Computers had shifted the very nature of graphics: all was now data, and the "remix" process in design was entering a new era.

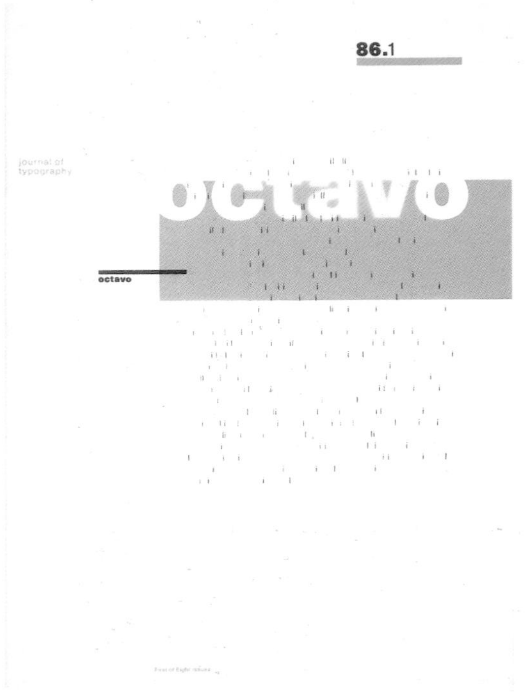

Opposite left: in 1986 the journal Octavo was launched by a group of designers in London called 8vo who were dedicated to arguing a Modernist case for higher quality in typography and against the "mediocrity" that they saw around them. Simon Johnston, Mark Holt, Michael Burke and Hamish Muir set out to publish eight, 16-page issues, which took them until 1992, by which time Johnston had left. Despite having only a small circulation, the journal was a marker for retaining the spirit of the Modernist pioneers. Opposite right: the European cultural poster tradition was the refuge of many leading designers. In Germany, Uwe Loesch (born 1943) combined minimal messages (this poster headline reads "Survival during war") with concept-based layout. Right: titles for a UK television programme, 1988, by English Markell & Pockett. New post-production systems were allowing designers to incorporate type into dramatic film and video effects. Here the words streamed in projections on faces and in abstraction before spooling into the words of the programme title.

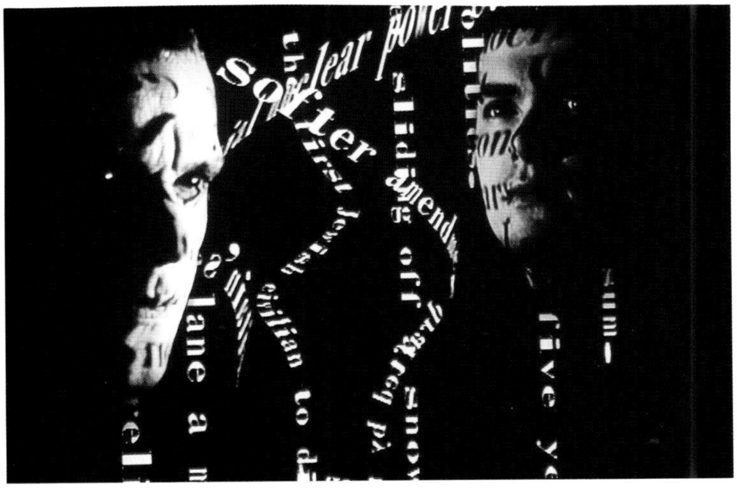

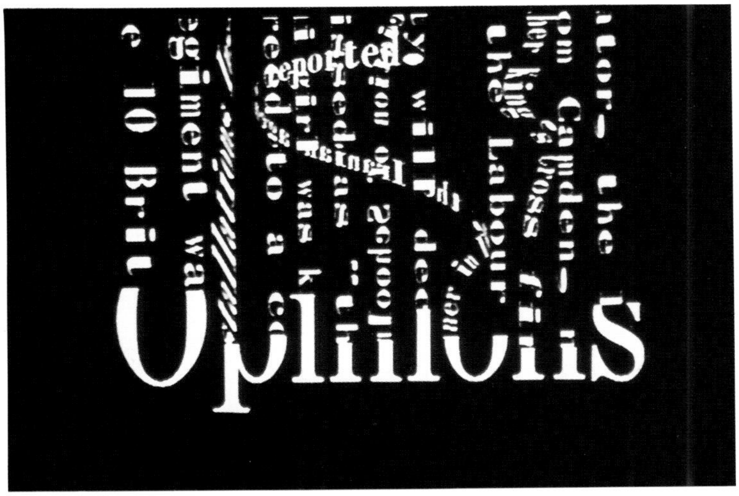

1990

As we approach the end of the century in this chapter, we will step out of history and into a sense of what the future may bring. We are near to "now", with the people and the processes covered in this chapter often those that are still at work and helping to drive the agenda – or, rather, as we shall see, multiple agendas.

It is worth taking a moment to consider how all that we cover in this book is actually about "now". Typography seeks to become invisible in the carrying of information – to create an immersive moment, an experience that goes beyond the mere appearance of an artifact, a document or sign, and instead *is* the message. Through such an illusion typography seeks to wire a viewer directly into the objective of the message, be it the data in a railway timetable or the ideas, images and characters in a piece of creative writing. But while this quest for "virtual reality" and transparency of message transmission is the main focus of typography and type design, from time to time there are periods of reflection, of inquiry, of deep self-consciousness in typographic design. The 1990s were just such a moment. The opportunities, questions and challenges raised by the shift to digital technologies gave birth to a period of intense creativity around typography, along with a period of self-expression and even self-indulgence. Given the explosion of type activity at this time, a result of the change in media technology, this is no surprise: there was much to be self-conscious about. As a result, type and typography increased in visibility.

A postcard issued in 1996 promoting the new typeface FF Schmalhans by Hans Reichel proclaimed itself as "the 3 million 285 thousand 467th font ever to be made in the Universe". It proposed that the universe could take up to four million fonts, so there was room enough for a newcomer. While the first figure was an exaggeration, the second figure was an underestimate of the infinite variety of fonts now possible. Reichel's little joke addressed the incredible proliferation of type design in the 1990s, a boom that blew apart the assumptions of what type involved. With a technology that allowed anyone with a personal computer to draw or customize their own typeface, or at least pick'n'mix an assorted font, the total user base of PCs suggested that a community in excess of one hundred million typographers and type designers existed by the late 1990s. As the PC (and its software with fonts ready-loaded) spreads in usage, that constituency of mostly untrained typographers continues to grow. This newly empowered group of people handling the arrangement of type contrasts with just a few tens of thousands of type specifiers (such as designers, art directors and printers) in previous generations. Fewer still of them were pure type designers – no more than a very few thousand worldwide who designed type in the days of hot metal, thanks to the concentration of activity in a handful of foundries. Now even the most basic PC comes with software that permits some routine reshaping and other abuses of the supplied typefaces, along with rudimentary drawing tools that might invite the sketching of new letters that could exist in the same digital space as the most sophisticated and traditional of fonts. Type design is now not necessarily a profession or a craft – it is something anybody can do, albeit rudely; it is similar to cooking – anybody can do it, after a fashion, but some do it with ready-meals, others create famous restaurants.

For all this new facility, most PC users did not (and do not) design or even play with type beyond perhaps changing the default font, using the bold and italic options, or increasing the type size and leading. And yet they work with letterforms and typographic controls that did not exist for the end user before the digital era. The PC brought together functions previously carried out by means of handwriting, the typewriter and professional typesetting. It took typography to laypeople – even if they did not necessarily want the responsibility that went with the power. But even if these accidental typographers did not actively think of typography, their computers would be doing it for them, producing typographic matter "on the fly" as they generated text or downloaded internet pages with a default font crudely "setting" the requested information.

Even within the professional design community, the quantity of new type design in the 1990s was unprecedented – on a scale that makes estimating the number of typefaces in circulation almost impossible. Every young designer seemed, and seems, to want to make a face or two, and many of the major type companies also went through rapid design exercises to convert to the new media and market their constantly growing "offer".

The major type vendors moved their large libraries to digital form and onto searchable CD-Roms and then the internet, offering thousands of fonts. They bought in new designs to put in the "shop window" of their marketing, and promoted the existing libraries widely. They reshaped their operations continually, moving into aggressive business-to-business marketing in a way that had been unnecessary in the context of the steady trade of pre-digital eras, when type was tied to the suppliers and their technologies. Business lunches gave way to direct mail drops as a way of selling type. The fact that the traditional big type companies were selling type rather than typographic systems marked the major shift. They also increasingly found business difficult, as the old steady state of affairs vanished along with the proprietary type technologies, and the new desktop age failed to offer a business model that supported the previous organization.

Type sales were subject to the rapid proliferation of illegal copying of fonts. By the beginning of the 21st century, it was likely that at least nine out of ten type usages were actually unlicensed. Traditional type companies also moved away from being focused on their own designs, and instead sought to outdo each other as distributors, with confusing lack of differentiation as they began to cross-license each other's fonts. Hot competition was provided by the explosion of small font companies and independent designers – hundreds of small companies able to use the web to promote and distribute their wares.

Type was now something that could be made in a one-person, one-bedroom design studio. A digital type "foundry"

With Emigre's "Starting from Zero" issue of 1991, the face Template Gothic gained its first official airing. Designed by Barry Deck and distributed by Emigre, it was quickly called "typeface of the decade" by one magazine and it became highly fashionable. While the aesthetic is derived from laundromat signage, the characters suggested screen-derived forms – an association to please a culture in which the computer had at last become "personal", and a friendly tool to use at work, rest and play.

could be set up with little more than access to a Macintosh computer, a copy of Fontographer software and, perhaps most importantly of all for business success, an understanding of the new marketing opportunity. The opportunity was to serve the new community of type buyers – professional designers and their clients or employers.

Emigre showed that type "brands" could be launched out of the new technology. Emigre started its existence as a music/style magazine but by the early 1990s it had gone on to become a byword for experimental fonts, to the point that a 1993 issue of the influential music magazine *Ray Gun* proclaimed on the cover "No Emigre fonts". This was an ironic gesture from its art director, David Carson (see below), to signal that he was not dependent on the company's designs for his creative expression. It was also interesting in that he could now assume readers actually knew what a font was.

Emigre traded its type at the top end of the market, with a small list of unusual fonts offered at a high price, in contrast to the "pile 'em high, sell 'em cheap" tendencies of larger companies. It was wedded to a policy that made each individual design seem as much a theoretical statement about the potential of type and the overall direction of design as a functional font. Emigre's extension into music and book publishing suggested the model of the business, which was more like a small record label or publisher than an old-style system seller. The type business was now clearly creatively focused, with the technology just part of the digital age. "Foundries" depended for brand image and business strategy on having a few hit typefaces for survival. Some were cash cows, some were more for the creative reputation. Some faces managed to be both.

Template Gothic by Barry Deck (1990) was a highly popular Emigre-distributed face that came to signal the zeitgeist to the point that design magazines proclaimed it (somewhat prematurely) "typeface of the decade". Through stencil-like structures seemingly unlinked to written forms, it combined the vernacular (drawn from laundromat signage) with a suggestion of new technology. Hi-fi brands and telephone companies found it perfect for styling their ads.

Through the 1990s the Emigre catalogue grew to include more than two hundred faces, with the "house" designer Zuzana Licko as the key contributor. By this point, Licko and Rudy VanderLans (the publisher/editor of *Emigre* magazine) had been pursuing their path for long enough and with sufficient purity of purpose to earn themselves a retrospective at the San Francisco Museum of Modern Art. Increasingly during the decade, Licko's work moved from overtly exploring the digital language to reinterpreting the classical tradition of typography with designs that responded to the engagement of, say, Baskerville with the digital age – out of which came Licko's Mrs Eaves.

A larger, more commercially motivated type design business than Emigre, FontShop International, also owed its existence to the digital revolution. Founded in 1990 by the graphic/type designers Neville Brody in London and Erik Spiekermann in Berlin, it was no less experimental in the nature of the typefaces it published and distributed, but grew much faster than Emigre thanks to a strong system of franchise distributors. FSI expanded over the decade into a library of more than one thousand faces, with a type catalogue that needed updating quarterly in order to take in all the new launches. Faces (such as Schmalhans, above) were branded under the FontFont "label" with "FF" appended to the name. More than 80 designers were represented, although (as with many businesses) a significant proportion of all revenue came through a small number of the overall faces. The earners were not the overtly creative showpieces, but those that had the robust possibilities of extensive licensing and application across corporate identities. They tended to readability with great flexibility of application, with multiple sizes and weights, with an aesthetic that inevitably tended towards neutrality with a twist. Scala and Thesis were two such faces, distinctive without being showy, as was Spiekermann's own Meta face, a leading earner across the decade. It was Spiekermann's typographic functional rigour that influenced the design of many of the most successful faces and that comes through also in the success of other fonts such as FSI's revived DIN and OCR (see picture captions for information on all three of these key 1990s faces). The FSI support for young designers ensured that character sets and the general build of a font had a robust quality that was sometimes lacking in the output of smaller independent foundries.

FSI worked through a network of distributors covering various parts of the world, although it had problems with the management and control of some of these, notably in the US and UK. At one point in 1996, Brody, as represented in FSI, was taking legal action against his UK distributor, FontWorks, where he had 51 per cent ownership, which was threatening a counteraction against FSI. This problem led to FSI partnering with Monotype as a new distributor of its fonts, bringing one of the old major "labels" in type design into collaboration with the new force.

FSI successfully focused on building its brand around innovative contemporary type design. Once again, the music or book business comes to mind as the model for this, rather than the old practices of type companies: instead of having an in-house studio as the drawing workshop for the latest faces, FSI worked as a publisher whose reputation drew in new designers and new designs from existing designers. The "cool" credential of its founders combined with the energetic marketing of its distributors (who also brought in new fonts and designers) to make a highly competitive operation unburdened by any pre-digital history or other business activity.

Typefaces were no longer being sold off the back of some proprietary system, as with hot metal or photosetting, nor was there the wholesale digitizing of existing familiar faces as with Bitstream. Instead, in the 1990s the emphasis was less on working within a technology (a photosetting or hot-metal system, or even Letraset transfer sheets) and more purely on the design content being marketed. While being by no means the leading distributors of fonts in total, FSI and

Emigre were the pioneers around which a whole new industry of type companies and type design practice emerged. Small foundries such as [T-26] or House Industries, or the designer/distributors such as Jon Barnbrook with his Virus label or Jean-François Porchez's Typofonderie, were only able to create and distribute fonts because of digital technology. Literally hundreds of small labels, many just one designer's own work, became available, some also represented through larger collections, some represented through internet-based aggregator sites, some represented through many distributors.

Although the industry rapidly switched to digital, issues such as the choice of computer platform (PC or Mac) or type format (PostScript or TrueType fonts) could still cloud the picture. Fonts tended to be released to cover all profitable eventualities, as the adaptations required software tweakings rather than any investment bound up in a physical product. The wave of new companies also worked as a further spur to the rejuvenation of more traditional type developers and distributors. However, they already had the motivation to get out of the fast-failing old technology where type was attached to proprietary systems.

The death and rebirth of Monotype illustrates this pattern: after some years of restructuring, matters came to a head at the Monotype Corporation in 1992 when the business was put into receivership. This was after an awkward period of shifting ownership, but the key problem was the speed of change to desktop publishing and the dying market for old typesetting systems. Out of this was born a new company, Monotype Typography, a software-based company which

domus
NUMERO 730
SETTEMBRE 1991
MASSIMO CARMASSI
TEATRO A PISA
J. PAUL KLEIHUES:
PER UN RAZIONALISMO POETICO
REM KOOLHAAS:
EDIFICIO A FUKUOKA
ISAO HOSOE:
TAVOLI MULTIPLI
J. LUIS MATEO A BARCELLONA:
UN PROGETTO COMPLESSO
VENEZIA: 10 PROGETTI PER IL PALAZZO DEL CINEMA
DESIGN:
JASPER MORRISON
UMBERTO RIVA
HEINZ TESAR
OSCAR TUSQUETS

Left: Emigre's fonts in the 1990s became increasingly varied – from technology-centred to the vernacular. This 1991 brochure puts black-letter back on the menu as Zuzana Licko argued for her Totally Gothic. "It seems curious," she wrote, "that black-letter typestyles, which we find illegible today, were actually preferred over more humanistic designs during the eleventh and fifteenth centuries. Similarly typestyles that we perceive as illegible today may well become tomorrow's classic choices." Above: cover of the magazine *Domus*, September 1991, art directed by Italo Lupi. Notable for its espousal of OCR-A as a headline face – once the manifestation of intermediate computer technology, by 1991 a post-modern reference.

went on to celebrate its centenary of “type making” in 1997 on the back of a business built on realizing the value of archives of classic fonts, along with custom design and consultancy work. The shift to living by intellectual property had started to happen before the liquidation of Monotype Corporation, with font-licensing deals struck with Apple Computer in 1989 and Microsoft in 1990. The next partnership saw the company issue a CD-Rom of its entire “classics” collection along with the Adobe Type Library – the fast-arrived leading force, a giant born of the ubiquity of its software. The Adobe Type Library grew to be a major typographic presence, helped by Adobe's dominance in providing the PostScript technology of type description. For Adobe, type was just a sideline, a way of selling something else, in the way that it had once been for Monotype. By the time of Monotype's hundredth anniversary, the double-CD font collection featured around five thousand typefaces and was not only marketing the Adobe and FSI libraries, but had launched the Creative Alliance with Agfa. It was a short step to merger, and in this anniversary year Monotype finally gave up its independence to Agfa. In 2000 Agfa Monotype went on to acquire ITC as the traditional suppliers converged further to provide a new font company, which by 2002 distributed its eight thousand typefaces through its own web portal, fonts.com.

Linotype and Berthold were other major traditional typesetting system companies that had a difficult passage in the 1990s as they fought to realign their businesses and to realize the value of their intellectual assets against the decline

Berliner *24pt*

X-Fuse Fontur *12pt*

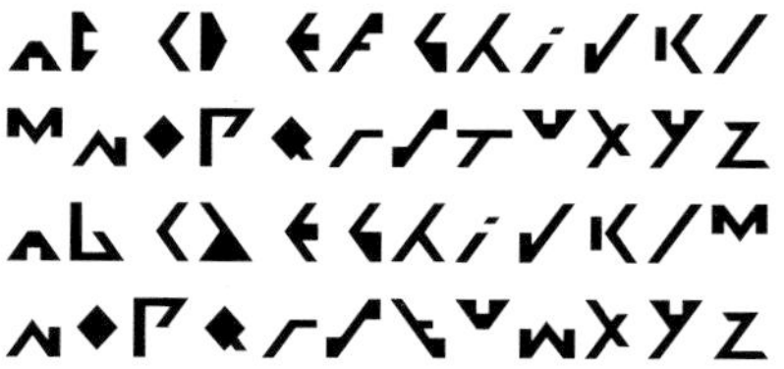

All images and faces on these pages are part of the Fuse project started in 1991 by Neville Brody and Jon Wozencroft. This has involved the publication of a small magazine with a disk containing experimental fonts and a set of posters by the font designers exploring their font. The new faces were not intended as useful, but questioned type and communication. Brody's State, 1991, seen in the poster shown left, set the tone of the investigation. It sought “to get inside the structure of the alphabet and to accentuate the shapes that are inherent in written language”. While Brody said it was not for day-to-day use, he added: “Readability is a conditioned state. I wanted to take the typography away from a purely subservient, practical role towards one that is potentially more expressive and visually dynamic.” The image shown opposite is by the Swiss designer Cornel Windlin with his font Moon Base Alpha – one that has begun to find its way into more everyday use despite its “unconventional” readability.

Whatthehell *18pt*

evil hate body vice disgrace

pain ecstasy ignorance take false no thanks weak a is not them things slavery answer question deceit fear chaos war

good love soul virtue honor pain knowledge give true thanks strong the is us ideas freedom question answer

honesty hope order peace innocent others

of their traditional business. Berthold retained its independence, albeit with a key distribution partnership for its typefaces with Adobe. Linotype also refocused into a type library business of some four thousand faces, which it increasingly distributed through other partners, from within the protection of the printing machine company that owned it.

In contrast, the purely software-based Adobe rapidly grew to having one of the largest and best-distributed type libraries, being in the useful position of controlling the use of the PostScript page (and font) description software. This gave Adobe room for leverage when it came to developing and licensing type and striking partnerships. However, by the end of the decade, the difficulties in continuing to revolutionize the software (along with the general downturn in technology stocks) had Adobe on the retreat. The lack of any particularly appealing type business model (difficult to defend intellectual property and a glut of product in the market) would ensure that investment in type was not a priority.

CD-Roms and catalogues were generally distributed free and in increasingly vast numbers during the 1990s. A phone call was all it then took to unlock a typeface on the disk, or to download it over the line, or to have it biked across town or prepared for next-day delivery. Contrast this with the pre-digital era in which the creative agency had to wait for a type specification to be turned around by a third-party typesetter, who in turn might be required to order up the face from the type foundry.
To give some "brand difference" to offers that were becoming increasingly similar, foundries turned their attentions to

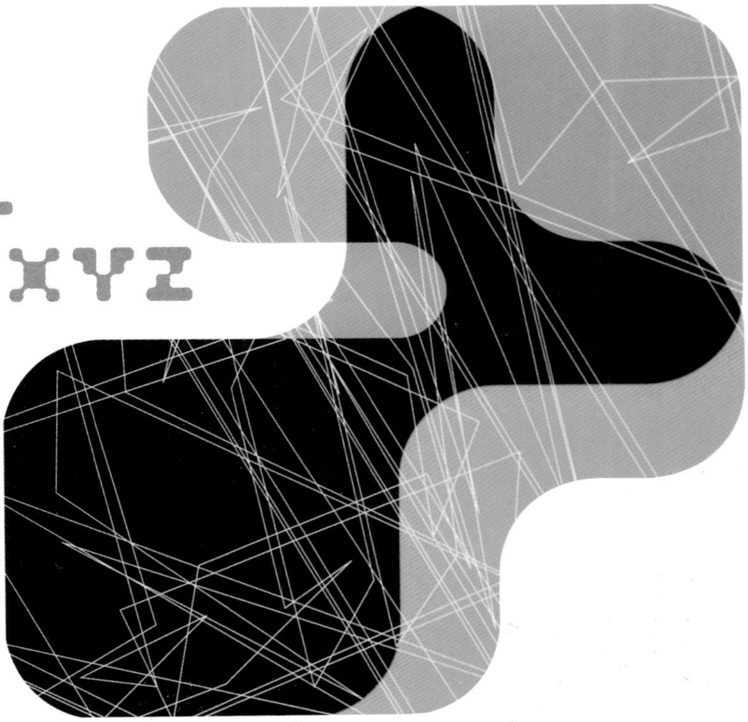

Moon Base *48pt*

Freeform One *24pt*

Atomic Circle *12pt*

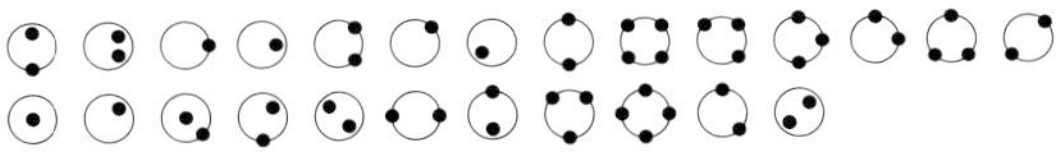

Flixel *18pt*

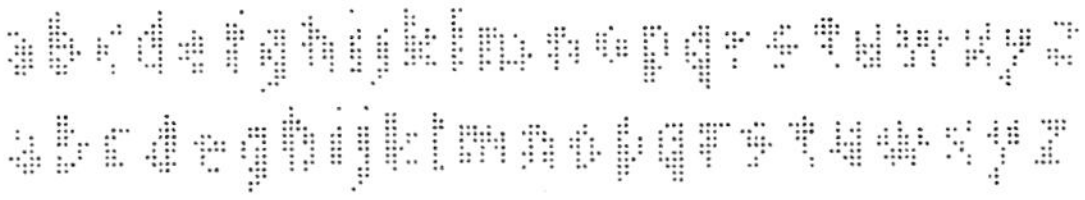

Bits *18pt*

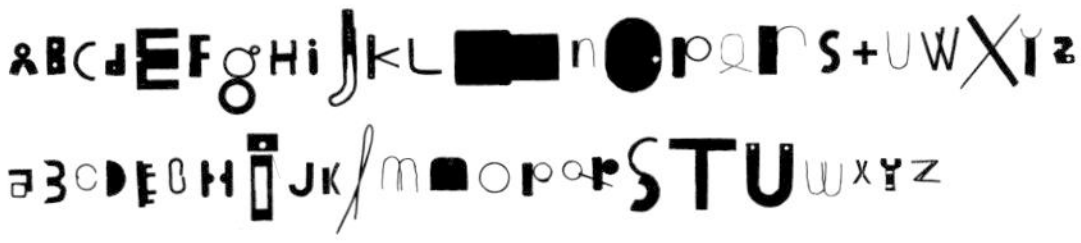

Crash *12pt*

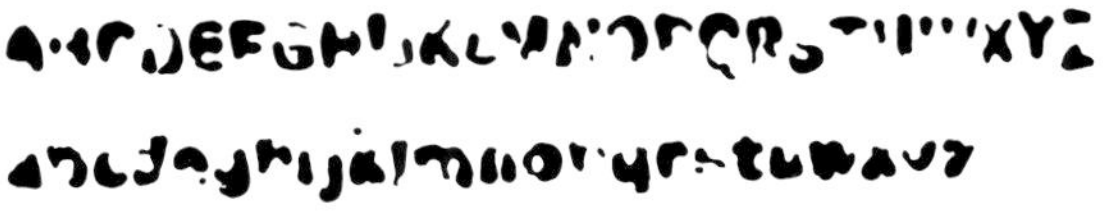

packaging. For example, considerable creative and physical resources were invested in the output of some of the new, small design-led type companies. The Chicago-based, Cuban-born designer Carlos Segura went to lavish lengths – his [T-26] presentation packages exemplify the baroque extremes reached, where typefaces were packaged in cute burlap sacks containing a host of printed sample material, while QuickTime movies were made to demonstrate the moving qualities of the type. Thereby [T-26] fonts assumed an air of physicality that belied the fact that the core products were invisible bits of information. Meanwhile, Plazm fonts, out of Portland, took the route of Emigre in that they made their fonts visible through *Plazm* magazine. It was hard to see which came first, the fonts or the magazine, but the general effect was to make music, writing and type design seem to be part of the same area of cultural exploration. Those were two of the more notable examples in the world's richest economy, but hundreds of other examples could be found worldwide.

The internet emerged as a means for promoting and distributing a font without requiring physical packaging or a distribution medium. This worked for commercial type companies, and also for the hacker world of computer activity. Many fonts were (and are) placed on the web for free or "shareware" distribution but, inevitably, these are less than complete in their character sets, functionality or quality. Plagiarism is more than a little in evidence, with software such as the leading type-design package Fontographer making it relatively easy to take in character forms, and adapt and rename them. Even less honourable was the practice of illicit

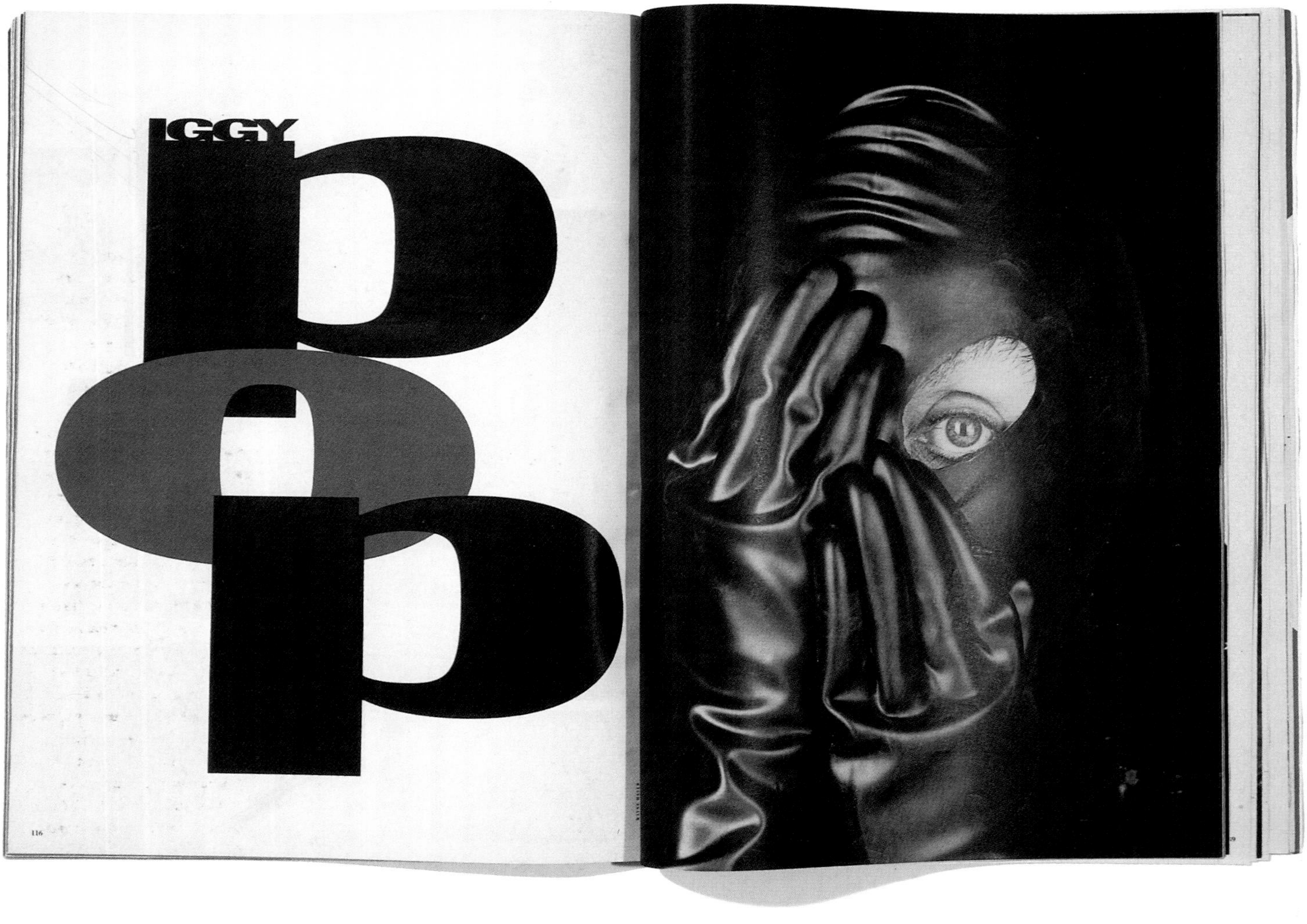

internet offerings of whole libraries of copyrighted fonts (along with other software) which could be downloaded for free. It became common in major cities to have illegal operators of software downloads who for a price would turn up and copy a whole archive of material onto a computer hard drive.

Such activities realized the darkest fears of the type-publishing community, who faced not only deliberate copyright infringement, but also confusion as to what was and was not permissible in the carrying and transferring of fonts. For designers and publishers, the need to buy a typeface not only for their own creative use but for the company that might carry out the subsequent imagesetting added an unpalatable increase to their costs, which often prompted them to give a copy of the font to the output company for free. Against this, developers have worked to raise awareness about copyright law, devise controls restricting digital copying (so far largely unsuccessfully) and have lobbied for stronger action to curb illegal copying. However, the lack of recognition of the differentiating factors of type design in law, rather than patents on names, has been a problem in bringing actions in the United States, and more generally is the problem in proving a copyright infringement without costly actions. Quite simply, the multitude of small infringements were and are impossible to police, and would not justify the costs of the numerous legal actions required to enforce copyright observance.

As a result, type developers have argued that digital technology could undermine the basis for serious type development. The

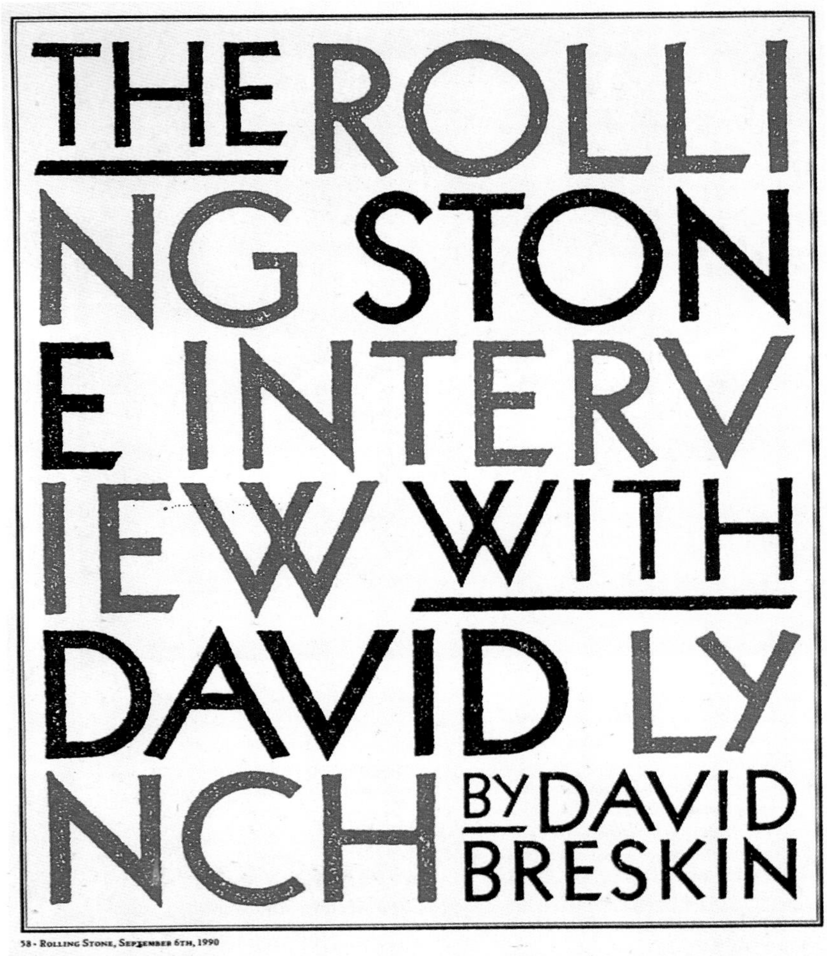

Expressive typography has spread across editorial and advertising worldwide in the 1990s, partly as a result of the ease and economics of the publishing technology now compared with pre-digital days. However, certain art directors are major influences – Fabien Baron's work on Italian *Vogue*, then *Interview*, shown opposite from April 1990, and subsequently *Harper's Bazaar* in the US, has pioneered typo-illustration as a powerful and elegant tool within fashion and style publications. And the strong typographic feature openers of *Rolling Stone*, as practised since 1987 by the art director Fred Woodward, have celebrated calligraphy, wood letter and more contemporary type as highly expressive editorial tools. Shown left is one page of an opener spread from 1990 that faced a portrait of the subject, David Lynch.

Federation Against Software Theft (FAST) agitated for a change in ethics around digital typeface use from the mid-1990s, but without any measurable success. When the product of years of work could be copied perfectly in a few seconds and then used without charge, the incentive to make a business out of high-quality type design disappeared. The fate of the major providers, the lack of investment in major type research programmes, the failure for type design to offer a decent reward for the skill invested – all of this followed from the failure of respect for the intellectual property involved.

Rudy VanderLans, founder of Emigre, grimly summarized the implications in the "frequently asked questions" on his site:[1]
"Question: What is the future of type design?
"Answer: The art and craft of typeface design is currently headed for extinction due to the illegal proliferation of font software, piracy, and general disregard for proper licensing etiquette. You can begin to solve this problem by properly licensing your usage of each and every font that you have in your possession. If you have copies of fonts for which you did not purchase a license, please, throw the fonts away, or better yet, contact the manufacturer and come clean."

It became apparent through the copyright and distribution dilemma of digital type that an important development would be the creation of a technology that allowed the viewing of a typeface without permitting the user to create with it or take it elsewhere. The OpenType standard being developed for the internet enables the user to embed type design code within web pages, delivering accurate

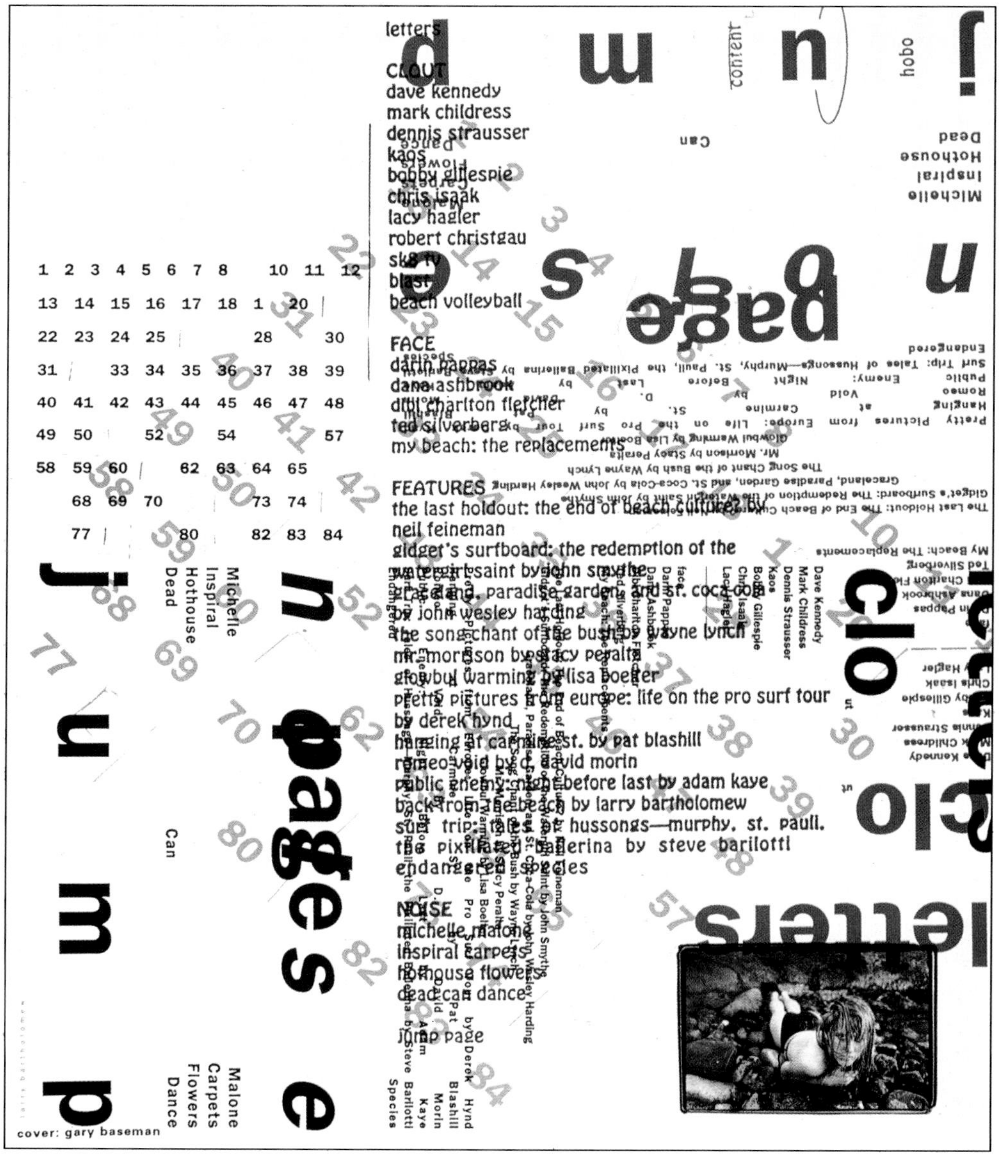

David Carson became the most widely celebrated graphic designer of the 1990s, thanks to his typographic pyrotechnics on the magazines *Beach Culture* (1990–1), right, and *Ray Gun* (1993–5), opposite top, and the subsequent bestselling books (both created with the current author) *The End of Print* and *2ndsight*, opposite bottom. His highly expressive use of type, which at times would be used more like paint or collage elements than for its linear reading sense, has won him many critics as well as fanatical support. His approach has been at the centre of a movement of younger designers towards making expressive, personally indulgent work, at the expense of any designer anonymity. His "Zapf Dingbat" spread, opposite, shows a whole magazine feature set in an unreadable font of symbols – Carson's personal reaction to the dull text. The *2ndsight* spread shows his move away from an early concentration on editorial and into work for advertising and, here, a website for MGM.

bryan ferry
photos:Peter Morello stylist: Jill Spector

LOG IN
colors
vault
go
events
ONLINE
MOV-
IES
BACK

images of the particular characters without having to download and hold the particular fonts used on each and every user's computer. However, this only goes so far. The larger challenge is for a technology that could make type available for sharing in typographic layout but without permitting unlimited distribution or final implementation and use. This is purely a philosophical construct, however, with no currently realizable means.

Digital technology has been partly responsible for many of the above changes, but these have also been driven by a new use and appreciation of type and typography in society. As ever, typography reflected society's myriad concerns, but ambiguity around the changing media invited diversity and deviations in the forms of innovation. With no single powerful aesthetic or political position driving a vision, every remembered form of graphic design from the past was recycled as style. In almost any country in the world you could pass from pseudo-traditional lettering on food packaging to techno-pop music typography, to some minimalist setting of words in fashion advertising. Typography became a powerful signifier of the diversity possible in a world that had largely capitulated to the power of the capitalist model of production – where competitive choice, or the illusion thereof, was the rule. Now typography aimed to clothe and promote, rather than transparently communicate, a truth (the sometime innocent purpose of typographers past).

Any cynicism about the marketing-led values of most typographic production should not obscure the real climate

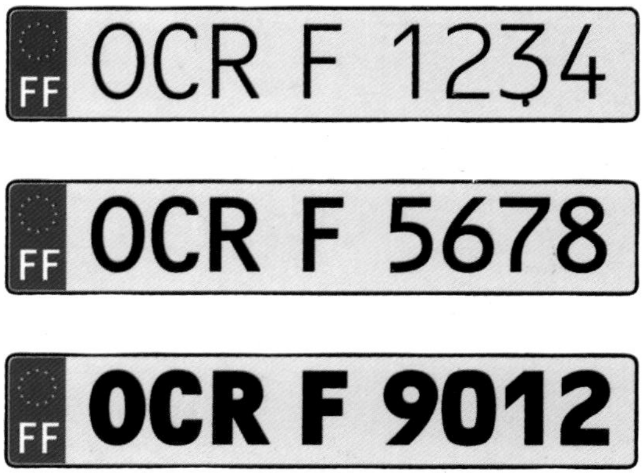

Left and above: since its inception in 1991, FontShop International has been to the fore in building strong distribution alliances and promoting its new releases with wit and commercial relevance – as seen here with a font sampler being shown applied to vernacular signage. Left is a range of weights developing the German standard DIN by Albert-Jan Pool, 1995, and Info, 1996, by Erik Spiekermann and Ole Schäfer, while above is an ingenious re-working of OCR by Pool in 1995 to provide it in differing weights. Opposite: Mark Farrow has been a prime exponent of minimalist typography in the 1990s, an increasingly credible route against the endless type design and typographic diversity brought about by the digital explosion. This poster was for the Hacienda club in Manchester, England, and gained its impact from being printed in fluorescent ink so that the type stood out at night.

for radical innovation in these years. The maturing of advances in computers and in global media delivered a new landscape for typographic activity and for type design. As suggested previously, it became customary over this decade for type to be designed, "set" and output using computers. In fact, this revolution essentially removed the notion of typesetting in most applications, thereby abandoning an area of craft skill along with the repetition of keystrokes. The lack of a trained compositor's eye on type led to a general decay in controls over much commonplace printing.

In 1990, desktop publishing techniques (digital authoring and transfer of materials for publishing) were still being pioneered and were starting to move rapidly beyond the stage of "early adopters" in the leading Western countries. By 1995 it was commonplace, and by the end of the decade it was a fundamental – taken for granted – part of the design business practice the world over. While hand-set, hot-metal and photoset practices remained to some degree available, sometimes through harsh economic circumstances and sometimes through an aesthetically motivated regard for the old craft, the core production switched to digital source and output of type and typography, and often digital delivery via web- or other screen-based communication.

A personal anecdote may illustrate how this revolution in communication plays out in both innovative and degraded realities, at one and the same time. I was due to visit a design college in the Siberian capital Novosibirsk in April 1997. No printed matter on this city was readily available before

I set off, but more than ten thousand internet sites existed, delivering a selection of sunny photographs and extensive data on the weather and suchlike, albeit thrown over the internet with my default font churning out long line-lengths of closely set Times. I could equally have seen the sites in other fonts or in alternative translations. In short, my own state-of-the-art type technology presented a picture of faraway Siberia that involved one culture mapping over the other. On arrival at the real (rather than virtual) city, it was clear that road and building maintenance programmes were short of funds. The state of civic pride was apparent in the lack of postcards and rundown or non-existent signage, though I found a hidden stash of propaganda about 1960s Communist monuments and other showpieces in a cupboard just off the lobby of my hotel. However, at the college, powerful Macintosh and Sun computers matched the technology available in many Western schools, and within the design, advertising and print industries, similar technology was commonplace.

The point of this story is that while large differences in physical, cultural and economic conditions may exist between and within nations, the technology within which typographic activity largely takes place has linked (or is linking) around the world. Using earlier technologies is in many ways not an option. The digital technology is the only one that provides a gateway to the digital media of today – it is simply not possible to stick with an earlier technology and still contribute to most contemporary publishing, or the "new media" of the internet and multimedia. This has helped determine a "melting pot" of activity in the creation and delivery of

material as never before. The internet often goes further to iron out differences, producing an illusion of greater similarity than actually exists when participants step back from the computer monitor.

This is the reality where, at its most extreme, the end of the 1990s and early 2000s saw lone adventurers – single-handed sailors, or Pole explorers – able to "publish" to the world via email and websites from the most remote parts of the world. The information environment became more advanced than the physical environment – digital data floated free of physical limitations and borders, with the typographic process absorbed into the invisible "publishing" industry that such activities represented.

The material in this book has concentrated on an Anglo-American dominance in technology and typographic theory, since it is their imperialist communications culture that has led the evolution of type. The march of that technology and culture has worked with the development of a world where English has become the most international language – but now, just when the triumph of Western political, economic and cultural thought may be at its zenith, it is also most exposed to new influences. Even after a decade of decline, the second-largest advertising market in the world remains Japan, and it remains defiantly Japanese and non-Western in its signage. China has also started to open up, and will become another massive market that will not easily adopt Western scripts.

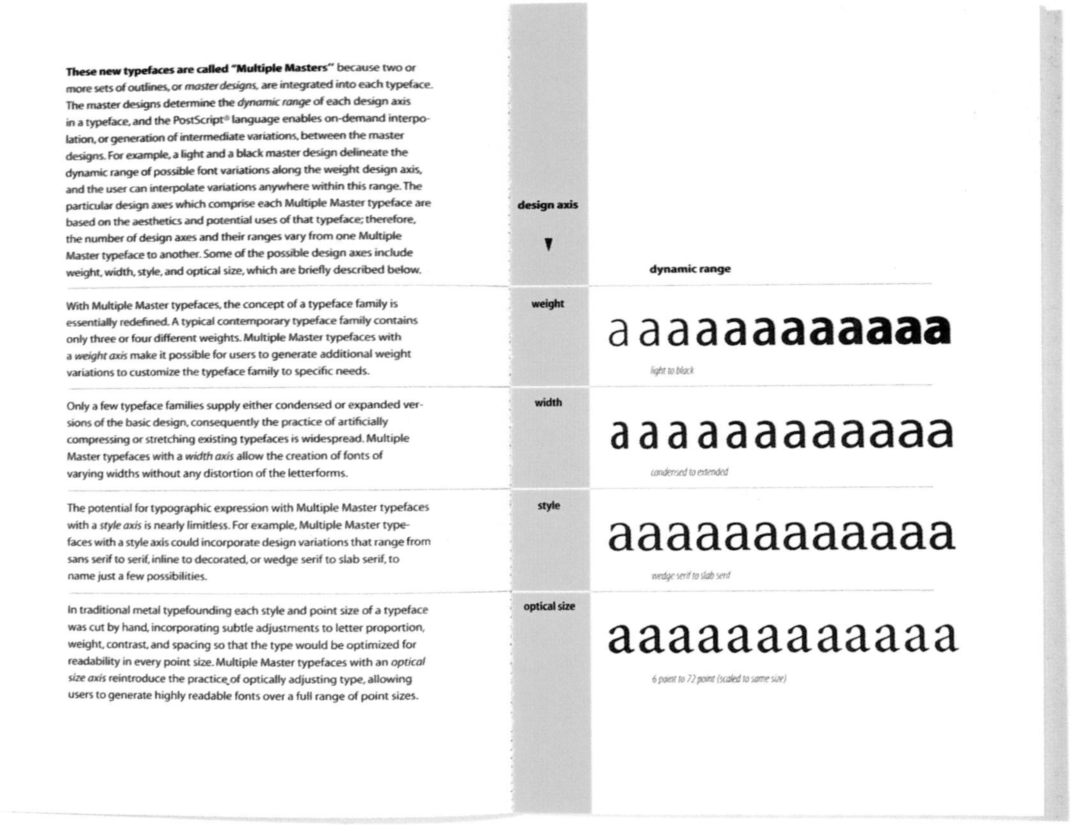

	design axis	dynamic range
These new typefaces are called "Multiple Masters" because two or more sets of outlines, or *master designs*, are integrated into each typeface. The master designs determine the *dynamic range* of each design axis in a typeface, and the PostScript® language enables on-demand interpolation, or generation of intermediate variations, between the master designs. For example, a light and a black master design delineate the dynamic range of possible font variations along the weight design axis, and the user can interpolate variations anywhere within this range. The particular design axes which comprise each Multiple Master typeface are based on the aesthetics and potential uses of that typeface; therefore, the number of design axes and their ranges vary from one Multiple Master typeface to another. Some of the possible design axes include weight, width, style, and optical size, which are briefly described below.	▼	
With Multiple Master typefaces, the concept of a typeface family is essentially redefined. A typical contemporary typeface family contains only three or four different weights. Multiple Master typefaces with a *weight axis* make it possible for users to generate additional weight variations to customize the typeface family to specific needs.	weight	a a a a a a a a a a a a *light to black*
Only a few typeface families supply either condensed or expanded versions of the basic design, consequently the practice of artificially compressing or stretching existing typefaces is widespread. Multiple Master typefaces with a *width axis* allow the creation of fonts of varying widths without any distortion of the letterforms.	width	a a a a a a a a a a a a *condensed to extended*
The potential for typographic expression with Multiple Master typefaces with a *style axis* is nearly limitless. For example, Multiple Master typefaces with a style axis could incorporate design variations that range from sans serif to serif, inline to decorated, or wedge serif to slab serif, to name just a few possibilities.	style	a a a a a a a a a a a a *wedge serif to slab serif*
In traditional metal typefounding each style and point size of a typeface was cut by hand, incorporating subtle adjustments to letter proportion, weight, contrast, and spacing so that the type would be optimized for readability in every point size. Multiple Master typefaces with an *optical size axis* reintroduce the practice of optically adjusting type, allowing users to generate highly readable fonts over a full range of point sizes.	optical size	a a a a a a a a a a a a *6 point to 72 point (scaled to same size)*

The long quest for a universal typeface did not disappear in the 1990s, but the precise objectives varied. Erik Spiekermann's Meta, 1993, opposite left, addressed the need for a highly durable and adaptable text font for wide use across differing print and screen environments. It offers extensive variations. Lucas de Groot's Thesis, 1989–94, opposite right, has three dramatic variations – TheSans, TheSerif and TheMix. Each of these is in eight weights. Each weight is in six variants (plain, italic, small caps, small caps italic, expert and expert italic). This made a total of 144 fonts and more than 32,000 characters in the initial release of the font. Meanwhile, Adobe's multiple masters technology has sought to put type choice into an intelligent engine, whereby users can manipulate a font to a suitable design through altering the nature of a font along sliding axes, such as on weight or width. Myriad (promotional book shown left) and Minion, launched in 1991, were the first faces to sport the new technology, which has been slow in being adopted.

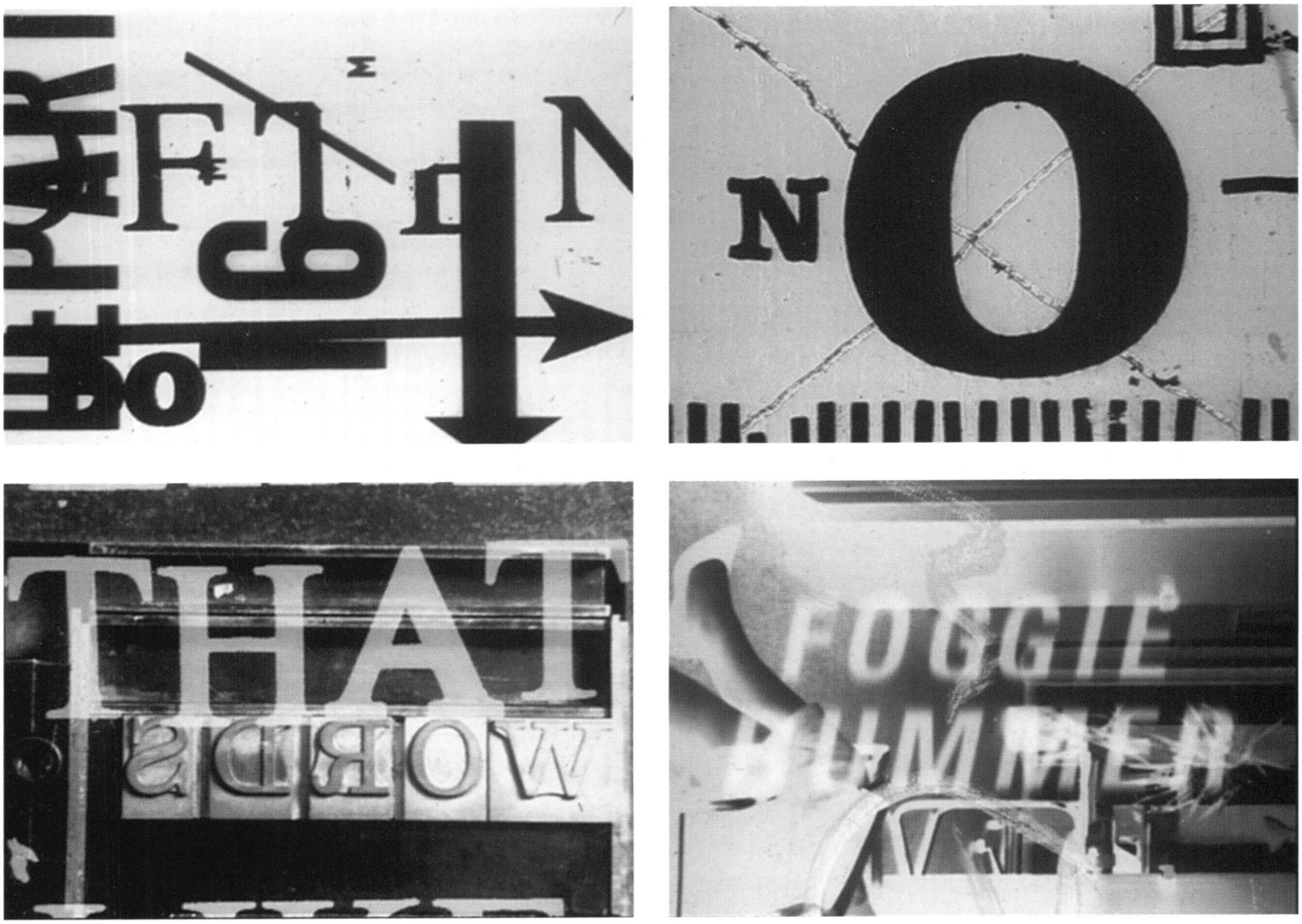

Bastard-Even Fatter *36pt*

ABCDEFGHIJKLM
NOPQRSTUVWXYZ
abcdefghijklmnopqrstuvwxyz

Above: stills from Foggie Bummer, 1995, for BBC Radio Scotland, designed by Jon Barnbrook. Animated typography on screen has proliferated in television titles and commercials, and this spot was one of six (three directed by Barnbrook, three by tomato) that were internationally recognized. The campaign asked the designers to animate the spoken word, concentrating on the power of the language. Left: an early font by Barnbrook, who now has his own "foundry", Virus.

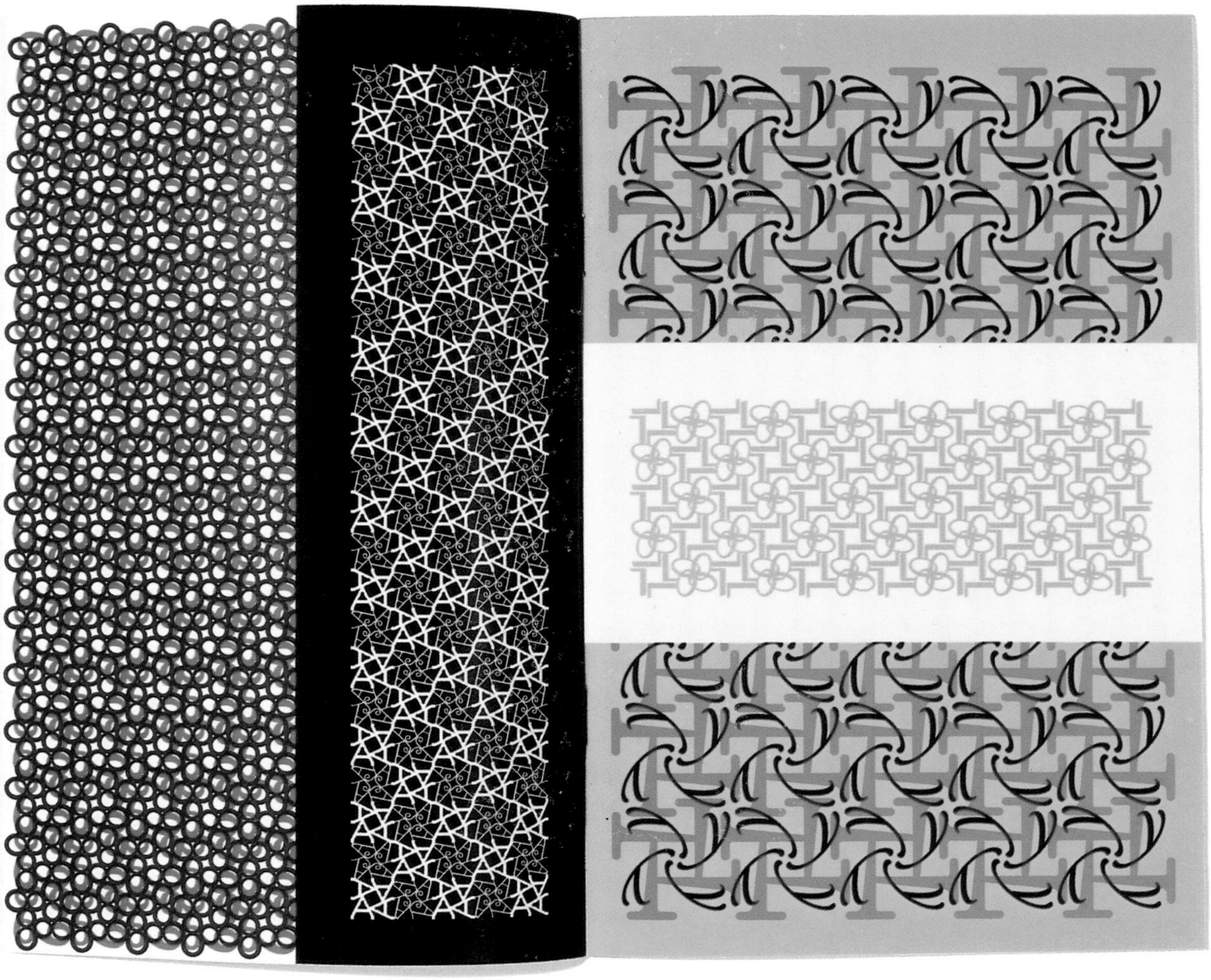

The diversity of 1990s design was matched by type makers – with Emigre as likely to publish a font of ornamental devices driven out of the typographic engine, such as Hypnopaedia by Zuzana Licko, 1997, launch promotion above, as add to its explorations of late modernism. Left: the Hoefler Type Foundry catalogue typifies how individual type designers moved into self-publishing and distribution, a late 1990s phenomenon that, thanks to the internet, could become the standard distribution method.

Right: stills from an interactive multimedia project by antirom with tomato and underworld, built around a font by Don Nendle, 1997, published by Creative Review, London. Type forms were attached to sound loops and three-dimensional movement, enabling the user to compose sound/image pieces with the software. Work such as this proposes an opportunity for type to move beyond the terms of its print or televisual life.

Below right: Jesus Loves You by Lucas de Groot, 1995, one of the new genre of fonts described by its distributor FSI as "destructives" for their deconstructive take on letterforms. This font was one of those taken in the Dimensional Typography project, 1995–6, example characters opposite, led by J. Abbott Miller of New York studio Design/Writing/Research. Jesus Loves You became Rhizome (the resulting lower case "j" is shown opposite top, viewed from above). The other character is from Polymorphous, a 3D development of Zuzana Licko's 1995 font Modula Ribbed. The line drawing is from the wire frame used to build such forms. "The ability to think of letterforms as having spatial and temporal dimension brings with it new obligations and opportunities to augment the visual and editorial power of letters," says Miller, who points out that the methods of visual development, such as extrusion, rotation, shadowing and more, are not new to the era of virtual environments, but lie behind the history of type design.

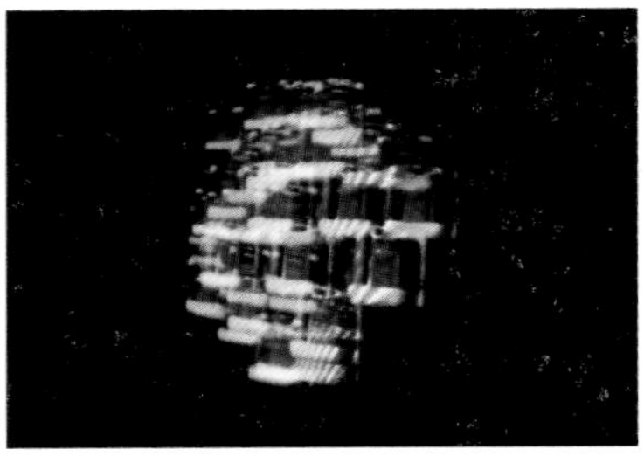

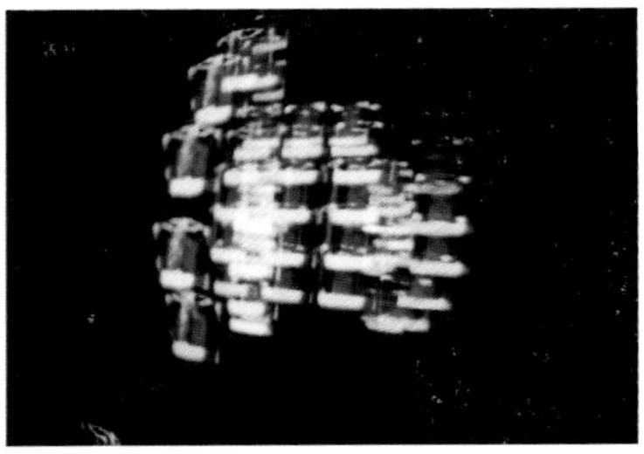

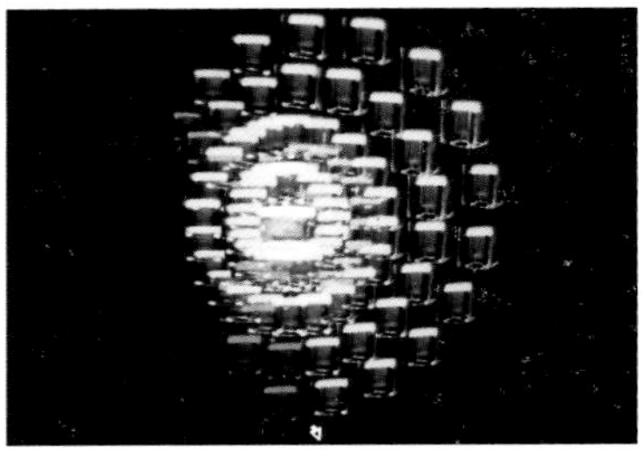

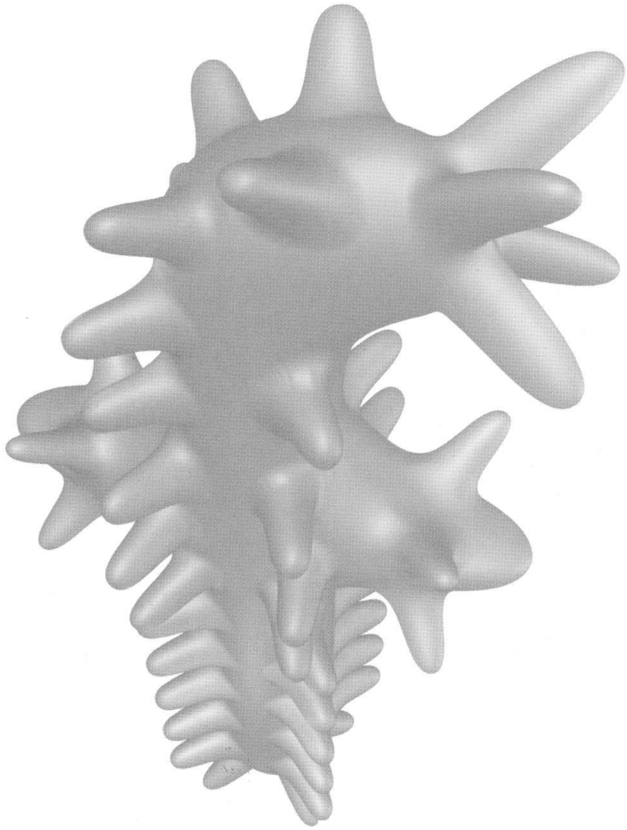

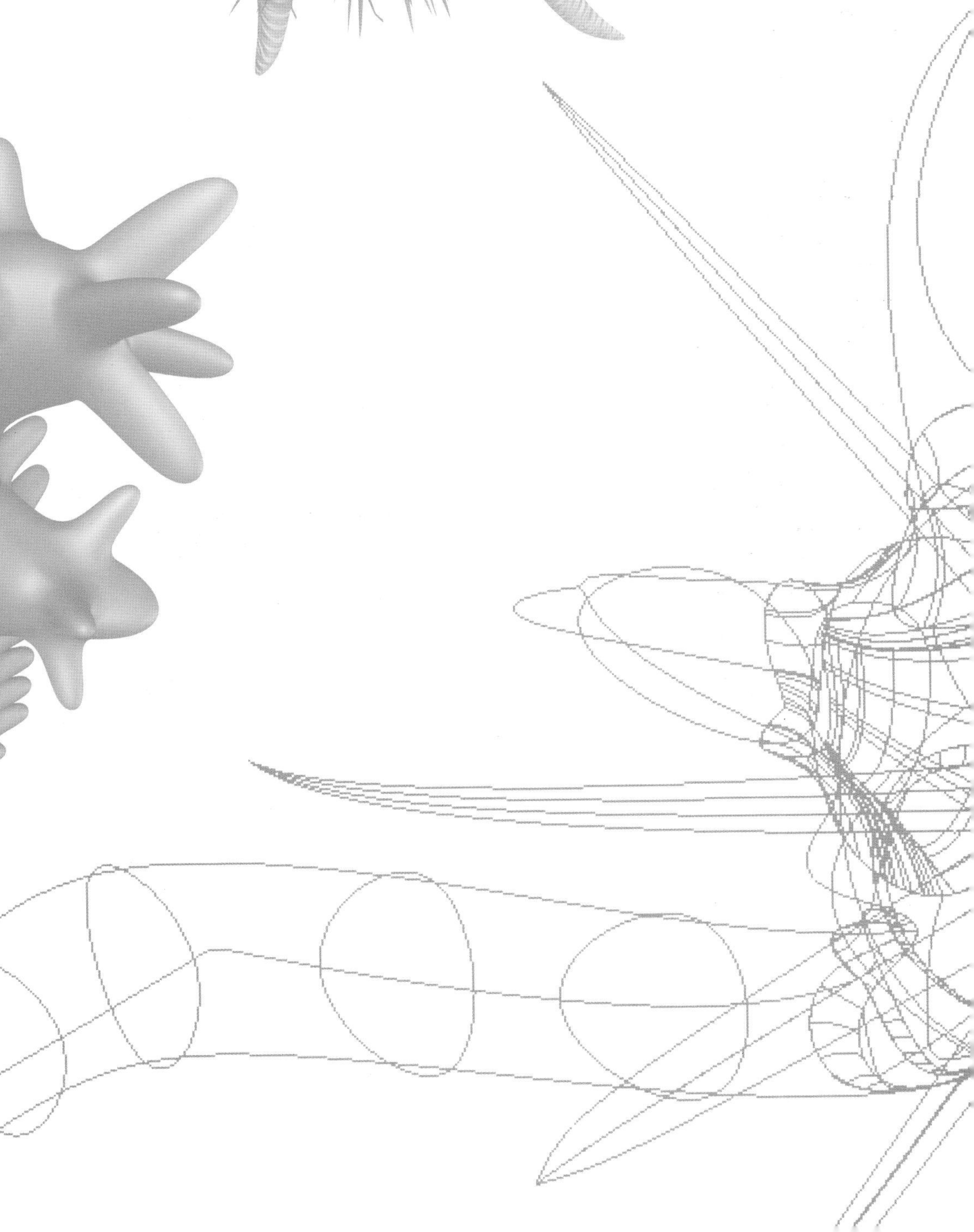

The project to develop Unicode,[2] a character-encoding standard, designed to enable a global interchange of multilingual information, could provide a global typography while supporting the retention of cultural diversity and preserving the world's variety of scripts. Unicode envisages a set of up to sixty-five thousand characters, drawing together the many different scripts and symbols that are used typographically around the world. Unicode-compliant software and hardware could enable keyboards to readily configure to the appropriate characters via a selection menu. A significant problem is the task of designing coherent fonts that carry the necessary characters. In practice, a system might assemble "font sets" that covered the options. The leading hardware and software companies have supported this and an International Standard has been written around Unicode.

However Unicode realizes itself, and whatever economic and social forces exist to retain multiple scripts, the counter-movement is that global communications bring an ever growing need for global sign systems. The media and world business activity push for more efficient systems that have coherence and can carry consistent messages, such as brand identities. Multinational corporations in the late 1990s moved to more rigorous and flexible management of their identity programmes by making the information available on intranets, centrally holding typographic and other data, which supported more accurate transcription of standards to all parts of the world. This was not necessarily a didactic, centralized process, unlike the central identity manual approach that preceded it. Identities increasingly tended to have areas of "play" allowing local options to be implemented

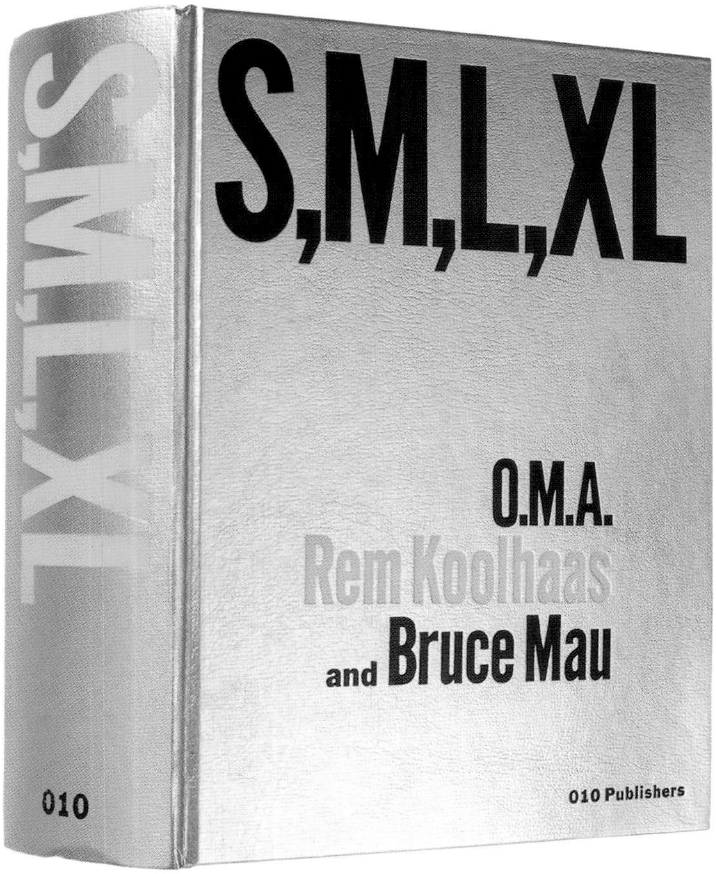

The two books shown on these pages were outstanding for their sheer scale and personality, each taking five years of design development. Left: in 1995 the Dutch architect Rem Koolhaas and Canadian graphic designer Bruce Mau completed a collaboration that explored the architect's work in a complex 1,300-page book. *S, M, L, XL* mixes type, image and other graphic elements in a multi-layered work that took the graphic object as a focal point for Koolhaas's interest in "bigness". Opposite: in 1996 the hundredth anniversary book for print company SHV Holdings was published. Designed by Irma Boom of Amsterdam, this 3.5kg (8lb), 2,136-page tome has special inks, die-cuts and finishes that make it a typographic object so challenging in its construction as to be in many ways unreproducible.

in keeping with a central philosophy, and also allowing local feedback into future central planning. The success of the large new font families such as Meta was born of their ability to respond to these typographic schemes.

With increasing globalized links in all aspects of society – from the media we watch and interact with, to the teams we support, to the organizations that go to war on our behalf – the needs of visual language tools have changed. "Transnational typographics" have a different dynamic from the old thoughts of an "international style", or the insensitivity of basic corporate identity. This is perhaps the most intriguing and socially significant area of typographic inquiry today. It needs to answer questions that engage with core political issues: notably, how do we communicate better, and how do we communicate in one fundamental sign language that we can all understand, and at the same time respect our cultural diversity and the range of meaning it carries?

Typography – both a language in itself and a means of representing languages – has an area of developmental meaning that sits between the totally understood and the totally incomprehensible. This is the area of meaningful creativity the 1990s drew attention to, and we continue to see the most experimental activity within it. It is where a global television network such as CNN or Discovery, a search engine such as Google, a pharmaceutical giant and a high fashion brand all have to operate. When they communicate, they seek to do so globally, adding new information to the user experience but always within a framework of the globally

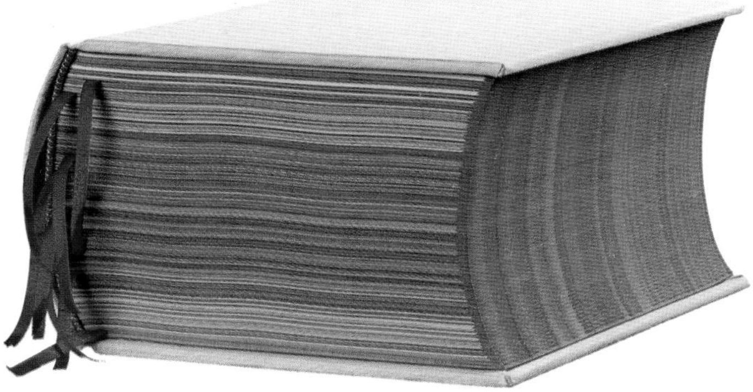

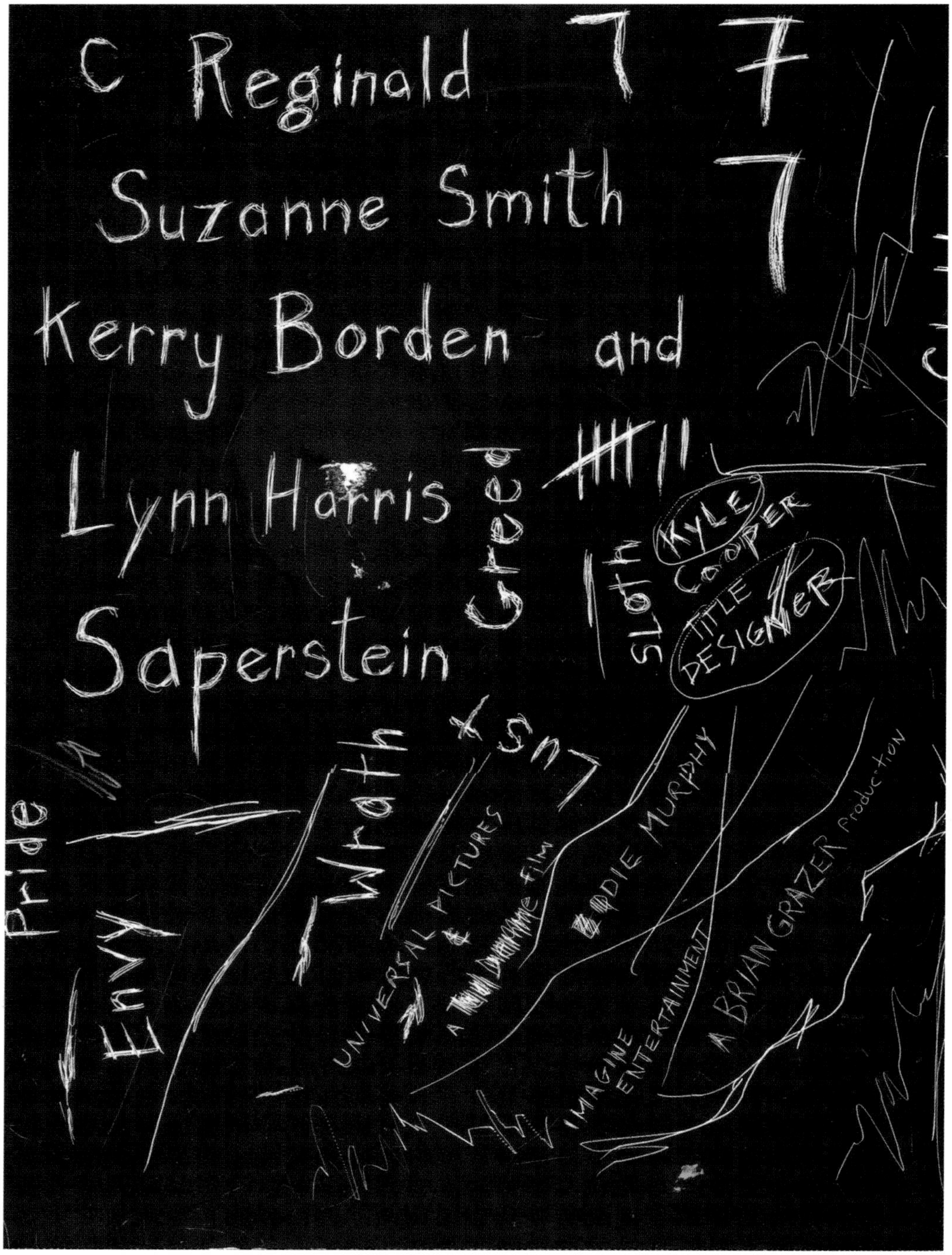

Left: in 1996 the titles to the movie *Seven* used handwriting and animation to create a disruptive sequence in which the nature of the lettering, its break from the familiar orders of typography, helped create a sense of unease – preparation for understanding the mind of a murderer. This image is from the preliminary sketches of the designer Kyle Cooper. Opposite left: in 1998, the cover of the previous edition of this book, designed by Angus Hyland, combined two emerging trends – a Swiss-revival shift away from expressive forms to minimalist typography, and a digital homage to Wim Crouwel's 1960s experimental typefaces (see page 121). Opposite right: the evolution of the Personal Digital Assistant (PDA) in the 1990s saw a reconnection of handwriting and typographic form, divided since the birth of moveable type. In Palm's Graffiti alphabet, users need to adapt handwriting so that it more easily separates and generates typographic forms.

understood. They cannot avoid the possibility of being global in the potential reach of their messaging, even if their intention is much more focused. As we converge existing languages, typographies and typefaces into a new, "transnational" one – one that could be understood at least in part in New York, Berlin, Moscow, Beijing or Tokyo, and places above and beyond – we face potentially the most exciting challenge yet for typography. It will not of course erase language differences, but it will help overcome them at some of the basic signing levels, whether that involves putting signs in the metro or on globally distributed medicine bottles, or carrying a global media brand to the world.

Of course, we have been doing this in an incremental way for a long time, but the global digital language and the media it has spawned have dramatically increased the pace of change, along with the increased globalization of capital markets through the 1990s. Now we engage with this culture, not view it as something that is somehow secondary to the local culture. It is not a by-product of the changes, it is in a significant way the driver. Rather like "world music", which has fed into individual music cultures around the world, global typographic information is coming together to influence its various parts in ways inconceivable before the current creative and media technologies.

While the sixty-five-thousand-character set proposed by Unicode might represent a lifetime's work for a type designer, the changed experience of type design in the 1990s also produced the opposite scenario: that a new font might

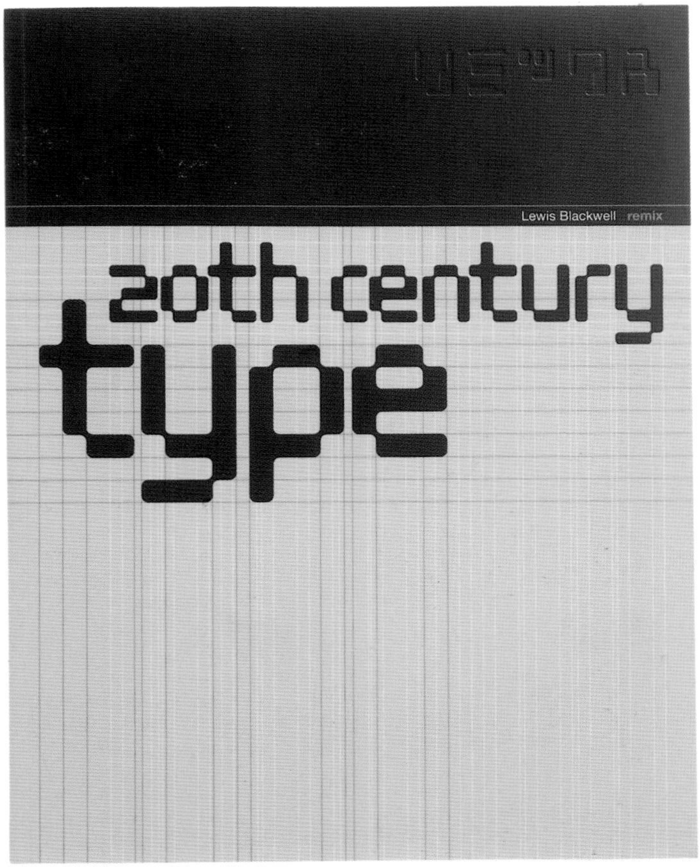

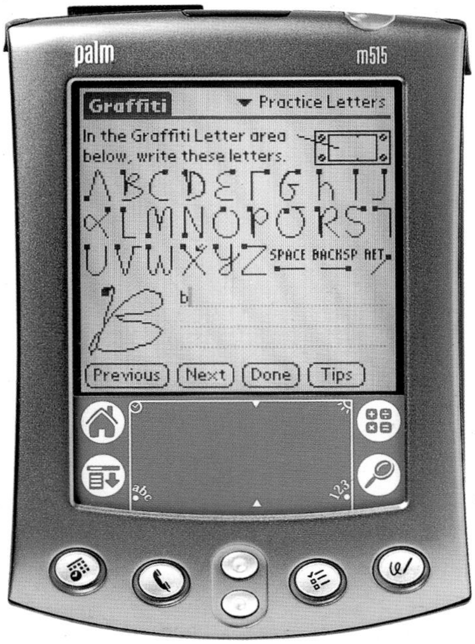

actually be knocked up in a day, and distributed globally via the web. It became possible, using desktop font design software, to draw or modify letterforms very quickly. Of course, instant letterforms were unlikely to result in a lasting, usable typeface, but no longer were the means of production and testing the factor in determining the time of type creation. Individual creation and global distribution of the typographic message were made possible, and built into this process was the means of localized manipulation and feedback.

The internet, of course, is the central element in this change, but its typographic controls were initially primitive. The instruction code for laying out pages (Hypertext Mark-up Language [HTML]) provided only rudimentary controls, such as setting left or right, and centring. The user's font selection or default fonts were (and often still are) either much to the fore, or else larger image files must be incorporated in the page where words are depicted as images, thus slowing down the delivery of the information. OpenType, mentioned above, might be the solution.
In 2003, as we close this edition, much of the world still has very slow modems: the world is multi-speed in its changes. While creative professionals and media types view the web world via broadband, others still struggle with a slow dial-up link to web pages. This transition sets restrictions for the richness of web graphics, and also engages the designer in an intriguing interplay with the localizing design of the user's computer on any web-page typography.

Pierre Bismuth. If/Then January 1999. Page 7

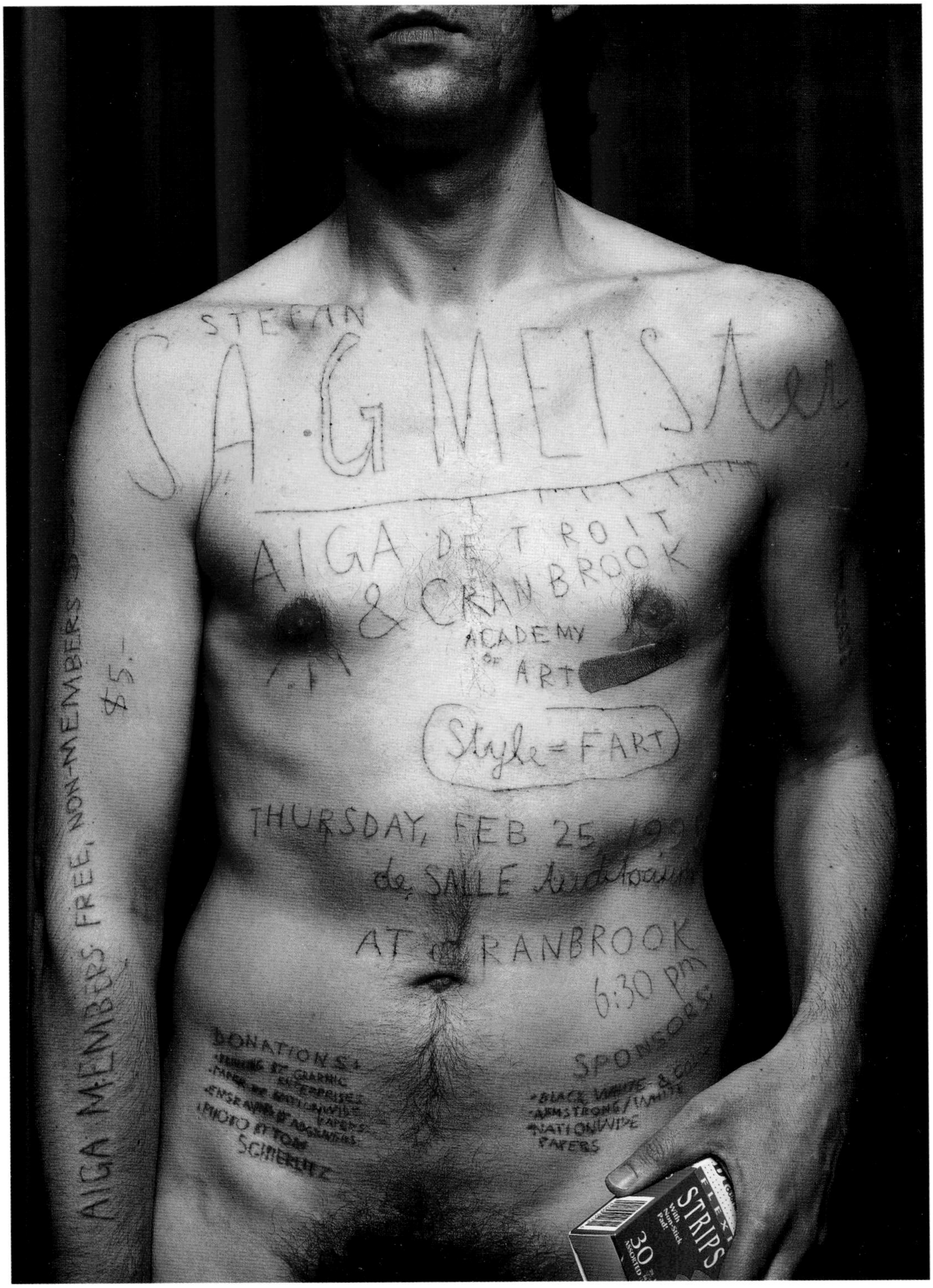

Opposite: spread from the one-off magazine *If/Then,* published out of Amsterdam in 1998. With its title referring to the conditional structures that drive computer code, the magazine broke its text into original hierarchies that questioned the usual construction of editorial. The conditional logic of programming was taken as the framework in which to articulate a manifesto commenting on the forces behind communication and design. This in turn drove the distinctive if anodyne typography by designers Mevis & Van Deursen for the Netherlands Design Institute. Left: Stefan Sagmeister took a razor blade and made an artwork of his own body in order to create the lettering for a 1999 AIGA poster. This was a celebration of creative process and an act of resistance to unseen technologies (the effect could have been digital, but is not) as much as a quest for a precise graphic solution.

In the 1990s, looking back over the century from near the end of the final decade in a millennium, there was an acute sensitivity to the benefit of hindsight. There was a temptation to draw portentous conclusions – to see ourselves at the end of something, or at the cutting edge of a new age. Many books did just that (many had "the end" in the title, including this author's collaboration with David Carson, *The End of Print*). Our raised position provoked the perhaps arrogant belief that the 1990s designer worked within a typographic context that could scarcely have been dreamt of by a previous generation, so fast had been the change. The boom-bust excitement around technology of the "dotcom" era, particularly from 1996 to early 2000, washed through design, with technophilia exciting thoughts around the future of the web and of design. Despite the downturn since in the technology industries, the effect of that shift has stayed in design: those tools and technologies may not have reaped the financial rewards for all industries that hooked up, but they did move the design industry forward. Even the naysayers of global capitalism, such as the highly designed and cleverly marketed anti-consumerism magazine *Adbusters*, operated using the tools and media that culture brought, or wrought. There was no meaningful other space to mass-communicate in and through. Change from within would seem to be the message in the manifesto.

Our current excitement over all things digital can also be read as the fulfilment of half-progressed experiments and the principles behind earlier movements. Imagine what the Bauhaus would have done with the internet! And wasn't

Left: the August/September 2001 issue of the anti-advertising, anti-globalization magazine *Adbusters*. The publication increasingly targeted graphic design, and used gestures of "anti-design", such as this cover, or pieces of elaborate pastiche, to make points about the links between typographic and other visual forms, their creators and the global capitalist agendas that in part drive them. In this it was a key mover in the new ethical movement that questioned the intentions of new typographies, among other matters. Opposite: the move to more calligraphic forms also found a synergy with the art-poster tradition of calligraphic form, which never died out in France and Eastern Europe. Here a theatre poster by Josef Flejsar (born 1922), which was created in 2000 and appeared on the front cover of the Paris-based *Etapes* magazine in 2002, fits into a great tradition and also accords with a new post-digital hand-crafted tendency.

Cubism just anticipating the four-dimensional explorations of multimedia? Futurism, excited by motion, war and energy in general, would have felt vindicated by the energy-based existence of information on the web.

This is, of course, to post-rationalize the past with the concerns and characteristics of today. To read the data assembled from our excavation of typographic history only in the terms that come easily to mind now obscures the complexity of matters past, as well as present. But it makes some telling points about the continuities, the connections and the value of historical inquiry in the design of our times.

The lesson from these connections for a designer is that we are condemned to always remix the past into the present forms. If we did not, we could not communicate, our messages would not be recognizable to the current audience whose interpretative abilities are built on the past, on their experience. But beyond this basic sequential connection with what the audience knows, there is the deeper thematic connection suggested above: that today designers are in a phase of rediscovering some of those lessons from the past, consciously reworking elements into “the sense of now”. In part, this might be a reaction to the deconstructive energy of the 1990s, where creative minds were carried away by the potential of the new tools to create something “new”. Now, less fuelled by naïve excitement at the potential of the tools or the media, we create carefully, with a greater sense of our place in history. Hence, perhaps, the tendencies in recent years to a Swiss style revival – a reintroduction of rigour and order after the

expressive disarray of some of the work of the past decade. This tendency was described to the author as "the sorbet course" in design by the American designer Paula Scher, a palate-cleanser and a deliberately understated moment before the next rich dish of design was served up. While apparent in media, identities, packaging and elsewhere, perhaps the key originating point for the revival could be the style magazine *Wallpaper**, launched in 1997. This captured the design zeitgeist. Just as the reaction to deconstructive design set in, it came out with a combination of clean, crisp design with some eclectic mixing of elements. The creative force behind the magazine, Tyler Brûlé, went on to launch the Winkreative agency which in 2002 helped create the Swiss International Air Lines branding, an enterprise formed from the collapse of Swissair. It is not only in the tradition of its predecessor, but is a deliberately "cool" and functional look that breaks with the cluttered friendliness of many other contemporary airline identities. The simplicity of the typographic identity stands out because of the overwrought clutter of those of its competitors. It is the sorbet course in airline design.

There is also another rewind, another conservative force at work in the late 1990s and early 2000s. While the flexibility of digital design and its output in print or on screen has created possibilities, in general it is highly backward-looking in how it appears on the most ubiquitous of screen displays, the user interface. Consider the conservatism of the internet browser interface designs as used by Netscape Navigator and Microsoft Explorer (the two overwhelmingly dominant products of the mid-1990s "browser war" that Explorer won

Left: a band logo from Twisted Nerve record label, one of numerous executions on the twistednerve.com site in 2003 that celebrate the hand over the mechanical in typographic compositions. All by Andrew Shallcross, aka Andy Votel. Right: modular three-dimensional type by Warren Corbitt of one9ine, developed for a special issue of *ESPN* magazine, 2002. The mutating forms go through transfigurations that reveal one complex but coherent root for all the letterforms.

thanks to Microsoft's near-monopolist muscle). These interfaces followed the graphical-user-interface (GUI) model pioneered by the Apple Macintosh and then largely copied by Microsoft Windows software. This was taken from technology pioneered at Xerox in the late 1970s, and derived in turn from computing-science thinkers in the 1960s (we have still only crudely realized the promise of Ted Nelson's 1965 dream of non-linear "hypertext"). The virtual desktop of mostly flat icons that has dominated the appearance of software tools from their inception is a graphic display derived from the print culture people are familiar with, rather than a language that originates from the fluid forms possible on screen.

Conservatism in form is the comfortable and perhaps inevitable path if communication and its typographies are to work. The tendency towards appropriating or emulating traditional forms in new media goes back to the first printed book, when Gutenberg drew on manuscript precedents for his Bible of 1452. Handwriting has continued to have some link to type form ever since. Now, on-screen type draws on print media. From 1997, the leaders in digital and web typography, Adobe and Microsoft, encouraged a narrow orthodoxy for web typography by promoting a special restricted palette of twelve or so web-friendly fonts on their internet sites. This was presented as a way of improving web typography, in that if web developers coded sites to work with these fonts, which were commonly available on users' systems, then crude type defaults would be less necessary. Nevertheless, the imposition of a new orthodoxy was involved. And while Adobe's "multiple master" fonts Myriad

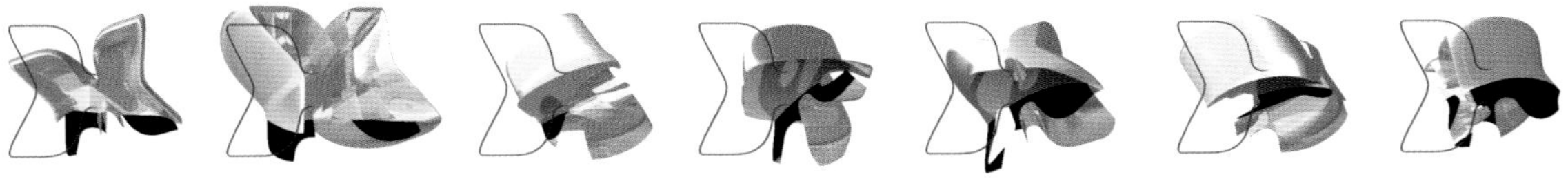

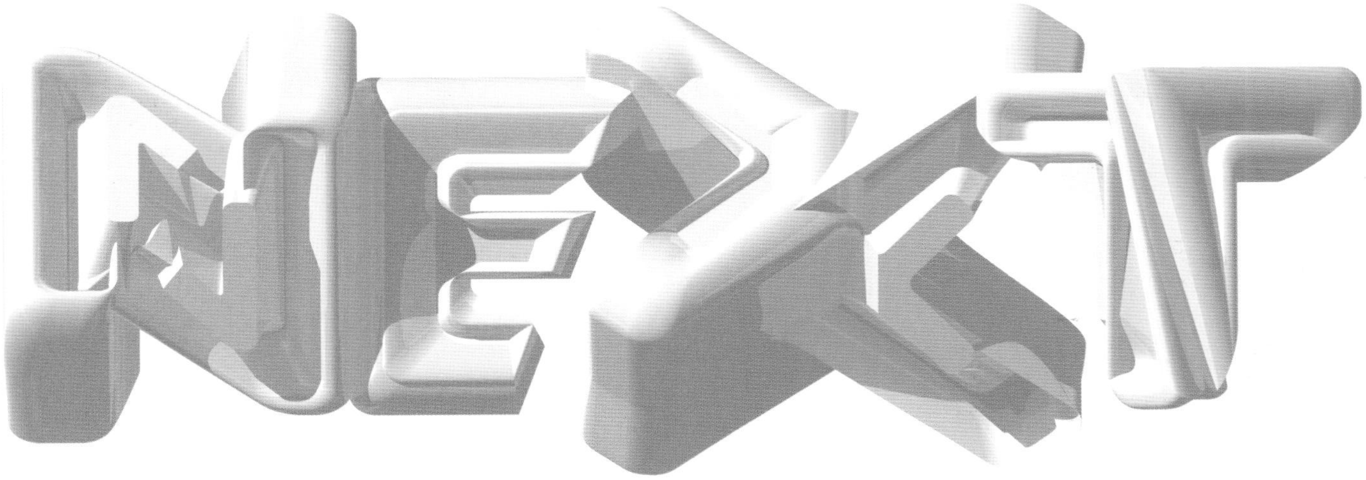

and Minion already had a popular following and a powerful range of expressive possibilities, the same could not be said for other faces proffered in the launch series. The free distribution of these fonts in part undermined those who (unlike Adobe and Microsoft) depend on font design and sales for their livelihood.

Such thinking at best seemed concerned with evolution, rather than revolution. It was in the advances made in the "typographic engine" and in probing three-, even four-dimensional typographic forms that we saw in the 1990s paths opening towards a new landscape of typographic form. These typefaces were not suitable for putting in type catalogues; they were activities rather than products. These experiments, ongoing, seek to understand how type can work on screen in a whole new way, how it can embrace the virtual three-dimensional graphic movement and live with the fourth dimension of time-based change. These major challenges for type designers and typographers were signalled by some experiments in the 1990s, mostly by non-typographer interactive designers who became interested in the issues raised by typography in their work.

The early experiments of three-dimensional and time-based modulating type forms, and those typographies which probe the organizational issues of virtual four-dimensional space, indicated that there is perhaps a revolution still to come as a result of our shift to digital. So-called "intelligent" fonts (whose form responds to the user in such a way that it modulates, randomly changes between options or

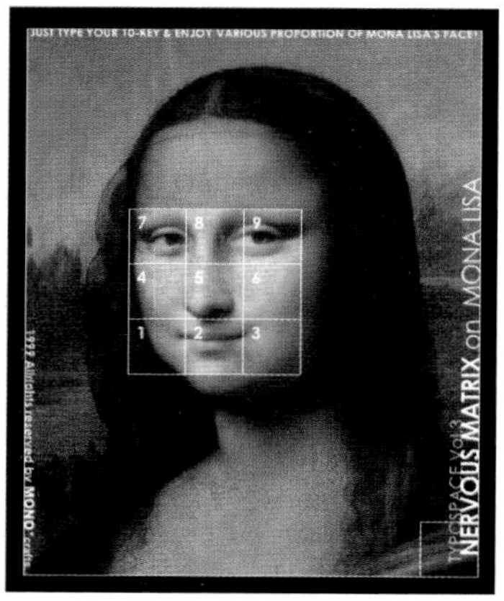

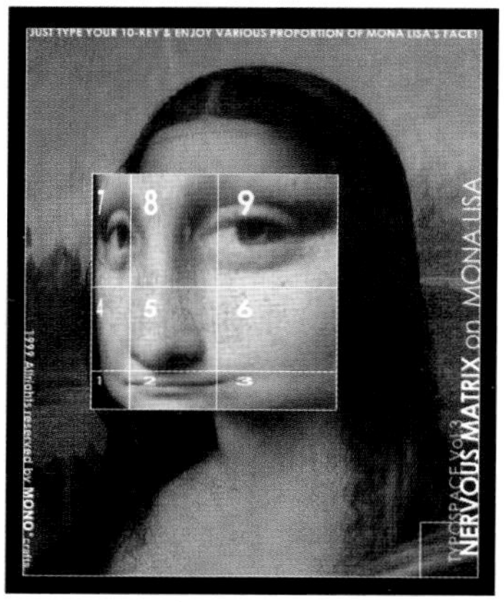

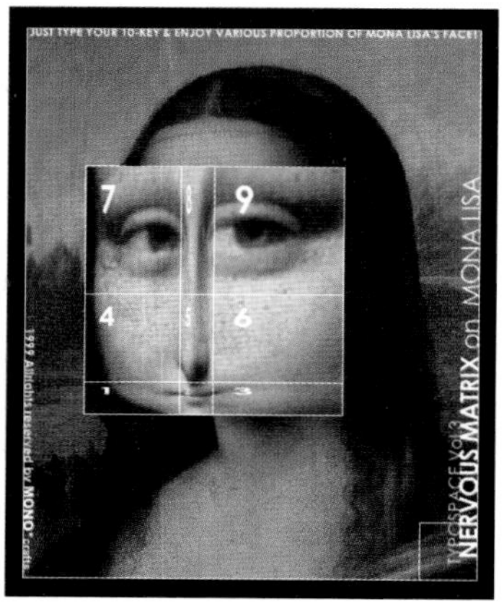

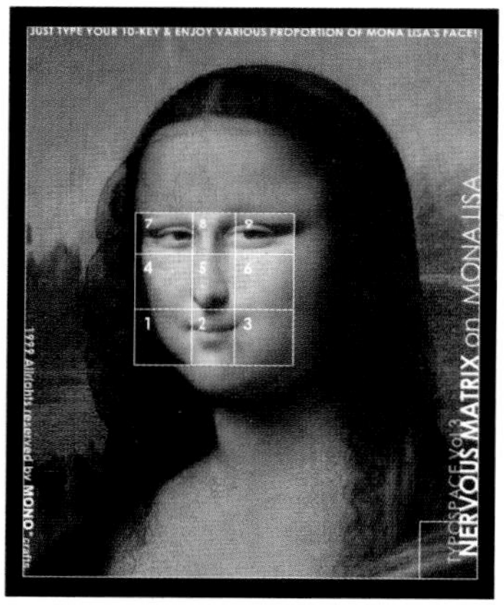

Left: Yugo Nakamura's "nervous matrix" is an experimental Flash animation work that uses the keyboard instructions to temporarily distort the *Mona Lisa*, in part showing that the typographic engine can step beyond two-dimensional type and interact in a time-based manner with other graphic elements. An infinite range of possibilities are generated by combinations of the keys. Opposite: Joshua Davis developed a late-moderrnist typography and typefaces within a tour-de-force exploration of Flash animation as presented in animated machines on his praystation.com site. These form a diary of explorations as the machines generate "art" within parameters defined by the designer, again rethinking how the typographic engine could be applied beyond typography.

destabilizes) were pioneered by Just van Rossum and Erik van Blokland with Beowolf in 1990 and have grown to become a new type classification. The three-dimensional experimental elaboration led by J. Abbott Miller in the Dimensional Typography project of 1996 also suggested the potential of the very different environment in which type and typography now exist on screen. The various experimental, often unreadable symbol-based fonts developed by the Fuse project (see page 156) also explored the dynamic of the typographic engine in a way that stepped beyond the expectations and strictures of our conventional alphabets.

Coming closer to the present, we can see in the "engines" created by the artist Joshua Davis a deep creative inquiry into the interactive potentials of computer-derived and represented graphic space. There are no conventional typographic marks here, but the activities displayed in the various experiments on Davis's praystation.com site (2000–) can be mapped back over typography, as well as over various other creative fields. In short, the digital realm that typography exists in opens it out to be in a flux of experimentation with all digital creativity.

It is this concept of type as a computerized organism for generating text that may be the most significant typographic development to emerge from the 1990s. Type can no longer be seen as a description of a static artefact, an immutable character or a font. In the 1990s, type changed from being something physical (metal, film) to being abstract information.

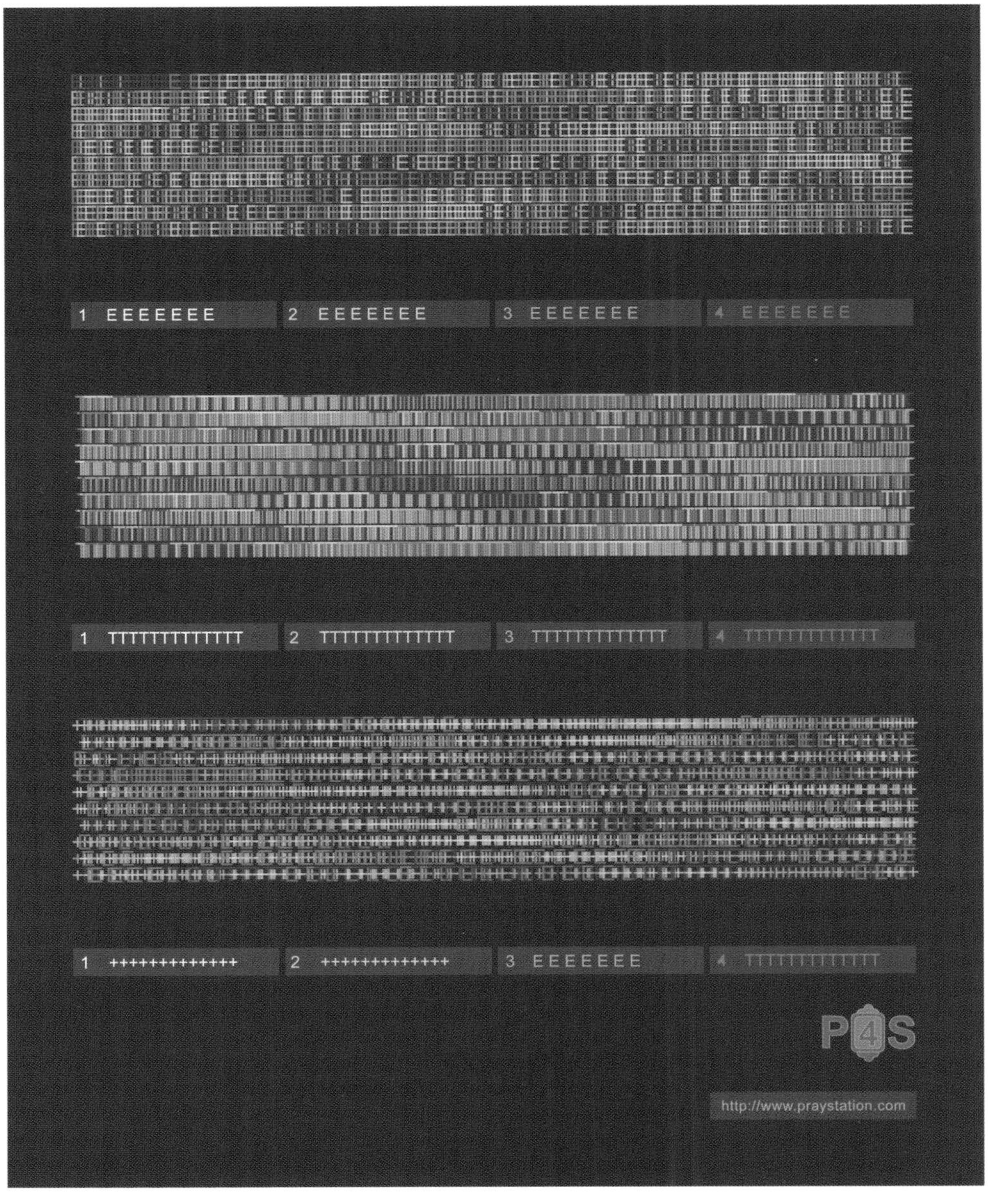

It now exists as instructions for bitmaps or bezier curves that construct the letter through mathematics. These maths can involve random elements as well as fixed data. What we commonly call type – the characters on the screen or on the page – is but one representation pushed out to a particular resolution by an imagesetter or laserwriter. Of course, this echoes and extends the fact that type has always ultimately existed as a piece of information, with any given metal or wood letter being just a means of suggesting through many variant impressions the unobtainable original intention of the carver or punchcutter.

The potential of screen-based communication suggests that intelligent fonts active across virtual space and time – anticipating, aiding and stimulating the reader/viewer – can become a basic tool for multimedia and internet content creation and use. Type is just starting to act and to move beyond the printed word.

The digital age has removed the physical, mechanical and aesthetic concerns of type from the development agenda. They are subsumed into wider issues pertaining to screen representation and the web-generated technologies by which type is increasingly delivered. In this movement type has followed a similar course to fine art, with a shift away from the "figurative" as the most meaningful way of talking about the potential of type. The figurative remains a reality, but is not the larger discussion. Instead, type is a conceptual issue. The questions are no longer fundamentally what a typeface or typographic composition can look like – they can

look like anything in this most diverse of times, in which there is no rule that is not open to question. It just depends how or what your kind of readability is. That is no longer the deep challenge, but is part of the mechanics of realizing a face. The deepest exploration now concerns the quest to define what type and typography might mean, and what they might engage with. The "why?" is more rather important than the "how?", as with so many inquiries. This questioning of the very meaning of type and typography has spawned the intelligent engines discussed above, and the subversive anti-type of calligraphic exercises that we have seen from the late 1990s to the present. It continues to spawn the seemingly endless variation of typographic engagement that is proposed today, and against which there is no true orthodoxy to measure it.

Five minutes ago the Google search engine on the internet gave 220,000 results pertaining to "type and typography". That is more matches than would have appeared five years ago, and most likely fewer than will be returned five years hence. Congratulations to *Serif* online magazine for momentarily being top of this search, although Microsoft floats to its head if the requirement is just "typography". Are we to assume from this that our subject is ubiquitous, grown large and pervasive in its importance? Is it significant, or is it just fragmented and flattered by this search statistic?

These and many more questions are still to be answered in our quest to understand more about typography, and to read all 220,000 entries would not necessarily provide that enlightenment. This book has set out just over a century of

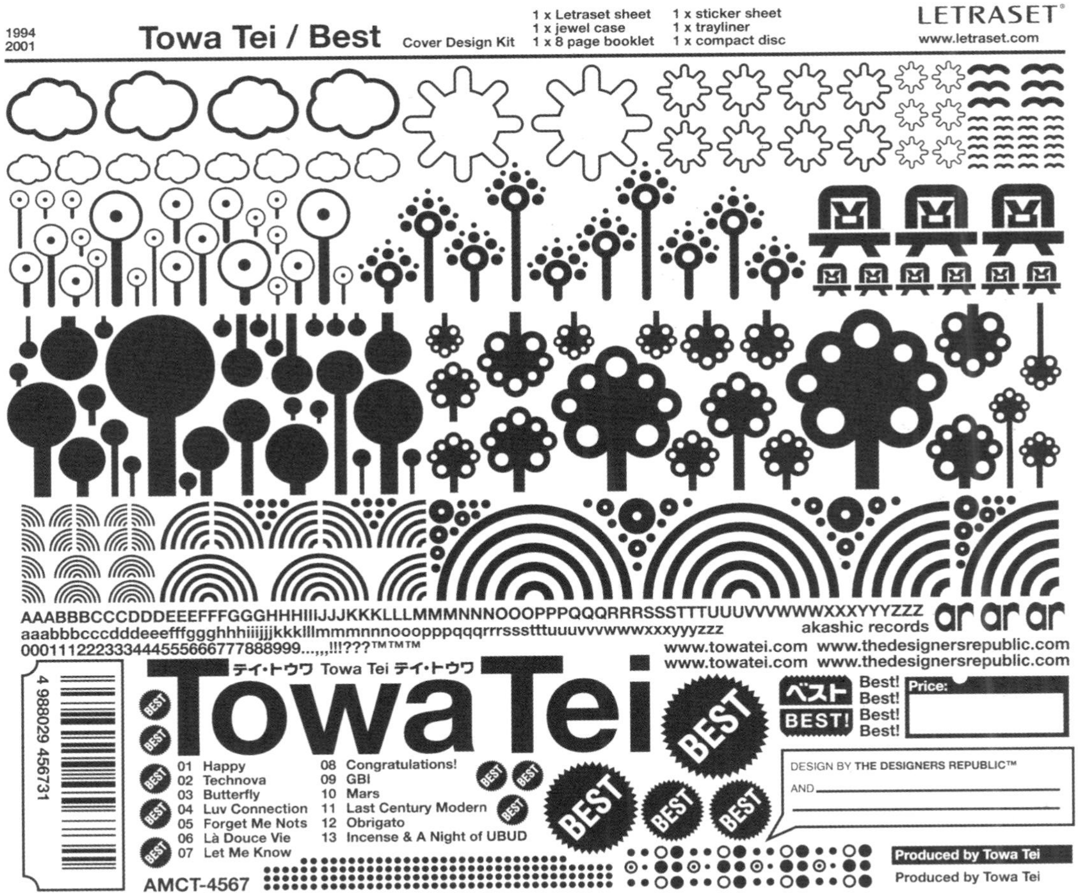

Opposite: a range of fonts created by Buro Destruct, Switzerland, from 1995 to 2001. The idea of the "constructed" typeface as the true nature of all digital typefaces was overtly explored in relation to many other letterforms (such as stencil and uncial). A disregard for readability is contrasted with a familiarity through the hint of retro forms. Left: Letraset rubdown lettering was revived by the Designers Republic to create promotions for Japanese music artist Towa Tei, with the transfer sheet being reborn and rethought for its intermediate technology qualities, rather in the way that vinyl has a continuing niche in the music scene.

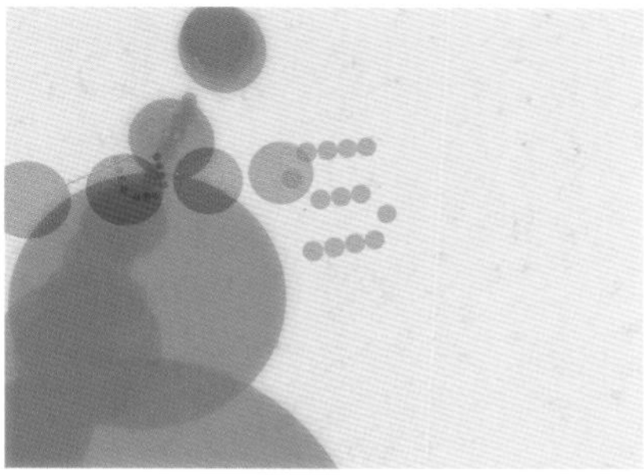

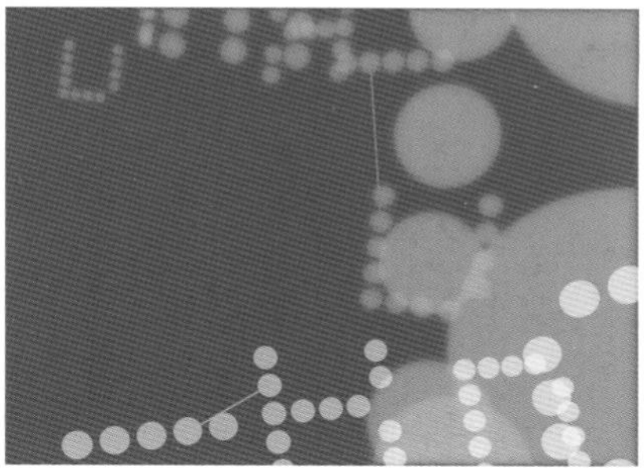

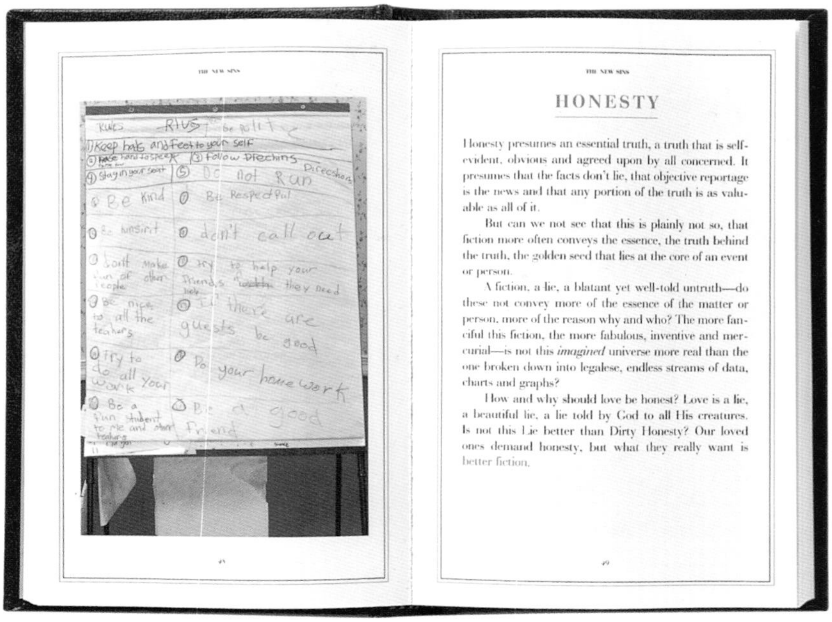

THE NEW SINS

HONESTY

Honesty presumes an essential truth, a truth that is self-evident, obvious and agreed upon by all concerned. It presumes that the facts don't lie, that objective reportage is the news and that any portion of the truth is as valuable as all of it.

But can we not see that this is plainly not so, that fiction more often conveys the essence, the truth behind the truth, the golden seed that lies at the core of an event or person.

A fiction, a lie, a blatant yet well-told untruth—do these not convey more of the essence of the matter or person, more of the reason why and who? The more fanciful this fiction, the more fabulous, inventive and mercurial—is not this *imagined* universe more real than the one broken down into legalese, endless streams of data, charts and graphs?

How and why should love be honest? Love is a lie, a beautiful lie, a lie told by God to all His creatures. Is not this Lie better than Dirty Honesty? Our loved ones demand honesty, but what they really want is better fiction.

49

LOS NUEVOS PECADOS

ADN a cualquier precio?

¿El concepto del pecado es tan solo un intento desesperado por mantener estas cosas, estos impulsos de insecto, bajo control? ¿Somos en el fondo tan amorales como los árboles, los perros y las cucarachas, sujetos bajo el influjo de un consenso social en permananente cambio, de sus reglas y códigos? ¿Y no depende ese consenso acaso de la situación económica, del clima político y la ubicación geográfica?

¿Entonces, quién es El Juez Supremo?

¿Quién sigue la pista? ¿Quién lleva cuenta de los cambios y alteraciones del clima moral? ¿Quién nos mantiene informados? ¿Serán los artistas y escritores que viven en sótanos de mala muerte y hacen comentarios desde fuera de la sociedad? ¿Serán los drogadictos, las estrellas porno, los raperos y los ejecutivos de las compañías discográficas promocionando el exceso como forma de vida? ¿Son ellos santos, experimentando con lo que sabemos que es nocivo y sacrificandose voluntariamente por nuestro bien? ¿Son los pobres, los apáticos, los desesperados y los desamparados los que han de juzgar al mundo, aquéllos para quienes la moral no significa nada?

¿ES CADA DÍA UN NUEVO MUNDO?

¿Reescribimos nuestros códigos morales cada vez que salimos a la calle, cada vez que besamos y con cada compra o intercambio de bienes? Vemos que cada día es diferente al anterior, y que aquello que era malo, despreciado y

17

Above: customizable logo for Sony by tomato. Users could download, adapt and then upload their own version of the mark, with the finished result becoming incorporated into the identity range. Right: in 2001 musician and writer David Byrne's *The New Sins/Los Nuevos Pecados* was designed with Byrne by Dave Eggers, novelist and publisher/editor of *McSweeney's* magazine. This volume displays Eggers' love of traditional book design, drawing on 19th-century bibles in particular, but combined with illustrative gambits derived from contemporary book-art traditions. This product is part of a self-published magazine and book culture, enabled by desktop technology and often driven by individuals who reject multinational publishing corporations. Opposite right: from the identity manual for Swiss International Air Lines, created by Winkreative and the Foundry, London, in 2002. Swiss style was self-consciously replayed with this scheme for the national airline. With its simple echo of the Swiss national identity (red cross on flag) and its use of an elegant sans serif arranged in strict modernist grids that continued the traditions of Swiss typography, the identity was fresh in its simplicity, and yet rich in how it drew on tradition.

the typographic quest, which would seem to have become more important and involved with society over the years, if more distant from any kind of final resolution. But for all the abstraction and the distraction of such a mass of information, we are all typographers now. This is not only down to the digital tools, but is due to our collective interest in working with them. In this past decade the typographic quest has slipped into everyday life.

Never mind the manifestos, the aesthetics, the systems of previous eras – our age demonstrates a democratizing of typography and design. For all the good and bad that democracy brings, for all the questionable value of everybody being able to play with typographic layout rather than simply type their message, it is currently the way things are. The joint forces of capitalism and democracy have led to us all having a vast range of tools (if we buy in), if not always so much experience, knowledge or craft. This is the philosophy that has driven typography to its current state. We finger our keyboards in a state of flux, with many choices, possibilities, sources of information, but no firm orthodoxy as our guide. There is much to be discovered by our community of 21st-century typographers.

CH Sans Medium Sub Heading (9/9.5pt)
Non equidem in sector delendave carmina
CH Sans Light Main Text (9/9.5pt)
Livi esse reor, memini quae plagosum mihi parvo Orbilium dictare; sed emendata videri pulchraquet exactis minimum distantia miror. Inter quae verbum emicuit si forte decorum, et si versus paulo concinnior unet alter, iniuste totum ducit venditque.
CH Sans Light Main Text (9/9.5pt)
Livi esse reor, memini quae plagosum mihi parvo Orbilium dictare; sed emendata videri pulchraquet exactis minimum distantia miror. Inter quae verbum emicuit si forte decorum, et si versus paulo concinnior unet alter, iniuste totum ducit venditque. Terentius arteos ediscit et hos arto stipata theatro spe Roma potens; habet hos num eratque poetas ad nostrum tempus Livi scriptoris ab aevo. Interdum volgus rectum videt, est ubi peccat anteferat, niillis comparet, errat. Si quaedam nimis antiqusi peraque dure dicere credit eos, ignave multa fatetur, et sapit et mecum facit et Iova iudicat aequo.
CH Sans Medium Main Text (9/9.5pt)
swiss
Swiss International Air Lines
36mm
28mm
20mm
14mm
12mm
8mm
CH Sans Medium Caption Headings
Non equidem in sector delendave carmina
CH Sans Light Caption Headings
Headings size 1 (14/15pt)
Headings size 2 (22/23pt)
Headings size 3 (32/33pt)
Headings size 4 (48/50pt)
Swiss International Air Lines 32pt
Typography
Swiss International Air Lines 22pt
Typography
Swiss International Air Lines 14pt
Typography
Swiss International Air Lines 9pt
Typography
Swiss International Air Lines 7pt
Typography
CH Sans Light
abcdefghijklmnopqrstuvwxyz
ABCDEFGHIJKLMNOPQRSTUVWXYZ
0123456789 €$%&(.,;:#!?)
CH Sans Medium
CH Sans Regular
CH Sans Bold

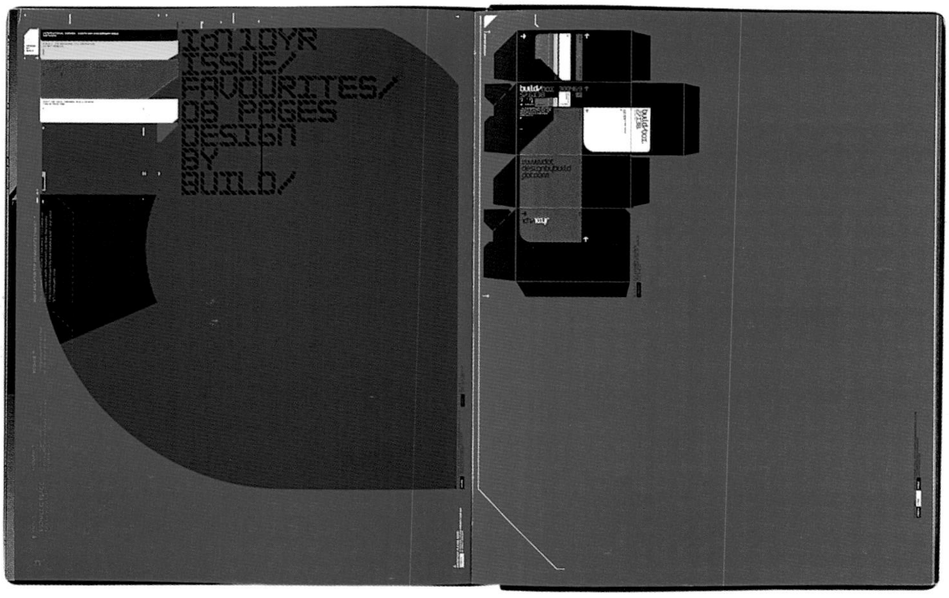

Above: from *Helvetica: Homage to a Typeface* by Lars Müller, 2002. The book records the ubiquity of the typeface in the environment, doing so as a fetishization of the face which it describes as "the perfume of the city". Left: by Michael Place/Build in London for *IdN* magazine of Hong Kong, 2002. Place pushes the boundaries of printable form with his highly constructed typeforms, highly contrasted type and object scale, and use of special colours and varnishes.

Below: one of a set of illustrated and lettered wardrobes for the retailer Howies. This one was designed by Marion Deuchars in 2002. The words are devised to question the "disposable society" with reference to automobiles. Cave art, poster art, graffiti – all are referenced in a rejection of polite forms as this recycled wardrobe gets repurposed for shop display.

Analysis of characters

Apex The outside point at which two strokes meet, as at the top of an *A* or *M*, or at the bottom of *M*.
Arm The projecting horizontal or upward stroke not enclosed within a character, as in *E*, *K* or *L*.
Ascender The lower-case letter *stem* that rises above the *x-height*, as in *b*, *d* or *k*.
Baseline The line on which the *x-height* rests.
Body clearance The space between the character and the edge of the unit.
Body size The unit height on which the character is mounted. See also *Point size*.
Bowl The oval stroke that encloses the *counter*, as in *b*, *p* or *O*.
Bracket A curving joint between the *serif* and the *stem*.
Cap height The height of the upper case in a font, taken from the *baseline* to the top of the character.
Cicero European unit of typographical measurement, equal to 12 *corps*. This is slightly smaller than the UK and US equivalent of one *pica* or 12 points, at 4.155mm.
Corps European measurement of *point* or *body size*, but slightly smaller than the UK and US equivalents.
Counter The white space within a *bowl*.
Crossbar The horizontal stroke in *A*, *H*, *f* or *t*; also known as a bar or a cross-stroke.
Descender The lower-case letter *stem* or lower part that falls below the *baseline*, as in *p* or *g*.
Ear A small projecting stroke sometimes attached to the *bowl* of the *g* or the *stem* of the *r*.
Leg The downwards oblique stroke of the *R* and *K*; can also be called the *tail*.
Link A connecting stroke when the *g* has a *bowl* and *loop*.

Loop The portion of the *g* that falls below the *baseline* when it is entirely closed.
Pica Unit of typographical measurement equal to 12 *points*, 1/6 or 0.166 of an inch or 4.218mm.
Point The basic unit of typographical measurement, approximately 1/72 or 0.0138 of an inch or 0.351mm.
Point size Equivalent to the body size, the height of body on which the type is cast (even if, with today's technology, it is rarely "cast").
Serif The small stroke drawn across and out of a *stem*, *arm* or *tail*.
Spine The main curved stroke of an *S* or *s*.
Spur The projection seen sometimes on the bottom of a *b* or *G*.
Stem The principal vertical or oblique stroke in a letter, as in *L*, *B*, *V* or *A*.
Stress The inclination suggested by the relationship of thick and thin strokes in a letter. Characters can have an inclined or a vertical stress.
Stroke The principal line within a character.
Tail The short stroke that rests on the *baseline* in *R* and *K*, or below it in *Q*. In *R* and *K* it can also be called the *leg*.
x-height The lower-case character height when *ascenders* and *descenders* are excluded.

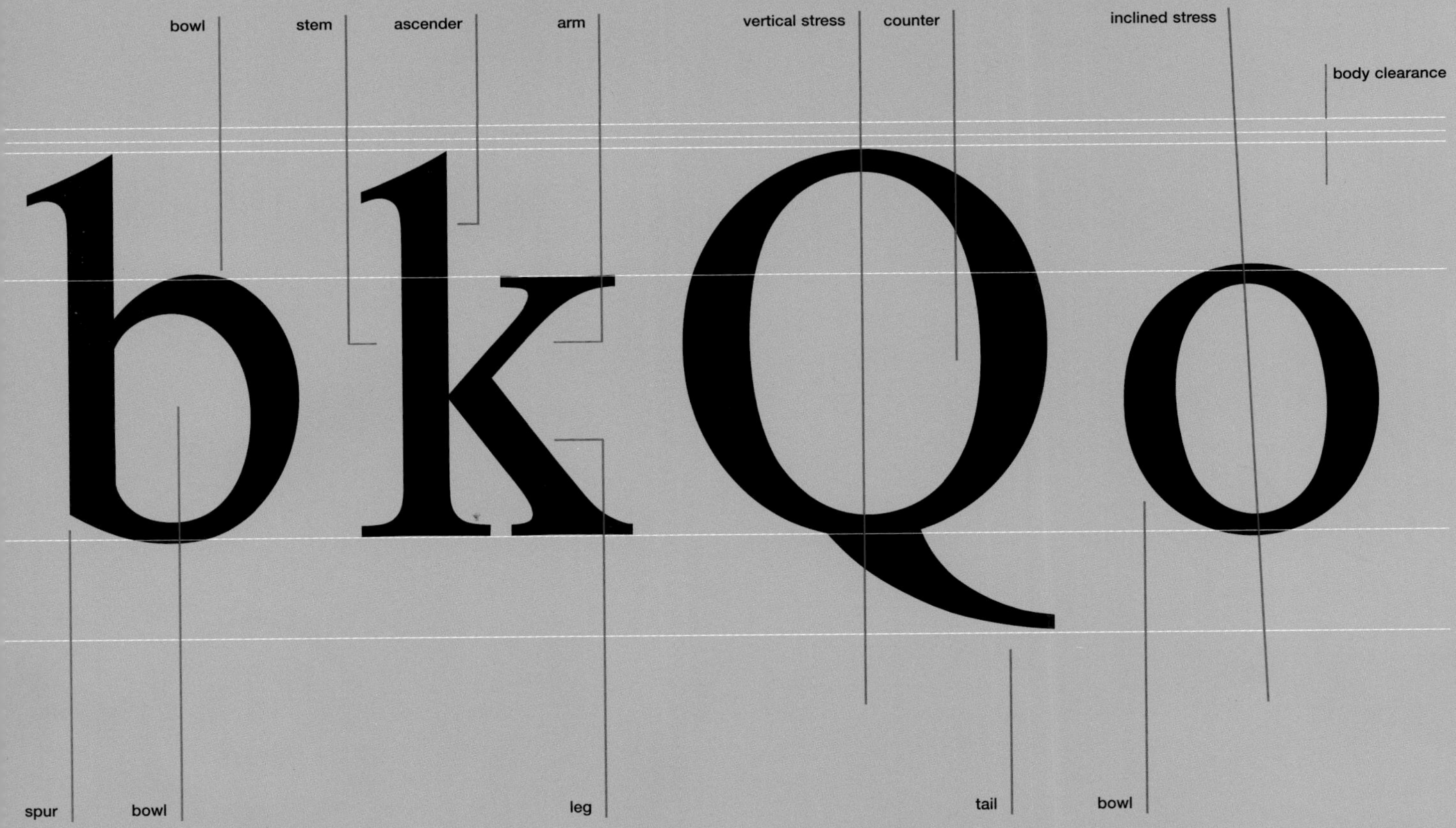

Type description and classification

All type samples are 18pt

Describing and classifying type has exercised many sharp minds, provoked many an argument, and led to continuing debate. The explosion in the variety of type design, and shift in its method of production and its purpose, has hugely exacerbated the problem of giving order to the world of type. So why bother? There are two principal reasons: one is practical, in that description and classification helps to make it possible to trace a typeface; the second is that this process of analysis enables us to see patterns within the forms, and possibly discern some directions, some meaning, behind the invention of new forms.

Various methods of analysis are used to identify the attributes of individual type characters, the fonts to which they belong, the families of fonts, and the contrasting and comparative groupings that can be made between them. While these methods try to explain matters, they can also be confusing. This is because differing terms, tables and systems of measurement have been devised over centuries of typographic evolution. As new ideas and new technologies have changed the nature of type, so new forms of typographic practice have emerged to challenge the classification systems. With a subject such as measurement, the issue is by its nature fairly precisely defined and different systems can be readily compared. The description of character attributes – stem, serif, bowl and so on – is also comparatively straightforward, although there are points at which verbal definitions of visual forms run into problems (for example, where does a serif simply become the flared termination of a stroke?).

The larger descriptive problem arises when typefaces are assigned to different categories. Typeface categories have emerged by evolution, one form developing from another and a range of faces being produced as a result, but their relationship is not explained by describing them only along historical lines. The revised categories devised by the typographic historian Maximilien Vox in the 1950s, which were widely adopted in various guises, now prove inadequate for explaining the huge number of new typeface designs since. A digital black-letter face, for instance, such as can be seen in the 1990s, has several reference points, while some modern re-drawings of earlier faces make changes (such as increasing the x-height) that effectively convert them into a different face from the one the name would suggest. Even the apparently simple split between serif and sans serif is complicated by designs with "flared serifs" such as Optima, or a face such as Copperplate Gothic, in which the minuscule terminus strokes are intended to assert the squared ends of the stroke rather than act as clear serifs. Adobe's multiple master fonts push out designs that can be altered by the user and range across classifications, while Beowolf began a culture of fonts that had an "organic" element within them of shifting design within set parameters. Classifiers have been challenged to find new methods of describing typefaces, and have yet to propose anything at all universally accepted. Different font distributors use different systems, and weaknesses can be easily picked in them. Some have no categories, some have titles that seem more led by their marketing considerations than by any rational structure. Meanwhile, research projects probe and suggest new descriptors. Our system draws on the Vox classification of historical groups, while adding subdivisions and extensions to cover less conventional forms and contemporary design. The categories are guidelines... redefine, remix the systems if you can.

All faces are presented here in 18 point, output from twentieth-century designs that have been digitized. They are indications of the faces, rather than definitive cuts – different technologies, different printing surfaces or output media, make different impressions. For a true idea of, say, the work of Manutius or Garamond, nothing matches seeing an original. In the original context it is possible to see why certain letterforms were designed – to cope with inkspread, to work in certain sizes and resolutions. These classifications cover the principal areas of typeface design discussed in the book, so do not include non-Latin typefaces or symbols. I suspect a further remix of the book will bring in new classifications, or indeed see a replacement of the essentially historical basis for this model by an altogether more synchronic analysis of content.

Humanist

Abefgor

Kennerley

Horley Old Style

abcdefghijklmnopqrstuvwxyz
ABCDEFGHIJKLMNOPQRSTUVWXYZ
1234567890

Jenson-Eusebius

abcdefghijklmnopqrstuvwxyz
ABCDEFGHIJKLMNOPQRSTUVWXYZ
1234567890

Cloister

abcdefghijklmnopqrstuvwxyz
ABCDEFGHIJKLMNOPQRSTUVWXYZ
1234567890

Kennerley

abcdefghijklmnopqrstuvwxyz
ABCDEFGHIJKLMNOPQRSTUVWXYZ
1234567890

A group of faces that take their inspiration from the early roman style, in particular the work of Nicolas Jenson (1420–80), a French printer whose most notable work was produced in the last decade of his life during which he lived in Venice. The face is based upon humanist writing seen in fifteenth-century manuscripts, as opposed to the black-letter hand that Gutenberg used for the first printing with movable type in the 1450s. Humanist writing was rounder and broader, and was produced with a broad-nibbed pen that helped give certain inflections. (The angle of stress in these faces matches the diagonal stress that would be given to, say, an "O" if it were drawn with a broad-nibbed pen held at an angle to the page.) The features that distinguish humanist faces from later romans are: a sloping bar on the "e", a marked inclination of stress backwards to the left, and little contrast between thick and thin strokes. Several foundries produced revivals of the face seen in Jenson's books. Cloister Old Style, by Morris Fuller Benton for American Type Founders in 1897, was the first revival of the mechanical composition era; William Morris's Golden drew on Jenson's face, as did Doves, but these were more loosely derived. Frederic Goudy's Kennerley of 1911 and Bruce Rogers' Centaur of 1914/1929 are based on Jenson, while having several differences: for example, Kennerley has noticeably shorter descenders and Centaur is generally lighter. The distinctive sloping bar characteristic of the group is displayed in Horley Old Style, a compact and robust face produced by Monotype in 1925, which in other respects is closer to a later garalde roman.

Garalde

Abefgor

Sabon

Sabon

abcdefghijklmnopqrstuvwxyz
ABCDEFGHIJKLMNOPQRSTUVWXYZ
1234567890

Garamond

abcdefghijklmnopqrstuvwxyz
ABCDEFGHIJKLMNOPQRSTUVWXYZ
1234567890

Bembo

abcdefghijklmnopqrstuvwxyz
ABCDEFGHIJKLMNOPQRSTUVWXYZ
1234567890

Times New Roman

abcdefghijklmnopqrstuvwxyz
ABCDEFGHIJKLMNOPQRSTUVWXYZ
1234567890

These faces, formerly called Old Face or Old Style, have a horizontal bar to the "e" but in other respects share features with the humanist grouping. Pen-influenced characteristics such as the oblique stroke on lower-case ascender serifs are still present and the characters tend to have a backwards slope (although not always as pronounced as in humanist). Contrasts between thick and thin strokes are more marked. The first models for garalde faces are those of the Venetian printer Aldus Manutius (1450–1515) and the punchcutter he worked with, Francesco Griffo. These faces were used in the Aldine Press books from the late 1490s onwards. The twentieth-century revival form Bembo (Monotype, 1929, and later other founders) takes its name from Cardinal Bembo's *De Aetna* of 1495, the book in which the Manutius/Griffo face was first noted. It was the sixteenth-century French typecutter and designer Claude Garamond (1500–61) who was the first to produce a notable reworking of the Aldine Press faces, creating a face seen from the 1530s onwards that has been redrawn by most foundries in the twentieth century for their own Garamonds. Granjon, based on the face associated with the sixteenth-century French type designer Robert Granjon, is close to Garamond, and the characteristics are still there in the eighteenth-century Caslon, itself modelled on seventeenth-century Dutch designs, such as those associated with Christophe Plantin. Stanley Morison's Times New Roman of 1932, while having short ascenders and descenders typical of newspaper type, in other respects takes its idea of stress and contrast from a Plantin-Caslon tradition.

Plantin

abcdefghijklmnopqrstuvwxyz
ABCDEFGHIJKLMNOPQRSTUVWXYZ
1234567890

Palatino

abcdefghijklmnopqrstuvwxyz
ABCDEFGHIJKLMNOPQRSTUVWXYZ
1234567890

Caslon Old Face

abcdefghijklmnopqrstuvwxyz
ABCDEFGHIJKLMNOPQRSTUVWXYZ
1234567890

Hermann Zapf's Palatino of 1950, named after a sixteenth-century Italian calligrapher, drew on Italian Renaissance lettering along with Roman inscriptions, which helps explain its generous counters and unorthodox serifs on the outside only of certain letters. Jan Tschichold's Sabon is a garalde that was designed to work across the various composition technologies (hand, hot metal and photocomposition when he drew it in the 1960s).

Transitional

Abefgor

Baskerville

Baskerville

abcdefghijklmnopqrstuvwxyz
ABCDEFGHIJKLMNOPQRSTUVWXYZ
1234567890

Caslon

abcdefghijklmnopqrstuvwxyz
ABCDEFGHIJKLMNOPQRSTUVWXYZ
1234567890

Fournier

abcdefghijklmnopqrstuvwxyz
ABCDEFGHIJKLMNOPQRSTUVWXYZ
1234567890

Perpetua

abcdefghijklmnopqrstuvwxyz
ABCDEFGHIJKLMNOPQRSTUVWXYZ
1234567890

Transitional faces are so called because they have characters that show the transition from the "old style" garalde to the "modern" didone faces that first emerged in the late eighteenth century. Transitional typefaces tend to be more upright than garaldes, with either a vertical or only slightly inclined stress. They may also have more contrast. Serifs may be bracketed and oblique as before, or horizontal and tending towards the starkness of the didone serif. The faces of the English typographer John Baskerville (1706–75) and the French founder Pierre Fournier (1712–68) are central to this grouping, while its links with what came before are suggested by the inclusion in the category of some twentieth-century reworkings of Caslon and Garamond. W.A. Dwiggins' Caledonia of 1938 is a transitional that incorporates aspects of the didone style: horizontal serifs are lightly bracketed and shade into an unbracketed "t".

Didone

Abefgor

Bauer Bodoni

Bauer Bodoni

abcdefghijklmnopqrstuvwxyz
ABCDEFGHIJKLMNOPQRSTUVWXYZ
1234567890

Bodoni

abcdefghijklmnopqrstuvwxyz
ABCDEFGHIJKLMNOPQRSTUVWXYZ
1234567890

Torino

abcdefghijklmnopqrstuvwxyz
ABCDEFGHIJKLMNOPQRSTUVWXYZ
1234567890

Walbaum

abcdefghijklmnopqrstuvwxyz
ABCDEFGHIJKLMNOPQRSTUVWXYZ
1234567890

Here the contrast between thick and thin strokes is extreme; lower-case serifs are horizontal and often unbracketed; the stress is vertical. These characteristics were exemplified in the work of Giambattista Bodoni (1740–1813) of Parma, who took the French types of Fournier and the Didots and refined them to the characteristics outlined above. Firmin Didot had produced the first didone – hence the name for the group – in Paris in the 1780s (the printing company bearing the name still exists on the Left Bank). Didot's thin serifs and abrupt contrasts involved hairline strokes that took advantage of improved paper and printing to create a more elegant typography. Bodoni's cuts made the most of this approach to typeface design, and his layouts displayed a generous use of white space that drew out the sparkling, high-contrast qualities of the face. Several twentieth-century revivals of his face attempt to retain these qualities while making it more efficient in its demands on space (for example, while the ATF cutting was the first and most commonly followed, the Bauer Bodoni is a more refined but less robust version). Torino is an early twentieth-century revival from the Nebiolo foundry with exaggerated serifs and other terminal flourishes, while Didi ITC is an exaggerated form of didone created for display purposes by Bonder and Carnase in 1970. Walbaum, a wider and less rounded didone, is based on designs by the German punchcutter Justus Erich Walbaum (1768–1839), who favoured the Didot style rather than that of Bodoni.

Abefgor

Bookman

Bookman

abcdefghijklmnopqrstuvwxyz
ABCDEFGHIJKLMNOPQRSTUVWXYZ
1234567890

Century Schoolbook

abcdefghijklmnopqrstuvwxyz
ABCDEFGHIJKLMNOPQRSTUVWXYZ
1234567890

Cheltenham

abcdefghijklmnopqrstuvwxyz
ABCDEFGHIJKLMNOPQRSTUVWXYZ
1234567890

This group covers those serif faces that display a complex, hybrid mix of features that do not feature in the previous historical evolution of form. They are sturdier faces than the thin didones, often originally cut in the nineteenth century to overcome problems of reproduction as larger print runs, poorer-quality papers and the demand for more compact faces put the typefaces of finer printing under stresses they were not capable of meeting. Bookman was originally a mid-nineteenth-century face, revived again in the 1920s; originally called Antique Old Style, it boasted a composite of features rather than being a straightforward garalde. Century Schoolbook, designed by Morris Fuller Benton and released in 1915, was – as the name suggests – intended for schoolbooks and is based on Century, the slightly condensed face designed by Linn Boyd Benton in the 1890s for the *Century* magazine. Upright stress, short ascenders and descenders and heavy serifs are all elements that make for its compact but legible letters. Excelsior, a newspaper face of 1931, has similar features since it strives for maximum legibility under stressful printing conditions. The massive popularity of the Cheltenham family, originally begun in the 1890s, was based upon its robustness and maintenance of character across many weights, widths, sizes and other variations.

Slab-serif

Abefgor

Memphis

Clarendon

abcdefghijklmnopqrstuvwxyz
ABCDEFGHIJKLMNOPQRSTUVWXYZ
1234567890

Memphis

abcdefghijklmnopqrstuvwxyz
ABCDEFGHIJKLMNOPQRSTUVWXYZ
1234567890

Serifa

abcdefghijklmnopqrstuvwxyz
ABCDEFGHIJKLMNOPQRSTUVWXYZ
1234567890

Calvert

abcdefghijklmnopqrstuvwxyz
ABCDEFGHIJKLMNOPQRSTUVWXYZ
1234567890

The name says it: those typefaces with heavy, square-ended serifs, with or without brackets. Clarendon, released by R. Besley & Co. in 1845, was the prototype slab-serif – indeed, "Clarendon" was used as a general descriptive for similar faces. Its clarity and sturdiness made it suitable for emphasis in text setting as well as for widespread use in display forms, such as posters. Robert Harling's Playbill of 1938 was an extreme form that made the serifs heavier than the main strokes in an imitation of Victorian playbill style. The late 1920s and early 1930s saw a major revival of slab-serif forms, with Memphis by Rudolf Weiss (1929) leading the way and proving the most lasting, along with Monotype's Rockwell. Serifa, by Adrian Frutiger and launched in 1967, is a slab-serif version of his earlier sans serif Univers. Calvert, by Margaret Calvert and released by Monotype in 1980, was based on signage lettering she designed for the Tyne and Wear Metro.

Lineale a. Grotesque

Abefgor

News Gothic

Franklin Gothic

abcdefghijklmnopqrstuvwxyz
ABCDEFGHIJKLMNOPQRSTUVWXYZ
1234567890

News Gothic

abcdefghijklmnopqrstuvwxyz
ABCDEFGHIJKLMNOPQRSTUVWXYZ
1234567890

Trade Gothic

abcdefghijklmnopqrstuvwxyz
ABCDEFGHIJKLMNOPQRSTUVWXYZ
1234567890

The first lineales, or sans serifs, can be found in catalogues at the beginning of the nineteenth century; they were bulky and tended to exist only in the upper case. Wood-letter forms existed, but were restricted to large-scale display use. At the beginning of the twentieth century there was interest in the form with the growth of display print needs, and Morris Fuller Benton was quick to cover the market for ATF with Alternate Gothic (1903), Franklin Gothic (1904) and News Gothic (1908). The strokes have contrast and there is a squared-off crudeness to the curves. The later Trade Gothic, by Jackson Burke (1948), is altogether smoother; however, Franklin Gothic has more than stood the test of time to remain immensely popular in editorial and advertising.

Lineale b. Neo-grotesque

Abefgor

Univers

These are similar to the grotesque grouping of lineales, but the stroke width contrasts are less marked. This means that the characters show more signs of being designed than of retaining any pen-drawn characteristics. The jaws of letters such as "C" tend to be more open than with the grotesques. The most marked distinction between the two groups is that the neo-grotesques do not have a lower bowl to the "g", but an open stroke. Akzidenz Grotesk, released by Berthold in 1896 and also known as Standard, became popular with the Swiss Style typographers; in the 1950s it underlay the design of Neue Haas Grotesk/Helvetica by Max Miedinger and Edouard Hoffman and also of Univers by Adrian Frutiger. Folio, by Konrad Bauer and Walter Baum of 1957, follows the same pattern. Venus, a Wagner & Schmidt design for Bauer of 1907, had some popularity with the Modern Movement and exists in a wide range of variations.

Akzidenz Grotesk

abcdefghijklmnopqrstuvwxyz
ABCDEFGHIJKLMNOPQRSTUVWXYZ
1234567890

Folio

abcdefghijklmnopqrstuvwxyz
ABCDEFGHIJKLMNOPQRSTUVWXYZ
1234567890

Helvetica

abcdefghijklmnopqrstuvwxyz
ABCDEFGHIJKLMNOPQRSTUVWXYZ
1234567890

Univers

abcdefghijklmnopqrstuvwxyz
ABCDEFGHIJKLMNOPQRSTUVWXYZ
1234567890

Lineale c. Geometric

Abefgor

Futura

Futura

abcdefghijklmnopqrstuvwxyz
ABCDEFGHIJKLMNOPQRSTUVWXYZ
1234567890

Kabel

abcdefghijklmnopqrstuvwxyz
ABCDEFGHIJKLMNOPQRSTUVWXYZ
1234567890

Eurostile

abcdefghijklmnopqrstuvwxyz
ABCDEFGHIJKLMNOPQRSTUVWXYZ
1234567890

Avant Garde

abcdefghijklmnopqrstuvwxyz
ABCDEFGHIJKLMNOPQRSTUVWXYZ
1234567890

Sans serif faces that follow the rule of being constructed from geometric shapes make up this group. Stroke widths tend to the constant. Chief among them is Futura of 1927, by Paul Renner, a face that quickly grew and kept popularity as it expressed both Modernist ideas and a sense of classic proportions within and between letters. It was widely copied. Erbar (1922), by Jakob Erbar, slightly predates Futura and is similar. Kabel (1927), by Rudolf Koch, is a more individual design that departs at times from the minimalism of its contemporary geometrics. Eurostile (1962) by Aldo Novarese, is sometimes grouped with neo-grotesques, but is essentially geometric in its interpretation of letterforms in relation to the square. Avant Garde Gothic, by Herb Lubalin and Tom Carnase of 1970, developed the geometric model for a face that would have a high degree of legibility in different uses, the numerous upper-case ligatures giving the opportunity for a distinctive character in display applications.

Lineale d. Humanist

Abefgor

Gill Sans

Gill Sans

abcdefghijklmnopqrstuvwxyz
ABCDEFGHIJKLMNOPQRSTUVWXYZ
1234567890

Optima

abcdefghijklmnopqrstuvwxyz
ABCDEFGHIJKLMNOPQRSTUVWXYZ
1234567890

Goudy Sans

abcdefghijklmnopqrstuvwxyz
ABCDEFGHIJKLMNOPQRSTUVWXYZ
1234567890

Rotis Sans Serif

abcdefghijklmnopqrstuvwxyz
ABCDEFGHIJKLMNOPQRSTUVWXYZ
1234567890

These faces do not so much follow nineteenth-century sans serif precedents as go right back to Roman inscriptions for their roots as well as drawing inspiration from the lower-case hand of humanist writing, which is apparent also in the seriffed humanist and garalde faces. They have some contrast of stroke width. Gill Sans of 1928, by Eric Gill, drew on Edward Johnston's type for the London Underground as well as Gill's signwriting and stone carving that brought him intuitively close to the inscriptional base of the roman forms. Optima, by Hermann Zapf (1958), and Pascal by José Mendoza y Almeida (1960) have notable variations in stroke width that break with the more monotonous line of the geometric and neo-grotesques that were prevailing at the time. Goudy Sans, by Frederic Goudy (1925), is something of a sport, offering variant letterforms and with a pronounced tendency to the inscriptional in the "chiselled" junctions, placing it closer to the glyphic group of faces. The problem of definition is further complicated when considering Rotis, designed by Otl Aicher and released in 1989. The wide range of fonts in the family sit together with design similarities while alluding to different historical roots, the Sans Serif drawing on the humanist lineale tradition.

Glyphic

Abefgor

Albertus

Albertus

abcdefghijklmnopqrstuvwxyz
ABCDEFGHIJKLMNOPQRSTUVWXYZ
1234567890

Friz Quadrata

abcdefghijklmnopqrstuvwxyz
ABCDEFGHIJKLMNOPQRSTUVWXYZ
1234567890

Trajan

ABCDEFGHIJKLMNOPQRSTUVWXYZ
1234567890

Amerigo

abcdefghijklmnopqrstuvwxyz
ABCDEFGHIJKLMNOPQRSTUVWXYZ
1234567890

Instead of the calligraphic base, these faces suggest more that they are chiselled than written. They refer back to inscriptional texts rather than the effect of the pen on paper, often taking their inspiration from Roman stonework. The characters tend to be comparatively uniform in width, as if measured out on the page – or stone – before being inscribed. Sharply cut, large, triangular serifs are often used. Albertus, by Berthold Wolpe for Monotype (1932), takes a different approach in that the serifs are more thickened terminals than separate strokes, tending towards the look of a humanist lineale, but the effect is still to suggest the stone-carved inscription rather than writing. Curiously, Albertus has found favour from time to time as a face for food packaging (for example, Cadbury's chocolate in the 1930s), the very opposite of the timelessness of its design root. Friz Quadrata, by Ernst Friz for ITC and released in 1978, is typically ITC – a very high x-height gives a curious distortion of the glyphic form; in the lower case the flaring stroke on bowls and on the spine of the "s" catches the eye and may impede readability. Gerard Unger's Amerigo of 1987, for Bitstream, is something of a hybrid, with similar tendencies towards high x-height as Quadrata, but slightly condensed. The more authentic glyphic is Trajan, 1989, by Carol Twombly, which takes the lettering of Trajan's column in Rome – a set of capitals that has been literally a touchstone for many type designers over the years – and produces a highly refined cut.

Script

Abefgør

Snell Roundhand

Snell Roundhand

abcdefghijklmnopqrstuvwxyz
ABCDEFGHIJKLMNOPQRSTUVWXYZ
1234567890

Shelley Andante

abcdefghijklmnopqrstuvwxyz
ABCDEFGHIJKLMNOPQRSTUVWXYZ
1234567890

Coronet

abcdefghijklmnopqrstuvwxyz
ABCDEFGHIJKLMNOPQRSTUVWXYZ
1234567890

Mistral

abcdefghijklmnopqrstuvwxyz
ABCDEFGHIJKLMNOPQRSTUVWXYZ
1234567890

A wide-ranging group that is drawn together around the idea that the typeface is an imitation of handwriting. The florid twirls of Robert Hunter Middleton's Coronet (1937) can be seen to ape a fine hand, but Roger Excoffon's Choc (1955) and Mistral (1953) are more painterly, Mistral being remarkable for the manner in which the lower-case joins up. Excoffon's brush-technique arguably moves the fonts right out of script and into the broad stylized area that so many contemporary faces fall into. Matthew Carter's Snell Roundhand (1965) also manages some effective junctions and takes as its basis the work of the seventeenth-century writing master Charles Snell (his rules for consistency in writing help the product to be imitated in type). Carter's 1972 Shelley Script, also for Linotype, came in three exotically named variations – Allegro, Andante and Volante – which referred to the degree of calligraphic flourish involved. Hermann Zapf's Chancery for ITC (1979) was an altogether more restrained and readable face that has proven popular, while still displaying pen-drawn inflections.

Abefgor

Fette Fraktur

Fette Fraktur

abcdefghijklmnopqrstuvwxyz
ABCDEFGHIJKLMNOPQRSTUVWXYZ
1234567890

Goudy Text

abcdefghijklmnopqrstuvwxyz
ABCDEFGHIJKLMNOPQRSTUVWXYZ
1234567890

Wittenburger Fraktur

abcdefghijklmnopqrstuvwxyz
ABCDEFGHIJKLMNOPQRSTUVWXYZ
1234567890

Wilhelm Klingspor

abcdefghijklmnopqrstuvwxyz
ABCDEFGHIJKLMNOPQRSTUVWXYZ
1234567890

The original of movable type forms – the type style Gutenberg derived from the manuscript tradition – black-letter would seem an impossible distance from ever reclaiming in display or text the dominant position that it once held across Europe and retained in Germany until between the wars. Now it tends to be used only as a stylized and near unreadable flourish, giving a nod to tradition for a newspaper masthead. What better proof could there be of the 1990s maxim “we read best what we read most”? There are four principle groupings of black-letter – fraktur, textura, bastarda (Schwabacher) and rotunda. Fette Fraktur is from 1867–72, Offenbach, designer unknown. Heavy and yet with a romantic flourish, it suggests a freely drawn pen stroke. Wittenburger Fraktur is a variation on the angular but flowing form of fraktur. In contrast, Goudy Text is a textura, displaying more fixed angles but still taken as if from the movement of the pen, although Frederic Goudy's 1928 design for Monotype is inspired by the 42-line bible of Gutenberg. Wilhelm Klingspor is a highly ornamental textura by Rudolf Koch, for the Klingspor foundry in Offenbach, 1920–26. It features exaggerated terminal flourishes, and in the hairy effect this gives the final type, one can see a source for such a modern experimental face as Jesus Loves You (see page 168).

Aefgor

Cooper Black

Broadway

abcdefghijklmnopqrstuvwxyz
ABCDEFGHIJKLMNOPQRSTUVWXYZ
1234567890

Arnold Böcklin

abcdefghijklmnopqrstuvwxyz
ABCDEFGHIJKLMNOPQRSTUVWXYZ
1234567890

Cooper Black

abcdefghijklmnopqrstuvwxyz
ABCDEFGHIJKLMNOPQRSTUVWXYZ
1234567890

Copperplate Gothic

ABCDEFGHIJKLMNOPQRSTUVWXYZ
ABCDEFGHIJKLMNOPQRSTUVWXYZ
1234567890

It sounds like a loose term, and it is – but how do we describe the rapidly increasing number of fonts that do not draw on one particular historical tradition or form of production, but are distinguished by being sports that draw on the varied visual culture of their time? The flagrant borrowings of visual form from aesthetic tendency can explain such fonts as Arnold Böcklin, which is emblematic of Art Nouveau (but this font also draws on black-letter). Frederic Goudy's Copperplate Gothic of 1902 is actually a highly functional design (holding up as a crisp form in small sizes on titling cards and the like). Its purpose, though, would seem to be decorative, if not its construction. Cooper Black is a loud character of a display type, designed 1921–5 by Oswald B. Cooper, sometimes very in but often out of fashion ever since. Like Morris Fuller Benton's Broadway of 1929, a dramatically contrasting quasi-geometric design that comes from but also helps define the American Art Deco aesthetic, Cooper Black has intimations of calligraphic origins but is clearly drawn. And perhaps it is this factor – the notion of letters being carefully assembled to wear a particular look or idiosyncrasy – that marks a group here, albeit these faces could also be put into other groups relating to the presence of serifs, or the intimation of cut letters with Copperplate Gothic.

Contemporary

Abefgor

Blur

Blur

abcdefghijklmnopqrstuvwxyz
ABCDEFGHIJKLMNOPQRSTUVWXYZ
1234567890

Beowolf

abcdefghijklmnopqrstuvwxyz
ABCDEFGHIJKLMNOPQRSTUVWXYZ
1234567890

Trixie

abcdefghijklmnopqrstuvwxyz
ABCDEFGHIJKLMNOPQRSTUVWXYZ
1234567890

Exocet

ABCDEFGHIJKLMNOPQRSTUVWXYZ
1234567890

Note that terrible label on this classification: contemporary... what overblown rock music became called in the 1970s shortly before punk tried to flush it away. However, 1990s fonts have become increasingly hard to classify and show up the inadequacies of classification systems. The analysis largely followed over the previous pages was generally accepted until the 1980s. It mixes historical, formalist and even intentionalist readings of type (who says a type is supposed to be script?). These help us understand some connections, but they miss and even obscures other links. Can the thousands of new digital fonts find their place within the existing analysis? It has become impossible to do this, but just what will replace the old structure is uncertain. Type companies have failed to produce credible groupings in their catalogues. For example, is Blur, 1992, by Neville Brody a geometric sans serif, albeit a bit fuzzy? Fontshop International call it "amorphous", but it has links with Trixie, also 1991 by Erik van Blokland, in the same group, which gets dubbed an "ironic". And both link with Beowolf, by Blokland and Just van Rossum, 1990, which with its random changes is dubbed an "intelligents" font. Jonathan Barnbrook's Exocet from Emigre Fonts, 1994, has black irony in its name, but draws inspiration from Greek stone carving. Ironic glyphic, then? The serifs and hard geometry (note the U or Y) would tax a stone cutter, lacking some kind of refined power tool. In the opposite column, we come to a provocative conclusion.

Abefgor

Template Gothic

Template Gothic

abcdefghijklmnopqrstuvwxyz
ABCDEFGHIJKLMNOPQRSTUVWXYZ
1234567890

Emigre Ten

abcdefghijklmnopqrstuvwxyz
ABCDEFGHIJKLMNOPQRSTUVWXYZ
1234567890

OCR-A

a b c d e f g h i j k l m n o p q r s t u v w x y z
A B C D E F G H I J K L M N O P Q R S T U V W X Y Z
1 2 3 4 5 6 7 8 9 0

New Alphabet

abcdefghijklmnopqrstuvwxyz
ABCDEFGHIJKLMNOPQRSTUVWXYZ
1234567890

The faces on this page have forms heavily influenced by technologies. Barry Deck's Template Gothic, 1990, is from laundromat sign lettering; Emigre Ten is one of Zuzana Licko's early Emigre fonts that explored the bitmap; OCR-A is a design driven by engineers looking for computer-readable type; Wim Crouwel's New Alphabet of 1967 reduced letterforms to minimal structures suitable for an early computerised photocomposition system. But as New Alphabet has been digitised, made into a useable face for the 1990s by The Foundry, and as OCR-A has become a fashion item, and as Template Gothic and Emigre Ten are filed for a late 1980s/early 1990s revival due along soon, so we have to reconsider the terms of description – the faces clearly draw on technological contexts, and are in histories. But it is apparent that to map the location of a typeface, to pin it down in history and in formal properties, requires a system of multiple criteria, plotting the nature of a design on more than one axis. It is no longer credible to propose a closed system of classification, because we can now see that the creative nature of the subject determines that new forms will seek to step outside existing structures. There is no rule book, only a series of possible readings to be made of each new font and from which its coordinates may be plotted. But these are never fixed. There was once one 42-line printed bible, but there is no longer a bible for classification, if there ever was. And should we miss it? We can just remember what we like... and then ask why.

Glossary

Note: some terms relating to characters and type groups are explained on preceding pages.

Baseline
The line (not printed) on which letters tend to sit and align. Descenders fall below this line.

Bezier curves
Curves created by drawing lines in relation to a series of coordinates. At the heart of the *PostScript* page description language.

Bitmap
The dots that make up a *digital* image. Digital typefaces have a bitmap image for screen display, each size having a separate cluster of bitmap information. This screen bitmap is low-resolution, and an accompanying printer font in high-resolution information, encoded in a form such as *PostScript*, enables the generation of a high-quality output.

Black-letter
Typefaces that are based on the gothic, medieval script. Textura, Fraktura, Old English, Rotunda and Bastarda (or Schwabacher) are groups of black-letter faces.

Body type
The type used for a main text, as opposed to headline or display usage; also known as text type. It is most often seen in sizes between 6 and 14 point.

Broadband
Refers chiefly to web-based communications that are able to allow the viewing of more substantial communications, such as multiple picture files, moving imagery and sound.

CD-Rom
Compact disc, read-only memory. In the 1990s, type libraries have been transferred complete on to CDs capable of being read by computers with CD drives. Several thousand faces may be in a library and accessible to view, but users only have to buy faces as and when they need them; this is possible through the use of codes that unlock just those faces on the disc that a user wants to pay for. Online search engines on the internet with payment systems seem likely increasingly to replace CD-Rom technology as a way of promoting and distributing fonts.

Chase
The metal frame in which the *galleys* of metal type were locked as pages ready for printing or for a *stereotype* plate to be taken.

Cold type
Printing which is not produced by the *hot-metal* process, but involves the use of *founders' type*, *photo-setting* or electronic processes.

Colour
In typography this can apply to purely monochrome pages, as it refers to the density of black/grey/white generated by the mass of type on the page. Choice of type, line length, leading, tracking – all these factors and others can affect the colour of the type.

Composition
The process of assembling individual characters of type into set matter of words, sentences and pages. This can be done by hand, *hot-metal* machine, *photosetting* or electronically through *digital* information.

Condensed
A typeface is condensed when the character form is compressed to a narrower width than is normal; the opposite is extended (or expanded). New technology of the *photosetting* and computer era enables characters to be condensed or extended by machine rather than specially *cut* as was required with metal setting.

CRT
Cathode ray tube, the technology central to television projection which also has an important part in the development of image-setting systems for type. Initial digital typesetting systems used a CRT to generate the type image as a series of pixels (picture elements) that were exposed on to a light-sensitive film, as with *photosetting*. *Laser setting* has now superseded CRT as the prime technology behind typesetting/image-setting. CRTs have been central to the display (and hence evolution) of screen type in the age of television and the personal computer. LCD (liquid crystal display) and other screen technologies are starting to replace the CRT, but the move to a radically higher resolution screen is still awaited.

Cut
Often used to define a particular font; a term dating from the days when a design was cut into a punch that was then used to form the matrices from which individual pieces of type were struck.

Digital
The term for the electronic technology that has taken over print and image manipulation systems since the 1980s. At the root of all the computer systems is the notion of sorting information digitally, as a mass of binary data.

Display Type
Type set larger than surrounding "body type" as in headlines or advertisements.

DPI
Dots per inch, usually applied to output devices, such as printers and image-setters, to define the resolution of the image that is available. Dot matrix printers have a low dpi, hence the visibility of the dots and the crudeness of the resulting characters and graphics. Inkjet delivers higher resolution, and laser higher still. Rapid developments in printer technology mean that even a cheap personal computer printer offers 300 dpi or greater. High-end systems for quality reproduction, as in book printing, are in excess of 2000 dpi. The resolution seen on a personal computer screen, however, is equivalent to 72dpi.

Dry transfer
Process behind the development of companies in the 1960s such as Letraset and Mecanorma, where sheets of lettering were sold as transfers to be rubbed down and transferred as ready-made artwork, replacing the need for some setting. Originally the system was wet transfer, a messier and more awkward process.

DTP
Desktop publishing, the computerized design and production of print that was made possible by the introduction of small, low-cost computer systems offering a *wysiwyg* screen image that enabled designers to work on screen effectively. It has been available from the early 1980s.

Electrotype
A printing plate formed by the electrolytic deposition of copper on a wax mould of the original printing plate. See also *stereotype*.

Em
A unit of measurement that is normally the square of a given point size of type. It is based on the letter "m", which tends to form a square piece of type, its width the same as the height of the face.

En
A unit of measurement half the width of an *em*.

Extended/expanded
Terms to describe the stretching of a typeface to a larger width than the normal dimensions of characters; the opposite is *condensed*.

Family
In type, a term given to a range of typeface designs that are all variations on one central design. Principal variations are roman, italic, bold, light, condensed and extended/expanded.

Font/Fount
The meaning has changed over time; the current usage defines the complete character set of a particular typeface in a particular size and style.

Founders'/foundry type
Setting based on the use of pre-cast metal characters of type composed by hand from a tray of type.

Foundry
The place of manufacture for type, dating from the days when a type foundry was a place for serious metalwork. Now sometimes used to describe the small digital type studio/distributor.

Furniture
As in "page furniture", those regular elements of a layout that are not type, but are part of the typographic arrangement, such as rules and bars, fleurons and the like.

Galley
Strip of set type, either in hot metal when arranged on the *stone* or as a bromide strip output from *photo-setting* or image-setting.

Half-tone
Blocks or pieces of film converted from images into a form ready for printing. They consist of a greater or lesser number of dots that depict light and dark areas.

Hardware
The physical machinery in computer systems, as opposed to the *software*, which is the particular operating system and the other *programs* carried on the equipment. The CPU (central processing unit) is at the heart of any system, with the screen and printer being described as peripherals.

Hinting
A function within digital type, whereby a range of automatic adjustments are made to simplify and clarify characters when they are produced in very small sizes or on low-resolution output. These adjustments guide the output so that it retains key characteristics. Most, but not all, digital fonts were hinted, but the development of Adobe Type Manager software in part decreased the need for hinting.

Hot metal
Term for type and the printing process that involves casting type from hot metal in order to print.

Inline/outline
Characters are inlined when part of the character stroke is cut away to create a white area within the letter other than a bowl. They are outlined when a line is put on the outside edge to create an open aspect to the form. This is different from adding a shadow effect, although they may be combined.

Justification
The ranging of type on both left and right sides; see also *ranged left* and *ranged right*.

Kerning
The spacing of letters closer than is standard, usually in order to create the optical effect of consistency of space between characters by allowing part of one letter to "kern" into the white space of another; see also *tracking*.

Laser setting
Lasers fire flashes of light according to the information of the character outline (which could be *PostScript* encoded, or some other page description, or *bitmap*). This light either records an image on a light-sensitive surface (laser typesetters/image-setters), or generates an electrostatically charged image that is put directly on to paper (laser printers). The former have high resolution, the latter lower resolution.

Leading
The space between lines. Prior to photocomposition, this was created by physically inserting a strip of metal called a lead into the page make-up in order to give more white space between the lines of type.

Legibility
In typography, legibility and readability are two terms that have precise and separate meanings. Legibility is usually taken to mean the quality of distinction between characters – the clarity of the individual letters. Readability is the quality of reading provided by a piece of typography, in which kerning, leading and other factors will have a bearing on the function of the type.

Letterpress
The most traditional printing process, which goes back to Gutenberg and the invention of movable type. Ink is placed directly from raised type onto the paper.

Letterspacing
The insertion of greater than normal spacing between characters.

Ligature
The joining of two or more letters for optical purposes (as with æ, fl or fi), a feature common in metal setting but less so with *photosetting*, where the enlarged character set thus required is undesirable for the manufacturers. There are signs, however, that ligatures are returning with digital typography.

Linotype
Describes a company, machine, system and type library. Linotype was the original hot-metal system, launched in 1886, and involved the setting of a line of type in hot metal by an operator working a keyboard directly attached to the setting machine. In contrast, the *Monotype* machine set one character at a time.

Lithography
Printing process that works on the principle of having an image on metal (or, originally, stone), parts of which will take ink, and parts of which (those not intended to print) reject ink; the surface to be printed is placed against this lithographic image. Water can be used to create the process of the attraction and repelling of ink. Offset lithography is where the image is first offset on to another surface (the "blanket") and this then transfers on to the surface to be printed.

Matrix
In metal setting, the mould from which the type is cast; it carries an impression of the type character which has been struck from the *punch*; it is made from copper or brass. In *photosetting*, the term used for the grid of characters that often carries the character set of a face.

Mechanical composition
The process of selecting and arranging type by machine rather than by hand. Prior to the *Linotype* and *Monotype* machines at the end of the nineteenth century, there was no commercially viable method of mechanical setting that could select, cast and re-sort (or melt down) type.

Monospace
A term applied to those typefaces, such as typewriter faces, where each character is allotted the same space.

Monotype
A company, machine, system and type library developed in the 1890s shortly after the *Linotype*. It offered a system based on setting individual pieces of type in hot metal, following instructions punched into a spool of tape by a keyboard operator. Monotype has been associated with the development of a fine type library, along with later type and print technology.

Multiple masters
Technology developed by Adobe Systems that allows the generation of a wide variety of fonts from one typeface – condensed and extended, or light and bold, even serif to sans serif. The software takes up a comparatively small amount of computer memory, providing a sophisticated range of options on relatively small systems at much lower costs than buying all the fonts. The first faces, Myriad and Minion, were launched early in 1992.

OCR
Optical character recognition; OCR devices can scan, or read, type so that it can be processed by computer. From the late 1950s onwards the issue of machine-readable faces has been important; this led to specially designed faces, as well as being related to the development of scanning technology.

Offset lithography
See *lithography*.

Outline
See *inline/outline*.

Pantograph
An instrument capable of transferring a design by tracing the master drawing. Linn Boyd Benton's pantographic *punchcutter* made it easier to convert a design for type on to the *punch* and made possible the development of *mechanical composition*.

Photosetting/phototypesetting
The setting of type by exposing the image of a type character on to light-sensitive film, with the photosetter outputting a bromide that is then used for paste-up on a page. The resulting artwork, when proofed and combined with other graphics, goes through a further film process to generate plates for offset *lithography*.

Pica
Typographical measurement comprising 12 points and thus amounting to roughly $^1/_6$ of an inch; also formerly the term applied to 12 point type.

Point
Typographical measurement; in the US and UK it is 0.0138 of an inch or 0.351mm; in Continental Europe it is 0.346mm.

PostScript
The digital page description language developed by Adobe Systems and widely adopted as a standard for digital page software. It is device- and resolution-independent, requiring only a PostScript-compatible system, and is thus able to work on a wide range of equipment. Type is described in a series of mathematical formulae that generate *Bezier curves* which are then filled in with dots to the output-system resolution.

Press
The printing machine, so-called because it traditionally works by pressing a piece of paper against the surface carrying the image, whether a relief image of metal type or a rubber blanket carrying an offset lithographic image. For each colour a separate plate exists and a separate impression is made. A flatbed press carries the image on a flat surface at the base and moves the paper against it, while a rotary press wraps the image as a plate round a rotating drum under which is passed the surface to be printed.

Program
The computer software carrying the instructions and operating methods of a particular system. A typesetting program has to be loaded on the hardware – the computerized equipment – before it can work as a typesetter.

Punch
Metal bar containing the master design of a type character used for striking a *matrix* for casting the type for printing.

Punchcutter
The highly skilled craftsman who physically inscribed the design of a typeface on to the metal bars of the *punch*. Prior to the *pantograph* this was a job of such individual skill that the punchcutter was often the same as the type designer, or was regarded as contributing to the design.

Ranged left
Ranging of type at the left side, leaving the right side ragged; also called unjustified. See *justification*.

Ranged right
Ranging of type at the right side, leaving the left side ragged; such a setting is unjustified. See *justification*.

Readability
See *legibility*.

Reversed out
Type which is the unprinted area, standing out of black or a coloured background.

RIP
Raster image processor. Device for converting ("rastering") the information from, say, a *PostScript* encryption into a series of dots, produced to a density determined by the output device.

Software
Programs in computer systems carrying typefaces and other typographic information, as well as the programs within which type will be worked with (such as QuarkXPress or Fontographer) and the operating system of the computer itself. They work on the system hardware, such as the central processing unit and the printer.

Stereotype
A duplicate metal plate made from a relief printing plate by taking an impression in a soft material (such as papier-mâché plate) and then casting the duplicates from this mould. This was often the process for converting a page of set matter into a plate suitable for printing.

Stone
The flat surface on which metal type was imposed (laid out) before being tightened up in the *chase* ready for printing or plating.

Stress
The angle of thickening across a curved letter. For example, modern faces are distinguished by a pronounced vertical stress, whereas humanist faces have an inclined backward-sloping stress, imitative of a pen-drawn character.

Swash
The flourish that may extend a stroke or replace a serif on a letter; characters with fancy flourishes are known as swash letters.

Tracking
The spacing standard set between characters in a text. *Photosetting* and digital setting made it much easier to play with tracking, either "negative" tracking, where characters have closer *kerning*, or "positive" tracking, whereby a word, line or text is given *letterspacing*. Digital typography introduced even greater flexibility into the manipulation of character relationships.

Wysiwyg
What you see is what you get; computer systems that reproduce on screen a working simulation of the graphic information that could be output by the system.

Notes

1910

1 Filippo Marinetti, translated in *Futurismo e Futurismi*, Bompiani, 1986.

2 Filippo Marinetti, translated in *Marinetti: Selected Writings*, edited by R.W. Flint, Secker & Warburg, 1972.

1920

1 László Moholy-Nagy, in *Staatliches Bauhaus, Weimar, 1919–23*, translated in *Bauhaus 1919–28*, catalogue edited by Herbert Bayer, Walter Gropius and Ise Gropius, The Museum of Modern Art, 1938.

1930

1 The complete text of this speech from 18 April 1959 was reprinted in *Print* magazine, volume 18, number one, 1964; also in Ruari McLean, *Jan Tschichold: Typographer*, Lund Humphries, 1975.

1940

1 Jan Tschichold, "Glaube und Wirklichkeit", *Schweizer Graphische Mitteilungen*, June 1946, translated as "Belief and Reality" in Ruari McLean, *Jan Tschichold: Typographer*, Lund Humphries, 1975.

1950

1 Information from *Advertiser's Weekly*, quoted in Kenneth Day, *The Typography of Press Advertisement*, Ernest Benn, 1956.

1970

1 Adrian Frutiger, *Der Mensch und seine Zeichen*, Weiss Verlag, 1978, translated as *Signs and Symbols: Their Design and Meaning*, Studio Editions, 1989.

2 Paula Scher, quoted in Hugh Aldersey-Williams, *New American Design*, Rizzoli.

1980

1 Matthew Carter, *PC Computing*, January 1989.

2 Grafix National Conference survey, reported in *U&lc*, summer 1991.

3 Matthew Carter, *Communication Arts*, January–February 1989.

1990

1 This quotation is taken from the FAQ at emigre.com. It is quoted with permission and was highlighted by Rudy VanderLans to the author in an email exchange in 2002 on how type design can cope with illegal copying. He also commented: "The tendency, as Napster and MP3s have shown us, is that people want everything that lives on the internet to be free. I simply cannot think of a licence model that can satisfy this want and keep creators in business."

2 Unicode assigns a unique number to each individual character that appears in the various character sets so as to allow precise recognition, whatever the home system. The project is much larger than type – it seeks to unify a global standard for programming to allow easy interchange of information. Various type creation teams (including Microsoft, Adobe and Agfa Monotype) have working on creating Unicode fonts. For further information, visit www.unicode.org.

Bibliography

If you have read this far, you might want to head off for in-depth coverage of a particular movement, technology, individual or perhaps something altogether more lateral. An exhaustive list covering all the subjects and issues touched on in these pages would be... exhausting, for reader and writer alike. So here is a relatively brief, eclectic list. These recommendations are in part complementary, in part contradictory, and some are just personal favourites. They often contain extensive bibliographies.

Books

Printing Types
D.B. Updike (second edition, Harvard University Press, Cambridge, Massachusetts, 1937, republished Dover Publications, 1980). A seminal earlier history.

An Introduction to Bibliography
Philip Gaskell (Oxford University Press, Oxford, 1972). Excellent on the history of letterpress printing and the making of books. Note appendix on Elizabethan handwriting which illustrates the evolution of letterform.

The Elements of Typographic Style
Robert Bringhurst (Hartley & Marks, Vancouver, 1992/1996). Immensely knowledgeable (written by a practising typographer and poet) and yet often infuriating in its presentation of "rules". Question it to death.

Modern Typography
Robin Kinross (Hyphen Press, London, 1992). An intelligent and opinionated essay on the nature of the "modern". Part of being modern is to eschew colour pictures and insist on the unending quest for rationalism. Stimulating.

Anatomy of a Typeface
Alexander Lawson (David R. Godine/Hamish Hamilton, Lincoln, Massachusetts/London, 1990). Avuncular trawl through the history of many classics.

Letters of Credit: A View of Type Design
Walter Tracy (Gordon Fraser, London, 1986). Another personal guide.

Die Neue Typographie
Jan Tschichold (Berlin, 1928; facsimile reprint Brinkman & Bose, Berlin, 1987; English translation as *The New Typography*, translator Ruari McLean, University of California Press, 1995). An attempt to summarize the 1920s innovations in one small book... and a highly influential one.

Type, Sign, Symbol
Adrian Frutiger (ABC Verlag, Zurich, 1980). Type in its mark-making context from the creator of the Univers.

An Essay on Typography
Eric Gill (second edition, Dent, London, 1936). Characterful, quirky, brief.

Dimensional Typography
J. Abbott Miller (A Kiosk Report/Princeton Architectural Press, 1996). Intriguing proposals of three-dimensional forms from previously two-dimensional type.

Stop Stealing Sheep & Find Out How Type Works
Erik Spiekermann and E.M. Ginger (Adobe Press, 1993). Witty guide to recent practice.

Typography on the Personal Computer
Sumner Stone (Lund Humphries, London, 1991). Interesting to read in the light of subsequent developments.

The Monotype Recorder: One Hundred Years of Type Making 1897–1997
(Monotype Typography, 1997). Useful summary that gives another slant on the period and subject through the history of one key company.

Pioneers of Modern Typography
Herbert Spencer (second edition, Lund Humphries, London, 1982). A few key designers are elevated to heroic status.

Frederic Goudy
D.J.R. Bruckner (Harry N. Abrams, New York, 1990). Human interest through words.

Alfabeta: Lo Studio e Il Disegno del Carattere
Aldo Novarese (Progresso Grafico, Turin, 1965/83). Human interest through drawings.

Typography: A Manual of Design
Emil Ruder (Arthur Niggli, Teufen AR, Switzerland, 1967). A Swiss style primer.

About Alphabets
Hermann Zapf (MIT Press, Cambridge, Massachusetts, 1970).

The Graphic Designer and his Design Problems
Josef Müller-Brockmann (Arthur Niggli, Teufen AR, Switzerland, 1983). Perhaps the most revered of the Swiss style masters.

Moholy-Nagy
Krisztina Passuth (Thames & Hudson, London, 1985).

Amusing Ourselves to Death: Public Discourse in the Age of Show Business
Neil Postman (Viking Penguin, New York, 1985). A sobering analysis that suggests our literacy has moved beyond (or backwards from) joined-up sentences.

The Gutenberg Galaxy: Making of Typographic Man
Marshall McLuhan (Toronto University Press, Toronto, 1962). It didn't make much sense... and then it did.

Being Digital
Nicholas Negroponte (Basic Books, New York, 1995).

The Elements of Typographic Style
Robert Bringhurst (Hartley and Marks, 1997). Well-written, rather didactic tome that evangelizes the rules for late-20th-century orthodoxy.

Finer Points in the Spacing and Arrangement of Type
Geoffrey Dowding (Hartley and Marks, 1995). Classic manners observed and celebrated at a time of rude change.

The Alphabetic Labyrinth: The Letters in History and Imagination
Johanna Drucker (Thames and Hudson, 1995). Fascinating insights into the origin of form in typography.

Type and Typography
Phil Baines and Andrew Haslam (Laurence King, 2002). A good primer and a practical user guide. Could work as a course companion with this book for students.

Annuals

The Type Directors Club in New York and the Tokyo Typodirectors Club both have well-produced and usually stimulating annuals. Also dig out old Penrose Annuals, a faithful record of printing industry innovation for over 80 years from 1895.

Magazines

Emigre, 4475 D Street, Sacramento, CA 95819, USA. <www.emigre.com>. Essential if sometimes painful reading for the contemporary typographer.

Fuse, Unit 2, Whitehorse Yard, 78 Liverpool Road, London, N1 0QD, England. Consistently innovative in its themed packs of new fonts, posters and a booklet. Distributed by Fontshop International worldwide and FontWorks in England. Or <http://www.research.co.uk/fuse/fuse-home.html>

Creative Review, 50 Poland Street, London, W1V 4AX, England. More typographic context than kerning tips... but the magazine and CD-Rom are your platform as well as information source. Note my personal bias here.

U&lc, 228 East 45th Street, New York, NY 10017, USA. The ITC/Letraset promo magazine is also widely read, diverse in subject matter and design.

Idea, Seibundo-Shinkosha, 1-13-7 Yayoicho, Nakanoku, Tokyo 164, Japan. What's hot in the West from a sharp Japanese viewpoint.

Seybold. The Seybold series of reports and conferences provide an expert running commentary on the development of digital publishing. <seyboldreport.com>

Octavo 1986–1992. Produced by the design group 8vo and now ended. Just eight issues (the last one a CD-Rom), so very much a collector's item. Read them as a manifesto for respecting the modern.

Type manufacturers and software companies

Catalogues, CD-Roms and online information are the primary way of finding out the choice in type today – information that is usually free. Online catalogues for browsing and downloading fonts are increasingly prevalent, with search engines that advance – or at least provide alternatives – to conventional systems of tracking down a typeface.

Monotype Typography, Salfords, Redhill, Surrey RH1 5JP, England.

Emigre, Inc.
As for the magazine above.

FontShop International, Bergmannstrasse 102, D-10961 Berlin, Germany. <www.fontfont.de>

Adobe Systems, Inc., 1585 Charleston Road, PO Box 7900, Mountain View, CA 94039-7900, USA. <www.adobe.com/prodindex/webtype/>

Microsoft. For Microsoft's extensive resources on typography, go to their typography home page for extensive information that goes beyond purely Microsoft matters. <www.microsoft.com/typography>

Apple Computer. <www.apple.com>. This large website has a useful search engine up front which will give you thousands of matches for terms like "typography" or "TrueType". Be specific.

The Foundry, Studio 12, 10–11 Archer Street, London, W1V 7HG, England. Producers of the Architype series of fonts, digital re-creations of "classic" avant garde typefaces.

Futures

<www.w3.org/> The consortium running the World Wide Web. Links here to important papers, developments about the basic history, structure and technology of the web, including information on hypertext and Ted Nelson.

And for more

Since the previous edition of this book was published in 1998, the web has moved from "a source" of information to the starting point. Whether you end up in a bookshop, library, studio or photographing signs on the street, a good starting point for inquiry will be the web. Try keying into an internet search engine such as Google any reference (name, typeface, movement, etc.) that interests you here or any book from the above. See what you get and then refine the search. A general search such as "typographic resources" would have given you *c.* 26,000 entries at August 2003... so you might want to be a little more specific. There are many typophile sites out there, full of mostly useful, but occasionally misleading information. Handle with care and enjoy.

Divider credits

1900 Vince Frost, London. **1910** Fernando Gutierrez, Barcelona. **1920** Irma Boom, Amsterdam. **1930** Chip Kidd, New York. **1940** Cyan, Berlin. **1950** Angus Hyland, London. **1960** M+M, Paris. **1970** Graphic Thought Facility, London. **1980** Naomi Enami, Tokyo. **1990** tomato, London.,

Picture credits

Many of the illustrations in this book are courtesy of the St Bride Printing Library, off Fleet Street, London, which generously allowed items from its vast and important collection to be photographed. The St Bride Printing Library has been abbreviated to SBPL in the following list.

22 left Rudhard'fche Giekerei in Offenbach-am-Main, *Behrens Schriften-Initialen und Schmuck nach Zeichnungen von Professor Behrens*, 1902–3, p.20. SBPL. **22 right** AEG Archives, Frankfurt-am-Main. **23** Österreichisches Museum für Angewandte Kunst, Vienna. **25** American Type Founders Company, *American Specimen Book of Type Styles*, 1912, p.179. SBPL. **26** *ATF Specimen Book*, op. cit., pp700–1. SBPL. **31** Mattioli Collection, Milan/Scala, Florence/© DACS 1992. 15 x 11.8in/38 x 30cm. **32 left** Lucien Bernhard, *Das ist der Weg zum Frieden*, 1915. Lithograph 33.85 x 22.44in/86 x 57cm. Museum für Gestaltung, Zurich. **33** © DACS 1992. **39 top right** London Transport Museum. **39 below** The Trustees of the Victoria & Albert Museum, London [# E47-1936]. **43** *Offset Buch und Werbekunst*, number 7, Leipzig, July 1926, cover. SBPL/© DACS 1992. **44** above Bauhaus Archiv, p.397. SBPL/© DACS 1992. **46** Annely Juda Fine Art, London. **47** Annely Juda Fine Art, London. **49** Mikhail Anikst, *Soviet Commercial Design of the Twenties*, London, 1987, p.55/Calmann & King Archives, London. **50** The Trustees of the Victoria & Albert Museum, London (Library 95.JJ.96)/© DACS 1992. **51** The Trustees of the Victoria & Albert Museum, London (Library II. RC. M. I I)/© DACS 1992. **52 above** Stedelijk Museum, Amsterdam. **52 below** Haags Gemeentemuseum, The Hague/© DACS 1992. **54** *Futura* (promotional pamphlet), circa 1930. SBPL. **55 above** *Futura* (promotional pamphlet), circa 1930. SBPL. **56 right** Theo H. Ballmer, *Norm*, 1928. Lithograph 49.9 x 35.6in/126.7 x 90.5cm. The Museum of Modern Art, New York. Estée and Joseph Lauder Design Fund. **57** Stedelijk Museum, Amsterdam. **60 left** *The New Yorker*, 21 February 1925. Cover drawing by Rea Irvin © 1925, 1953 The New Yorker Magazine, Inc. **61** *The Broadway Series* (American Type Founders promotional pamphlet), 1929. SBPL. **62** A.M. Cassandre, *Nord Express*, poster for French Railways, 1927. Lithograph 41.33 x 29.13in/105 x 74cm. Museum für Gestaltung, Zurich/© ADAGP, Paris and DACS, London 1992. **63** *Words* (Deberny & Peignot brochure advertising Bifur), circa 1930. SBPL. **64** Fortunato Depero Museum, Rovereto/© DACS 1992. **65** © DACS 1992. **69 below** Retrograph Archive, London/© DACS 1992. **70 above** Royal Institute of British Achitects, London. **70 below** *De Onafhankelijke* (Amsterdam Type Foundry Promotional Pamphlet), circa 1930, cover. SBPL. **71** Campo Grafico. Private collection, London. **73** *The Peignot: A New Type Drawn by A.M. Cassandre* (Deberny & Peignot promotional booklet), circa 1938. SBPL. **74 below** *Libra medium and light* (Amsterdam Type Foundry promotional pamphlet), circa 1938. SBPL. **75 below** Max Ernst, *Kunsthaus Zürich*, 1934. Letterpress 39.37 x 27.55in/100 x 70cm. Museum für Gestaltung, Zurich/© SPADEM/ADAGP, Paris and DACS, London 1992. **80 above** Reproduced by permission of Penguin Books Ltd. **80 below left** *The Picture of Dorian Gray* by Oscar Wilde, Tauchnitz Edition, Leipzig, 1908. Private collection, London. **80 below right** *The Albatross Book of Living Prose*, 1947. Private collection, London. **81 above** Herbert Matter, *Für schöne Autofahrten die Schweiz*, *En route pour la Suisse*, 1935. Gravure 39.76 x 25.2in/101 x 64cm. Museum für Gestaltung, Zurich. **81 below** SBPL. **82–83** SBPL. **87 below right** Courtesy Paul Rand, Weston, Connecticut. **88** *Introduction to Typography* by Oliver Simon, 1946; photograph Ferdy Carabott. **89 above** From *Alfa-beta* by Aldo Novarese, published by Progresso Grafico Torino, 1983, pp.310–11. **89 below** *The Buildings of England*, 1951; *Dante: The Divine Comedy*, 1949. Reproduced by permission of Penguin Books Ltd. **90 right** © The Upjohn Company & Lester Beall. **91 below** © The Upjohn Company & Lester Beall. **93** Max Huber, *Gran premio dell'Autodromo Monza 17 Ottobre 1948*, Offset lithograph 27.56 x 19.29in/70 x 49cm. Museum für Gestaltung, Zurich. **97** *Mistral* (Fonderie Olive, Marseilles promotional pamphlet), circa 1955. SBPL. **98 below right** Courtesy Franco Grignani, Milan. **99 above** Courtesy Saul Bass. **99 below** *Banco* (Fonderie Olive, Marseilles promotional pamphlet), circa 1955. SBPL. **100 left** Westvaco, New York. **102–03** *Neue Grafik*, 15th issue, March 1963, pp.54–55. SBPL. **104** *Univers* (Deberny & Peignot promotional booklet), 1954. SBPL. **106** *Neue Haas Grotesk* (Haas Typefoundry promotional booklet), August 1958, front and back cover. SBPL. **107 below** *Helvetica* (Haas Typefoundry promotional book), updated. SBPL. **108** Paul P. Piech, Porthcawl. **109** Courtesy Franco Grignani, Milan. **113** *right now Jackie McLean*, 1965. **114 above left and right** *Jackie McLean "it's time!"*, 1964; *Joe Henderson in 'n out*, 1964. **114 below** From *Alfa-beta* by Aldo Novarese, published by Progresso Grafico Torino, 1983, pp.316–17. **116 right** The Herb Lubalin Study Center of Design and Typography, New York. **117 above left** The Herb Lubalin Study Center of Design and Typography, New York. **117 above right** James Moran (ed.), *Printing in The Twentieth Century: A Penrose Anthology*, London, 1974, p.293. **118 above right** Lee Conklin, concert poster for Procol Harum at the Fillmore, 1967. Offset lithograph 21.26 x 14.17in/54 x 36cm. Museum für Gestaltung, Zurich. **118 below left** B. McLean, concert poster for The Yardbirds, The Doors and others, 1967. Offset lithograph 21.26 x 14.17in/54 x 36cm. Museum für Gestaltung, Zurich. **118 below right** Victor Moscoso, concert poster for The Doors and others at the Avalon Ballroom, 1967. Offset lithograph 20.5 x 14.17in/52 x 36cm. Museum für Gestaltung, Zurich. **119 left** *Ad Lib* (American Type Founders Company brochure), circa 1961, cover. SBPL. **119 right** The Vintage Magazine Company Ltd, London. **121 left** Total Design, Amsterdam. **122 above centre and right** Reproduced by permission of Penguin Books Ltd. **123** Letraset UK Ltd. **127** DDB Needham Worldwide, New York. **128 left** Cover of *U&lc*® volume I, number I © International Typeface Corporation, New York. Reprinted by permission. **129 below** Covers of ITC typeface specimen booklets © International Typeface Corporation, New York. Reprinted by permission. **130** SBPL. **131** Peter von Arx. TM12. **132** Poster by A. G. Fronzoni. Private collection, London. **133** below right Chermayeff & Geismar Inc., New York. **134** The Robert Opie Collection, London. **135 left** Greenberg Associates Inc., New York. **139** Courtesy April Greiman Inc., Los Angeles, California. *Your Turn My Turn* 3d poster 1983, by April Greiman for the Pacific Design Center, 24 x 36in/61 x 91.5cm. **141 left** Studio Dumbar, The Hague. **142** Courtesy Neville Brody, London. **143 right** Vaughan Oliver, London. **144 left** M & Co., New York. **145** Courtesy Peter Saville; photograph Ferdy Carabott. **146** Institute of Contemporary Arts, London/Steve White. **147 above** London Transport Museum. **148 left** Octavo magazine. Private collection; photograph Ferdy Carabott. **148** right Uwe Loesch, *Survival during War*, for Ruhrlandmuseum, Essen, 1990. 33 x 46.85in/84 x 119cm. Courtesy Uwe Loesch. **149** English Markell Pockett, London. **153** Courtesy Emigre Graphics, Berkeley, California. **155 left** Emigre Graphics, Berkeley, California. **155 right** © *Domus* (Milan), number 730, September 1991. **156 left** Fontshop and Neville Brody, London. **157** Courtesy FontShop International. **158** photograph Ferdy Carabott. **159** *Rolling Stone*, 6 September 1990, pp.58–59. **160** From *The End of Print* Lewis Blackwell and David Carson, published by Laurence King, 1995. **161 above** From *The End of Print* Lewis Blackwell and David Carson, published by Laurence King, 1995. **161 below** Spread from *2ndsight* Lewis Blackwell and David Carson, published by Laurence King, 1997. **162** © FSI Fonts & Software GmbH. **163** Courtesy Mark Farrow. **164** © FSI Fonts & Software GmbH. **165** Promotional material, courtesy Adobe. **166** BBC Radio Scotland commercials, courtesy Jon Barnbrook. **167 above** Emigre Graphics; photograph Ferdy Carabott. **167 below** The Hoefler Type Foundry; photograph Ferdy Carabott. **168 above** Courtesy Anti-Rom, London. **168 below** © FSI Fonts & Software GmbH. **169** J. Abbott Miller, *Dimensional Typography* (A Kiosk Report/Princeton Architectural Press, 1996). 170 Rem Koolhaas and Bruce Mau, *S, M, L, XL* (Uitgeverij 010 Publisher). 171 *SHV Thinkbook*, design and research by Irma Boom, 1996. 172 © Kyle Cooper. 174 If/Then, editor: Janet Abrams; assistant editor: Julia van Mourik; art direction: Mevis & Van Deursen. © the authors and the Netherlands Design Institute, Amsterdam, 1999. 175 © Sagmeister Inc. Photography: Tom Schierlitz. 176 Courtesy www.adbusters.org. 177 Josef Flejsar, *Laterna Grotesca*, '40 Years of Black Theatre Prague'. 179 © ESPN The Magazine. 181 Courtesy praystation.com. 182 © Büro Destruct – Typedifferent.com. 183 © The Designers Republic Ltd. 184 left Connected_Identity. URL: www.sony.co.jp/en/SonyInfo/dream/ci/en. Design companies: One Sky Inc., Tokyo/Business Architects, Tokyo/ tomato, London/tomato interactive, London. Site builder/site manager: Sony Corporation. 184 right © McSweeney's and David Byrne. 185 © Swiss International Air Lines Ltd. 186 above Lars Müller, *Helvetica: Homage to a Typeface* (Lars Müller Publishers, 2002). 186 below Copyright 2002 Michael C. Place/Build. 187 Wardrobe by Marion Deuchars; client: Howies; design group: Carter Wong Tomlin.

Index

Figures in *italics* refer to captions. See also Glossary, pp. 208–09

Published 2004 by Laurence King Publishing
71 Great Russell Street
London WC1B 3BN

A catalogue record for this book is available from the British Library.

ISBN 1-85669-351-1

Designed by Pentagram

Printed in Singapore

Lewis Blackwell is the author of several acclaimed books on design and communication. These include editing and writing *The End of Print* (about the work of David Carson) and co-editing with Neville Brody *G1*, and with Chris Ashworth *Soon: The Future of Brands*. His principal activity, though, is to head creative direction at the world's leading imagery company, Getty Images. Previously he was editor and publisher of *Creative Review*, and he continues to write articles and lecture worldwide. His daughter Caledonia is modified Scottish.

Angus Hyland designed this book and many other things. Since April 1998 he has been a partner at Pentagram, London. Hyland designed the 1950s divider with Sharon Hwang.

Irma Boom, who created the 1920s divider, works mainly on books. She goes beyond the conventions of design, being involved at the concept stage, and also in research, authorship and editing. Between 1991 and 1996 she designed and co-edited a 2,136-page book weighing 3.5 kilograms on the 100th anniversary of a major company. She has had her own studio in Amsterdam, lectures widely, and is a visiting professor at Yale University.

Cyan is a Berlin-based group of designers, founded in 1992 by Daniela Haufe, Sophie Alex and Detlef Fiedler. They work chiefly for cultural and governmental institutions and are united in a respect and reference for the twentieth-century avant garde. They aim to "maintain the idea of reading as an occupation directed at the gaining of experience" and believe "reading needs engagement and awareness" which leads them to oppose "fast-food communication". The 1940s divider is their work.

Naomi Enami lives and works in Tokyo. He has created images on computer since the late 1980s (the divider he was asked to produce). Prior to this he was a magazine art director on leading magazines including *Elle* and *Marie Claire* in Japan. He works with his design company Digitalogue.

Vince Frost runs his own studio, Frost Design, in London and Tokyo. He has won many awards internationally, particularly for art direction on *Big* magazine and *The Independent* magazine. Recent clients include the Royal Mail, Sony and Magnum. "I have a strong interest in wood and metal type, anything dusty and dirty. I prefer to use three-dimensional type rather than electronic. So when I have a new job I visualize piles of trays of forgotten type. It's much more of a physical process." As things were in 1900, for which he designed the divider. In 1998 he was the launch art director for Japanese *Vogue*.

Graphic Thought Facility are Paul Neale and Andrew Stevens. Graduates of the Royal College of Art, they formed GTF in 1990 and are based in London. Their (joint) top five typefaces of all time are currently: 1, the Sony logotype; 2, Schriebmaschinenshrift; 3, Bunny Ears; 4, Girl; 5, Souvenir Monospace. They art directed the 1970s remix, with design and craft by Lizzie Finn, a freelance graphic designer.

Fernando Gutierrez is a partner in Pentagram, and previously co-founder of the Barcelona studio Grafica. Until recently he was the art director of *Colors* magazine. He once designed an issue with 359 pictures but only 442 words. He gave no words for this, but did create the 1910 divider.

Chip Kidd's book jacket designs for Alfred A. Knopf have featured in numerous magazines and won many awards. Descriptions include "Monstrously ugly" (John Updike), "Apparently obvious" (William Boyd) and "Faithful flat-earth rendering" (Don DeLillo). Kidd has also written widely about graphic design and popular culture and is the author of his own book, *Batman Collected* (Titan, 1996) in which he attempts to rid himself of his inner demons. To no avail – he is the co-author and designer of *Batman Animated* (HarperCollins, 1998). Batman was created in the 1930s – for which Kidd did the divider here.

M+M are Michael Amzalag and Mathias Augustyniak who have worked together in Paris since 1991 across many different kinds of media – books, fashion catalogues, stickers, art catalogues, towels, posters, record covers, advertising, magazines, postcards. "We spend our time trying to contaminate the world with our ideas. We do recommend to all readers to use Barthes/Simpson typeface (designed in 1994 by M+M and based on standardized McDonald french fries) to write their thoughts." M+M's contamination of this book is with the 1960s divider.

Dirk van Dooren and Karl Hyde, who created our 1990s divider, are two members of the London-based tomato collective of artists, whose output covers design, film, music and other media. Hyde is also a member of the music group Underworld.

Acknowledgements: many thanks to many people, including all the people mentioned in *20th Century Type*, plus Linda Jorgensen at Monotype Typography, David Quay and Freda Sack at The Foundry, FontShop International, Fontshop UK, Stuart Jensen of Fontworks UK, Neville Brody, David Carson, and especially the long-suffering editor of this book, Jo Lightfoot at Laurence King. That's what we said last time… and now she is more long-suffering. As is editor Robert Shore. Credit to all and any mistakes are probably mine.

In memoriam: Raymond Vincent Blackwell, 1925-93, father and printer